Then an Angel Came

Then an Angel Came

Carol Gino

Kensington Books
http://kensingtonbooks.com

KENSINGTON BOOKS are published by

Kensington Publishing Corp.
850 Third Avenue
New York, NY 10022

Library of Congress Card Catalog Number: 97-071434
ISBN 1-57566-231-0

First Kensington Hardcover Printing: December, 1997
10 9 8 7 6 5 4 3 2 1

Printed in the United States of America

Dedicated
To a world where
All children are precious
Elders can share their stories
and
Every soul can hear the whisper of an Angel

AUTHOR'S NOTE

A life is no small thing. No matter how small the life. The family we come into is not an accident. Nor is the experience it provides. The seeds of our potential are sown long before we're born and the plans we make then affect not only ourselves but all others. Each of us is unique and essential because each of us touches others on very deep levels. How we do is both a part of a life and a part of the Mystery.

A family is a soul's first view of the world, a world, in fact, in itself. Each family has a spirit, a soul, and a heart. The spirit of a family knows its plans. The soul of a family holds its secrets. The heart of a family beats its music as it dances in the world. Our family is our first partner in the dance of relationships. Some of the steps are simple, others are more complicated, but all of them are teachings.

The first step in the dance is finding the gifts hidden in life's hardships and tragedies. Each step we learn is important to others. Each individual's story, in the context of family and in the larger family of humankind, is significant. No one story more than another.

I have had the good fortune to find myself in the middle of a very good family. Not easy, just sometimes wonderful. Each member, though very different, has supported and complemented the others. But within this family's plans, we had some big dips in the dance; a chance to fall hard, to break. Often we had to lean on each other, sometimes we even carried each other. But we learned to see these times as opportunities for evolution, a chance to perfect the steps. Somehow we found the sacred in our sacrifices and that has helped us hear the music and dance on.

There was an angel; she was part of it too. Now what's sacred in my family is sacred in my life. And so I'd like to share my family with you. I'd like to share our gifts. But first I have to share the tragedy. If this story touches deep places within you, please be patient, stick with me, I won't let you fall. In the process, with some blessing, you will hear the music in the heartbeat of our family, and maybe hear the music in your own.

I offer it to you with love and hope.

Carol

Chapter One

I don't know how I got to the phone. Half asleep, I must have stumbled across the dark room. Finally I was jolted awake by my sister Barbara's voice. "Carol?" she asked. She was crying.

My heart stopped. A call in the middle of the night when I was in Los Angeles, so far from home in New York, could only mean big trouble. Something must have happened to my father, I thought. Then, immediately, something must have happened to my son.

"Carol?" she said again, but before I could answer, I heard the shuffle of the phone.

"Barbara?" I said urgently. "Talk to me. Tell me *who* it is."

But the voice that answered wasn't my sister's. It was my daughter, Teri. "Mommy," she said softly, "Gregory's dead."

"Gregory?" I repeated, holding dumbly on to the phone. Gregory was my grandson, Teri's child, but at that moment I felt as though I'd never heard the name before.

"Yes, Mommy," Teri said, her voice cracking, "the baby's dead. Come home."

Barbara got back on the phone. "Greggy was fine when Teri put him to bed last night, but this morning when she went in to wake him, he was blue."

As I listened, my mind automatically searched everything in my experience. Sudden infant death syndrome, I thought. SIDS. Crib death.

Barbara began to cry again. "What should I do until you get here?" she asked.

"Just keep everyone close," I said.

Gregory was dead. Now we had to worry about the living. "How are Mommy and Daddy?" I asked, my voice strangely calm.

"They're devastated," she said. "Mommy's walking around crying but Daddy isn't even speaking."

"And Gordon?" I asked. "Is he okay?" Gordon was my son-in-law, the baby's father. I didn't really expect him to be *okay*, I wanted to know if he was still sane or if he'd lost his mind.

"He was home this morning when Teri found the baby," Barbara said. "Gordon tried to bring him back. He tried to breathe for Greggy while Teri called for help. . . ."

Thank God for that, I thought. They were together. "I'll be home as fast as I can."

I sat on the bed, shock mercifully freeing my mind of any coherent thought. Instinctively I reached for the phone to call Danny, my twenty-one-year-old son.

Teri, Danny, and I were the triangle that formed our nuclear family for as long as I could remember. Danny was very close to both his sister and Gordon, and was a strong and stabilizing force in an emergency. When there was no answer, I held the phone for much too long.

Suddenly I was aware of Mario standing in front of me.

We had just arrived at the Beverly Hills Hotel the night before, filled with high spirits and big plans for the months ahead.

He asked, "What's happened? Can I help?"

Mario and I had been together for years, lovers and very good friends. We had come out to California, as we did every year, to spend the winter living together, writing.

Now I looked up at him and said numbly, "Gregory's dead. I have to go home."

Mario reached to hug me, to comfort me, but I was just too fragile. "Please don't," I said. "If you're too kind to me, I'll fall apart." He nodded as I added, "Just make arrangements to get me out of here as quickly as possible."

"You don't want me to come with you?" Mario asked, concerned. "Are you sure?"

"I'm sure," I said. "I need to be with Teri and Gordon. I want to be there for the family."

"Okay," he agreed. "But promise to call if you need me."

It was only two days after Christmas. As we arrived at the airport, lighted Christmas trees with hanging garlands of shiny silver bells and red ribbons greeted us. Inside, I was acutely aware of the cheery chattering of the crowds and the many Happy Holiday signs all around. Christmas was a time for celebration—the birth of the Christ child—and New Year's, the beginning of New Hope. I wondered if Gregory's death would seem any less a tragedy at another time of year.

At the gate I kissed Mario quickly and boarded the plane.

Inside the small cabin, after taking my seat, I suddenly felt a rush of panic. I couldn't breathe. My heart began to race and pound so loudly, I was sure everyone could hear it. I wanted to jump up, push through the door, and get out. Instead, I forced myself to fasten my seat belt. I had to get home. To Teri, to Gordon, to my granddaughter, Jessica . . .

The takeoff was rough, but I was too numb to care. As soon as the pilot turned off the Fasten Seat Belt sign, I struggled over the lady next to me to get to the bathroom. Once inside the tiny cubicle, I locked the door and leaned against it. Slowly, afraid of what I would see, I moved in front of the small stainless steel sink and looked at myself in the mirror. The pink sweatshirt I had thrown on with my jeans was wrinkled, but I didn't look half as bad as I felt. Though I was only forty-two, I had expected to look suddenly old, wrinkled, and gray. I'd seen how pain could show in a face and body. But my hair was dark and shiny and my skin no more wrinkled than before. Still, I seemed smaller, my shoulders narrower, my hands less strong.

Suddenly I felt light-headed and was afraid I was going to faint. *Don't you dare fall apart now,* I threatened myself, *or the family falls with you.*

I took some deep breaths, threw cold water on my face, and walked back to my seat. There in the dark, with the movie playing, I laid my head back against the blue velour seats and tried to stop my tears.

The first time a baby died in my arms, I was forced by my fury to face my God. I was a very young nurse then, still shiny with innocence and purpose, and he was nobody's baby, abandoned after he'd been abused. He was three months old, and I was working in the pediatric nursery. But as soon as I laid eyes on that little blond boy, I thought of angels.

Each night in the quiet darkness of the hospital, as I sat in the hard wooden rocker to feed him, I whispered words of love and encouragement. I kissed his bruises, touched his little nose, and let him wrap his tiny hand around my fingers. His grasp was never tight, he was too weak for that, but starlight shone from his light blue eyes whenever he opened them to look at me. No one had ever touched my soul as deeply. I called him Crissy—for Christmas, for Christ, for kisses—and before I went home each morning I prayed to the gentle God of babies to take care of him.

Crissy never seemed to grow; still, my love for him kept growing. For the next two months I dreamed of him when I slept, and when I was awake, he was first on my mind. I wanted to take him home with me, I wanted to keep him safe forever. If he was nobody's baby, then he could be mine. I would adopt him and he would live with me and my two children.

But God had different plans. And I had learned, those many years ago, that I, myself, was not a match for God. I was sitting in the rocker, holding that baby when he died, when the gentle God of children took him back to his real home to be the angel I'd always known he was.

I screamed that night, I raged at God, I even shook my fist. I cursed as I ran straight out of the hospital into the dark and starless night. I drove directly to the beach. The sand was wet, the water black, but I wasn't afraid, though I was alone, because my heart was already torn to shreds. What the hell could God do to me now? What the hell could hurt as much? I ran, fast and furious, across the wet sand toward the water, breathless from my pain and my rage. Finally I stopped, looked up at the heavens, and shouted, "One little kid, God, why couldn't you just save that one little kid? I hate you for this, I swear, I hate you for this. You'll never trick me again, God . . . not like this."

There was no answer from my God, no thunder or lightning, just the soft constant sound of the breaking waves. I stood there and looked up again at the black, silent sky. Suddenly, frightened by my own arrogance, I covered my face with my hands and tried to hide, terrified that my God would respond with even greater anger and rage. What about my own two children?

Repentant, I kneeled on the wet sand and I cried for His mercy. "I'm so sorry," I whispered. "I know that baby wasn't mine . . . that he belonged to you, but I loved him so. . . . Please don't touch my kids. You can do anything else to me and I won't complain. I'll spend my life in the service of others, I'll do anything you want me to, but please, God, let me keep my children."

That night we made a deal, my God and I. Since that time, God had kept his promise, and I had kept mine.

I had been a nurse for over twenty years, and because of that promise, I'd held and taken care of many more dying babies. Some I surrendered willingly, because they were in so much pain, others I let go of reluctantly. Always with sadness, but never again with anger. I'd found that there was a big difference between God's territory and mine. For my part, I learned as much as I could about nursing and medicine so I could do my very best in *my* territory. In some wacky way, I thought it was insurance.

Now I felt betrayed. As though there was something in the fine print I had overlooked. Yet, I had been warned. With my first glimpse of Greggy just born, something in me was instantly afraid. I should have been thrilled when I saw him, but all I could do was cry. He was too beautiful, too perfect, a chubby, fine-featured cherub. The warming lights of the hospital nursery cast a luminous glow around him, and I cried harder when I saw it. Confused by my reaction, I told myself I was acting weird. Even though I tried to hide it from myself, that first night when I saw him in the nursery, my heart and soul recognized that small angel all over again. And even God knows how hard I tried not to love that baby too much.

Once Teri brought Greggy home from the hospital, I carefully examined him, listened to his heart, checked his reflexes, and I felt a little better. He *was* perfect. Nothing supported my fears. Nothing except the nagging feeling that he was not only too beautiful, but he was also too gentle and certainly too good. He was a happy, placid, perfect baby with wise, clear blue eyes who hardly ever cried and demanded almost no attention. So everyone, especially Teri, found it a pleasure to shower him with constant attention. Gregory was such a change from Jessie, who demanded everything we had to give, all the time.

Of course, nothing kept me from loving Greggy. My heart reached out to him instinctively, and I fell in love with him totally and completely. My heart responded to his essential beauty as it did to a brilliant sunset, an exquisite painting, or a great symphony.

I closed my eyes as I leaned back against the airplane seat, and tried to prepare myself. "God," I prayed, "you got me again. But this time, I don't hate you. I'm older now, and maybe I even understand a little . . . so . . . I won't complain, I promise. I won't whine. I'll do whatever I have to. But, dear God, again I ask, please don't take my kids. Don't take Teri away. . . ."

The knot of fear in my stomach tightened. How did my gentle child Teri not go mad when she lifted her baby's stiff, cold body? Teri, my own child, always so afraid of sickness, so afraid of death. What had this done to her? How would it change her? What could I say when I saw her?

As the plane descended, I took a deep breath and tried to steel myself for what lay ahead.

When the taxi rounded the corner to my house, I saw parked cars lining both sides of the street. I suppose I paid the driver, but I don't remember. As I approached the front door, someone opened it for me.

There was a crowd of familiar faces, no one distinct. Several people approached me, but they moved aside as I frantically searched my living room for Teri.

Suddenly, as in a freeze-frame, I saw her. She was sitting at the dining room table, porcelain pale, her brown hair dull and limp. I had expected her to look different, somehow bruised and bloodied, with physical evidence of brutality that would indicate a mortal wound. But all I thought was, God, she's only twenty-four, she looks so young.

When Teri saw me, she stood up, and all I could see were her eyes . . . the eyes of a deer who'd been shot.

I walked quickly, almost ran to her. I put my arms around her, hugging her tight. "Oh, baby," I said, "I'm so sorry this awful thing has happened to you. I'm so sorry I can't make it better." Her head buried against my shoulder, she sobbed as I held her.

After a few moments a chair seemed to magically appear and I sat down. Teri sat across the table from me and someone placed a cup of hot tea in front of each of us.

"Oh, Mom," Teri said, wiping her eyes with the back of her hand, "this was such a low blow."

"I can't imagine how you lived through it," I said.

She shook her head. "I'm not sure I have," she said softly.

"Where's Jessie?" I asked. "And Gordon?"

"Jessie's inside with Jennifer," Teri said. "She was there. She saw everything. She was upset." Then she looked around the living room.

"I don't know where Gordon is," she said as she stood up. "Maybe with Danny. I'll find him."

The house I live in with my sister is an L-shaped ranch with the rooms one after the other like the cars in a railroad train. I got up to look for Jessie, Danny, and my mother and father, to see if any of them was going under. But at the junction where my house ends and Barbara's begins, the first person I saw was my sister. When I hugged her, I felt her body shaking. "Did I do everything all right?" she asked tearfully.

"Perfectly," I said, trying to smile. Her olive skin was streaked with tears and she had dark circles under her eyes. Though she was younger than I, she was taller. Still, I was the strong sister, Barbara was the gentle younger one. She was much more than Gregory's aunt; there had always been a special place in her heart only for him. He mirrored Barbara's innocence; he was a reflection of her vulnerability.

I turned to see my mother standing behind me, and when she put her arms around me, she said exactly what I had said to Teri, "I'm so sorry this has happened to you." My father stood stiffly beside her, a handkerchief held against his eyes. He said nothing, and when I hugged him, it was as though he were somewhere else.

All of us seemed to be walking around in slow motion, wandering aimlessly in some surrealistic dream. I walked over to Barbara's side of the house. Christopher, my seven-year-old nephew, was stacking Legos on the floor as I walked through his room. I tousled his brown hair as I passed. "You okay?" I asked.

He nodded. But never looked up.

Jennifer, my twelve-year-old niece, was sitting on her bed reading to my two-and-a-half-year-old granddaughter, Jessica. Jessie's fine blond hair fell like silk threads against Jennifer's dark sweater. Jennifer had placed a blanket over them, and so Jessie looked like a pretty doll, tucked in tightly next to her. "Hi," I said, bending down to kiss them. "How are you both?"

Jennifer, tentative and concerned, asked, "Are you okay, Aunt Carol?" Jennifer often took her cues from me. If I looked okay, she felt better.

I nodded and tried to smile a reassurance. "And, Jessie? How are you?" I asked, kneeling beside her.

Jessie looked up from her book. Her lips were tight. She frowned. "Mama Carol, I had a very hard day. My brother Gregory Thomas got sick and died today."

I bent over and hugged her. "I'm so sorry, Jessie," I said. What could she be thinking right now? I wondered. What could she be feeling? She was just a baby herself. She looked so sad, her whole body taut. I held her for a while before I stood up. There was nothing else to say. Jessie went back to reading her book with Jennifer.

On my way back, as I reached the hall on my side of the house, I saw Gordon and Danny walking toward me. Gordon was a head taller and much stockier than Danny, yet that day it was clear that Danny was the guardian, the trusted friend and brother—not only a brother-in-law.

"Hi, Mom," Danny said. "You got here pretty quick." But I saw a warning in his eyes to keep my distance, to be careful with Gordon or I would shatter his fragile composure.

Gordon looked up, and I saw the futility in his clear green eyes. It took everything I had to restrain myself, to say no more than "Tell me what I can do to help." I wanted to hug him, to stroke his hair and try to comfort him as I had Teri, but I knew I couldn't. Not yet. He was a young warrior, the protector of his family in the battle of his life, and he had just suffered an agonizing defeat.

Gordon had always been special to me, not only as my daughter's husband, but as a young man I recognized as authentic and honest. He was one of the rare good men who combined the best of male strength with sensitivity.

Danny could read my mind, and I could read his. *Don't say anything that will open more wounds,* his eyes warned. *Don't understand too much. This is a private thing, Mom. Gregory was his son, part of him, he's too hurt for words now. Don't make him say all he feels.*

"There was nothing you could have done, Gordon," I said, touching his arm lightly as I passed him. "There was nothing anyone could have done."

He nodded, but never said a word.

Teri was waiting for me. Together, we went into my study to talk. She looked lost sitting on my white leather couch. I sat in the chair opposite her, afraid to sit too close, as though she were burned and there was a chance I could hurt her more.

She sat silently for a few minutes, just staring down at her hands, then her body began to heave in deep, wrenching sobs. I sat, not moving toward her, feeling helpless. "Mom," she finally asked when the tears stopped, "did you know that the soul has a cry of its own?"

I nodded. I did know. Right now that part of me was hidden in some deep recess of myself, huddled in terror and howling with grief as I watched my own child struggle.

"Tell me what happened," I asked her. And so she began to explain. . . .

Teri had awakened that morning before the alarm rang and lay in bed snuggled under her down comforter. The cold air coming through the slightly open window made her want to stay in bed. She looked at Gordon, sleeping alongside her, and thought fondly that even with his dark curly hair showing some gray, he was incredibly handsome. She loved him even more now than when she had married him.

She glanced at the clock. She had about ten minutes before she had to get up. Teri then thought about Jessica. It was almost time to wake her up for nursery school. She wouldn't wake easily, she never did. She slept like she did everything else in her life from the day she was born, fully and with complete intensity. When Teri's mind wandered over to Gregory, she smiled. Her son. It was still hard for her to believe. That's why she carried him around with her all day, to make sure she wasn't dreaming. She had never envisioned herself having a boy. Only girls. In the delivery room, when the doctor announced it, she had asked, "Are you sure?" and the doctor had laughed.

She loved the smell of Gregory, the feel of him, the wise look in his eyes. He looked so peaceful when she held him that she often found herself laughing aloud. And she loved rubbing her nose against his as he rested his small hand on her cheek. When she nursed him she had a feeling of such closeness, it was as though they were one, he an extension of herself, a most precious part.

Not so with Jessica. Never. Jessie was another person, her own person, from the day she was born. Teri looked at the clock again. Time! she told herself as she slid from under the covers. Gordon stirred and asked sleepily, "Did Greggy wake up for his bottle last night?" Teri giggled. What a madman, she thought. Gregory had been sleeping through the night for weeks now, ever since she had started bottle-feeding him.

Jessie was lying on her back deep in sleep when Teri walked into her room. "Jess?" Teri called softly. "Time to get up for school." But Jessie slept on. Teri sat on the bed next to her and smoothed back her straight blond hair.

"Jessie," Teri cajoled, "you have to get up. Mommy will put on *Sesame Street* and then we can go wake Gregory." Jessie opened her eyes with effort, but they fell shut again. So Teri lifted her, thinking how big she seemed compared to Greggy. Laughing now and shaking her head at Jessie's reluctance to wake up, she carried Jess into the living room and laid her on the couch. Then she turned on the TV and went into the kitchen to make herself some coffee. With Jessie waking up and Gregory still asleep, Teri could take the time to have a peaceful cup of coffee before she began her hectic day.

After a few minutes Teri called in to Jessie, "Do you want to come with Mommy and wake up the baby?" It always worked. Jessie was off the couch in a minute. As Teri reached for the bottle that she had been heating, she felt Jessica's small hand in her own.

Teri and Jessie were laughing and talking as Teri's foot hit the threshold of the baby's room. Suddenly something stopped her short. A wave of fear, a flash of fright. Then terror.

Something's wrong! she thought, her heart racing. This room is empty. My baby's gone. Somebody's taken him! This can't be happening, her mind told her. The windows and the doors are locked. No one could have gotten in, she reassured herself. But still her knees began to buckle. It was Jessie tugging at her hand, Jessie's voice, that brought her back. "Mommy, come on," she said. "Don't stop. Let's get the baby."

Teri, with leaden legs, moved slowly toward the crib. Then she saw him, lying on his stomach, head turned away. He's here, thank God, she thought with relief, but only for an instant.

Before she even touched the baby, she knew. And when she finally lifted him, his arms straight as wood, his face blue as fading day, she *knew*. She began to scream then, heard the sound of her own voice as though the screams belonged to someone else, and ran frantically for someone who could turn time back to any moment in her life before now. "My baby's dead," she screamed, and it echoed through time. "Help me."

Gordon seemed to magically appear. "The baby's dead," she screamed at him. "The baby's dead." In slow motion he reached forward and took the baby from her. *Gordon, in his white pajamas, an ancient temple priest carrying his son to the altar of a savage god.*

He laid the baby on the couch, then bent over him and covered the tiny nose and mouth with his own lips. He began to blow gently. Life, love, hope, he blew. Between those breaths he lifted his head only long enough to say to Teri, "Call emergency! Call 911!"

But Teri was frozen, had rooted in the place she stood. No mind. Heart stopped. "Emergency?" she heard herself say. There's no emergency. It's all over. The thief of time has taken Greggy, he's already run away with our son. She glanced around the room. Her baby was nowhere to be found. From somewhere deep inside, she heard, "He never even said good-bye."

Jessie had gotten lost somewhere between Teri's last coherent sentence and her first frantic scream. Now, in a voice more of worry than of fear, Jessie asked, "Mommy, what's Daddy doing to our baby?"

Jessie jolted Teri back. She reached down and lifted Jessie in her arms. She held the child's face close against her own, then spun them both around to turn away from the couch. In Greggy's place there was a body, a stiff, cold blue thing that looked nothing like her sweet, warm baby. Spirit gone from matter, matter left alone.

"Call emergency!" Gordon shouted again. Now Teri picked up the phone. As she was giving the operator their address, she heard Gordon plead, "Please, God, give him another chance. Please give my son one more chance."

Time seemed to stop. Then the police were there. Several of them. One tall, kind-looking sergeant with a dark mustache whispered something to Gordon that Teri didn't hear. She was listening to the screaming siren of the ambulance pulling up outside their door. The sergeant quickly lifted Gregory off the couch and carried him outside. The red lights flashed and the sirens screamed again as the ambulance pulled away.

Teri, still holding Jessie in her arms, was numb. She felt Jessie shiver. The police had left the front door open. It was cold out. The first snow had fallen the night before and everything was covered with winter white.

"Gordon?" Teri said, then, "Gord, they took the baby out without a blanket."

The officer came back to the house and told them someone had to follow the ambulance to the hospital. Gordon offered to wait at home for Barbara to come stay with Jessie. Teri threw her clothes on quickly and was still carrying her shoes as she ran out to the patrol car. The whole ride there, her mind was blank. They rode in silence.

When they pulled up to the entrance of the emergency room, Teri noticed a van parked right next to them, a psychiatric transport van. Two paths seemed now to appear before her as she stepped from the patrol car. One led into that van, away from the real world, away from the hellish experience that was to follow. The other led through the emergency room doors into the real world, directly into that hell. The choice seemed simple. She could go crazy and she would never have to hear "Your baby is dead."

She imagined herself climbing into the van, she pictured herself letting it take her away. It seemed right. She turned her head, willing herself toward the van, but her legs, driven by the motor of her own destiny, without her personal consent, carried her straight through those emergency room doors. After what seemed like a very long time, sitting in the waiting room alone, Gordon finally came running in. Teri saw his eyes, knew he still had hope. She saw his vulnerability, and couldn't let him think, not for another moment, that there was a chance Gregory was alive. Before he even asked, she told him, "He's dead, Gord. He really is."

"How can you be so sure?" he asked. "How do you know?"

She knew, because when she had lifted her baby's still, cold body, looked at his outstretched arms, it was all wrong. The look of blue death, the feel of its stiffness, the sound of no breath in an innocent baby, was somehow repulsive, obscene. It so assaulted her senses that they shut down in defense. A sacred shroud of shock fell, severing her from the outer world, forcing her inside. She knew her son was dead, because that part of her was dead.

Gordon looked at her, and saw her certainty. He put his head on her shoulder and cried.

She and Gordon were called into the small white examining room by two nurses to hear the truth she already knew put in words. There, a black-robed priest held his hands out helplessly and said, "I'm sorry, sometimes a baby dies for no reason. It just happens and no one knows why."

The words hit her in the stomach, folding her in half. She grabbed for Gordon to keep herself from falling. From somewhere she heard a moan.

A nurse asked, "Do you want to see the baby?"

The baby? she thought. Then she remembered how he looked when she last saw him. "No, no," she said. "I can't."

She heard someone say, "Go home."

As I listened to my own child tell the story of the death of her child, I was afraid for her. I had always sworn that if something happened to my kids, I couldn't survive. Could she?

Teri didn't have my years of nursing behind her to help her understand. I had struggled with death, been steeped in human suffering. That kind of experience changed me, forced me to face my God, to face my fears, to face myself, to live my dreams. And in some way it strengthened my heart and thickened my skin. Teri had none of that. She'd had no dying patients to teach her about life. Teri and death were strangers.

I tried to take a closer look, to reassure myself. Teri did have a certain self-centeredness, a certain resiliency, a real ability to take chances and embrace change. At eighteen years old, she had torn herself away from an enmeshed Italian family to travel across the country. With only two hundred dollars, a backpack, and a bus ticket, she had moved to California on her own. She had set up home, found a job, enrolled in college, and made a life, without any external props for safety. And she was passionate about life. She felt comfortable in nature, and loved the landscape of the earth. She valued freedom and she valued intellect. But she had no time or patience for the more subtle landscape of inner worlds, or for my philosophical and metaphysical explanations. Those were very real tools I used on my inner journeys.

Now my mother-heart strained to comfort, but the only hope I could offer was "Honey, I know this isn't only a tragedy."

"Mom," she said, shaking her head with weariness, "Mom, let me tell you something. Right now, in this life, at this time, that's all it is. A tragedy. And I can't see it any other way."

"I know that, Teri," I said. "I know it's one of the most terrible things that can happen to a human being. I just don't want you to give up on life because you can't understand this yet."

"Mom," she said, "it doesn't make any sense. I always thought you had to be sick to die, to be old to die or at least to have some kind of accident. What sense does anything make when you can be healthy one minute and dead the next?"

I tried to reassure her. "Honey, a human mind can't conceive of the answers to life's mysteries. Those answers come from the heavens."

"Mom," Teri said, "that's bullshit. Platitudes. Stuff people say when they don't have the answers. It sounds like religion."

I shook my head. "Teri, it's not religion. . . ."

"I need facts now," she said, "I need concrete reasons, to understand."

"Teri," I said. "I've struggled for years with why babies get sick and die. Why good people suffer. Why life seems unfair. There are no concrete answers. I've seen wonderful little kids walking around with bald heads from chemotherapy, pushing IV poles down hospital corridors. Isn't it any comfort at all that Greggy didn't suffer?"

Teri sounded impatient when she said, "No, Mom, it isn't. This feels like shooting a perfectly healthy horse."

"Is there anything I can say that will help?" I asked, even though I knew in my heart that some hurts are too deep for words to heal.

Teri covered her eyes, shook her head, and started to cry. "The baby had a little cold, but I took him to the doctor's and got him medicine. It wasn't half as bad as the colds Jessie used to get." She looked up at me and asked, "How can I be sure I wasn't part of the cause? Try to explain it to me with medical facts. Why did Greggy die?"

I moved over and hugged her, smoothing her hair. "Honey, there are some things a heart can never understand. It's not possible. Death often feels like a failure. But *feeling* guilty and being guilty are two different things. As far as a *medical* diagnosis, my guess is he died of SIDS, sudden infant death syndrome. I've seen babies die in the nursery when all of us were watching. They couldn't be resuscitated. There was nothing you could have done," I told her.

"When I was in college," Teri said, "I read an article on SIDS. I remember thinking that the death of a baby was the most awful thing that could happen to a parent. But still," she said, "I was sure those parents had missed something. I was sure I was smarter. Now I'm not sure I didn't make a mistake. Maybe I gave the baby a little too much medicine."

"Honey," I tried to reassure her, "babies who are dropped in garbage cans live when they're supposed to and so do children who live on the streets during wars. Homeless kids who are practically starving survive and so do kids who are so handicapped, no one knows how they keep breathing. I don't believe in a random universe, so on some level I'm sure it all makes sense. For Greggy, maybe it was just time."

"Mom," she said, looking miserable, "he was only three months old. That's no time at all. It's hardly a life."

"A life can't be measured in time, baby," I told her. "If its value can be measured at all from here. It has to be measured by its effect on the lives of the people it touches."

We couldn't know it then, but behind the scenes, the karmic wheel was set in motion. Spirit was at play. One day Gregory's death would reach far across the world to touch someone to whom it would mean life itself. But that wasn't all. . . .

Chapter Two

*D*eath's ambush wakens primal memories. It forces us to our beginnings, brings us back in time. We seek the comfort of encampment, the safety of a fire to light the dark unknown. Someone to stand watch.

Italians are a tribal people, our family is our tribe. In times of grief, we gather. It's then we tell the stories, the myths that map our history, mark our journey, guide a path into the future.

The grandmothers on both sides of our family were very strong women. Risk-takers. My grandmother Catherine, a nurse and a mid-wife, drove a car, carried a gun, and got divorced before I was born. She was the only grandmother I ever knew. We lived with her until I was seven years old. She was my mother's mother, and my father loved her dearly and treated her with enormous respect. An air of mystery surrounded her, and the medical smells of birth and death clung to her white uniform like perfume. In her little black bag she carried amazing equipment she let me play with whenever we were home alone. It was through her shiny stethoscope that I first heard the fascinating rhythm of my own heartbeat. It seemed to me, as a child, that she was always involved in some big adventure, some important work, and whenever she came home to tell about it, she and my father talked long into the night. Sometimes in whispers.

My mother was devoted to her, and so was I. She was playful and eccentric, could anger as quickly as she could laugh, brought home friends of different colors, and was in all ways authentic. She was generous to a fault. I watched one afternoon as she took a pair of curtains off the kitchen window and right on the spot gave them to a friend just because she had admired them.

My sister and my cousins were afraid of her. They thought she was harsh and scary because she yelled so much, but I knew she wouldn't hurt me. I knew she loved me. Even when she chased me around the table with a broom because I was "fresh," I knew she would always give me time to hide before she whacked it against the table. She never talked to me as though I was a child, and answered all my questions frankly. Some things she told me would have made my mother faint, but I felt completely safe with her.

I was seven years old when she went to the hospital because she had a lump in her breast and had to have an operation. That day, before she left, she told me she wouldn't be back. She said that was a secret, our secret.

I didn't understand that she knew she was going to die. At seven, I thought it was "our secret" that killed her. Different people took care of me because my mother was so grief stricken that she locked herself in a room. I wasn't allowed in. Sometimes I'd sit outside her door, leaning with my ear against it, and listen to her crying. For the first time ever, my father spoke little to me.

I was furious then, angry at my grandmother for leaving *me*, angry at my parents for not making her stay. I was mad at God and even madder at the Blessed Mother. I smashed my statue of her and cracked her golden halo.

No one ever talked to me about my grandmother's death and I never saw her dead, so I didn't believe she was really gone. For years afterward I would catch sight of her walking along the street in her nurse's uniform. I'd chase after her, calling, until some other woman turned and I could see it wasn't my grandmother. I dreamed about her often and woke up shaking and sad. I'm convinced that one of the reasons I loved nursing so much was because of her: Each time I helped someone stay alive, I pretended it was my grandmother.

The mythology of our family, retold at every holiday dinner, included stories of very strong women, and from them I got my sense of self. One of my grandmothers was a pathfinder, and the other a pioneer.

My grandmother Justine, my father's mother, was always spoken about with a mixture of reverence and trepidation. She was born on the island of Sardinia, in Italy. She was very beautiful, and when she was only sixteen she married a man thirty years older. They had seven children.

Justine's husband, my grandfather, a village elder and the local judge, was known as Honest John Anthony. He was renowned throughout the surrounding areas for his compassion as well as his honesty. My aunt and all my uncles told us stories about him.

Once, a thief who had stolen a lamb from a rich village farmer was brought before Honest John to receive sentence. The thief explained that he was poor, and had stolen the lamb to feed his wife and children.

Honest John ordered the rich farmer to share the lamb with the poor villager and his family, because in a village where there was food, no one should go hungry. In return, the poor man was to work for the farmer. In order to prevent this from happening again, in the future the poor man would go to the farmer and offer to work his land. The farmer would then pay his wage with the food his family needed.

Like Honest John, most of the men on my father's side were strong, heroic, and caring. They were supportive and inspiring. Her husband, the judge, taught my grandmother Justine to read when no other woman in their village could. It was because of his belief in her, as much as her own will and vision, that when he died, she had the courage to take a boat to America. He taught her to stand as strong in the world of men as she did in the world of women. When she couldn't afford to take all her children, she had to choose three. With them she ventured forth into a strange and unknown world to start a new life.

Justine's youngest daughter, Josie, was only six years old when she battled with her older sister for the right to come to America. She insisted she be one of her mother's chosen children. She cried day and night for weeks and threatened to run away if her mother left her in Sardinia. Eventually Justine relented. She left her older daughter—whom she'd counted on to help—and took Josie instead.

But Justine died when Josie was just fifteen, and she was left to raise her younger brothers, Tony and Tommy, my father. It was Josie, little more than a child herself, who had to guide them through the traps and tragedies of the new world. She married early to support them, and give them a home, while she waited patiently for her oldest brother, Jimmy, to come to America to help. She sacrificed her own desire for an education for her mother's dream. To repay Justine for bringing her, Josie felt it was her responsibility not only to keep her brothers alive, but to make the dream come true.

Once her brothers were grown and had families of their own, it was to Aunt Josie's house that the extended family went each week to share an elaborate Sunday dinner. Aunt Josie, my mother, and my other aunts spent hours, starting early in the morning, cooking spaghetti sauce, huge roasts, and vegetables.

Aunt Josie's long dining room table was covered with a starched white tablecloth and dotted with several raffia-wrapped green glass jugs of Chianti wine. The large platter of antipasto was set out as soon as we arrived. Rolled prosciutto and salami alongside crisp stalks of fennel were complemented by chunks of provolone cheese. Long loaves of Italian bread overflowing their wicker baskets adorned the table. I remember the smell of the spaghetti sauce as Barbara and I eagerly ran to Aunt Josie's house after church each week. There, with my father's brothers and their families, my sister and I spent some of the happiest times of our early life. Our aunts and uncles doted on us, and we had cousins to play with. Aunt Josie's daughter, Rosemarie, was my favorite, and as we grew we stayed as close as sisters. Uncle Jimmy, my father's oldest brother, always brought several boxes of delicate Italian pastries, told us jokes, and gave out dollar bills to all the kids before we went back home. After dinner my uncle Paul, Aunt Josie's husband, pulled out his guitar to strum and sing Italian folk songs while all of us danced.

From the time I was a very small child, I understood that no one in our family had an easy life. All had "troubles," all worked hard, but each had struggled through adversity, even tragedy, to reach a personal victory. My father always said that ours was a pioneer lineage, bred for more than survival.

These were the ancestors whose blood coursed through our veins, whose will beat in our hearts. Their lives and the way they lived them held the promise of hope and victory for those of us who followed. Their courage and endurance were our legacy. Now I hoped Teri could draw on that heritage to find what she needed to survive.

When Teri and I came out of my study that day, the house was still full of people. Across the living room, Aunt Josie sat with her arm around my mother.

Even though it was many years later, Aunt Josie was still the matriarch of our family, still a warrior and a dream keeper. Her curling gray hair capped a lively intelligence and clever wit, but now, as she looked at Teri, her dark eyes shone with compassion.

Teri walked over to hug her.

"You'll be okay," Aunt Josie comforted, "you will."

Then, like a sacred tribal council, my aunt, my mother, and I went to sit with Teri around the dining room table. Aunt Josie was telling Teri, "Did you know that your great-grandmother Justine had a baby who died? And my own little Johnny died of meningitis when he was just a baby? In your mother's generation, her cousin lost a child. Remember?"

Teri nodded.

Aunt Josie continued. "In each generation, one of us has had to give up a child, a beautiful, wonderful child. And each of us has survived. Gregory was a beautiful little angel and nothing will replace him. But you will go on living."

Teri began to cry. "How, Aunt Josie? How?"

My aunt reached over to hold Teri's hand. She looked deep into her eyes. "You breathe. You just breathe. You put one foot in front of the other, and in each moment, you walk. You try to eat a little bit every day. You sleep whenever you can. The day will end. The night will come. And time will pass."

"Time?" Teri repeated.

Aunt Josie sat erect. "There's nothing else to do. You just wait for time to heal you. And you remember, you're not alone."

While Aunt Josie spoke, I looked across the table at my mother, but I couldn't look too long. She was Teri's other mother, had shared the care of her from the time she was a child. Now to see her pain was to stare directly at my own.

I had asked Teri earlier how my mother reacted when she found out. Teri had shaken her head and explained. "For the first few minutes I was sure we had lost her. She wailed and screamed and grabbed her heart. I thought she was going to have a heart attack. She cried, 'My baby . . . my baby . . . ' That cry echoed through the house so loudly, it seemed to move the walls. Danny and I actually hid in the bathroom. Then I heard Poppy telling her to stop, telling her that she was upsetting me. But it was strange, Mom, as long as Grandma was screaming, I didn't feel any pain."

My mind shifted to those ancient medicine women and shamans, those healers who healed by taking on the pain of another. And I wondered how often, over the centuries, grandmothers, mothers, and all those old women who had experienced life had taken on the pain of the younger ones.

I understood then that those screams were not screams of hysteria; they were the cries of mercy, compassion, and of strength. Those screams of old women were the songs of survival that carried their children toward healing.

Now Aunt Josie asked Teri about a funeral. When and where would it be?

Teri's whole body stiffened. "I don't want a wake. I don't want a funeral. I want Gregory cremated. Gordon and I want him thrown back to the wind," she said.

My mother objected. It wasn't a Catholic objection, not religious at all, it was strictly personal. She wanted ritual. Some prayers to ease the journey. A time to say good-bye. "Poppy and I will buy the casket. We'll have a service first. We can't just do nothing," she said as she wiped tears from her eyes.

Teri was quiet for only a moment before she said, "Gordon and I don't need a funeral for Greggy, Gram. We don't want Greggy buried, because if we ever move away, we don't want to feel as though we've left him behind. But you and Poppy can have a service if that's what you need. And for anyone else who wants to go." In our family we had learned that we didn't have to agree with each other, but we did have to honor what each of us needed.

My sister Barbara tentatively pulled up a chair next to Teri and joined us. She gently stroked Teri's back.

"Do you want to come to Greggy's funeral with us?" my mother asked her. Barbara's eyes filled. "I don't think I can," she said. And as quickly as she had appeared, she disappeared.

Then Jessie came in, walking softly toward her mother. She placed her head against Teri's shoulder. "Can we sleep at Mama Carol's tonight?" she asked.

"Yes, baby," Teri said, patting Jessie's hair as tears ran down her cheeks. "Yes, Jessie," she repeated.

Jessie looked up at her, stared into her eyes. "I love you, Mommy," she said. And then walked back inside to play with Jennifer again.

Teri looked incredibly sad. "What will this do to Jessie?"

My father had been pacing back and forth silently, walking from one side of the house to the other. Now, as he passed the table and heard Teri, he stopped, put his hand on her shoulder. "She'll be fine, Teri," he said, his voice hoarse with grief. "Jessie's special and she's a survivor. She'll be fine." But there was no conviction in his voice.

"Pop," she said, "she's not even three years old. She was crazy about that baby. How can she learn to trust again? How will she ever stop being afraid?"

My father raised his handkerchief to his eyes, shook his head, and swallowed hard. Again, he couldn't speak.

Aunt Josie frowned as she looked up at her younger brother, my father. She said something sharp, scolded him in Italian. I didn't understand the words, but she called him Octavio instead of Tommy, a name he hadn't used since they left Sardinia.

Then Aunt Josie looked directly at me. And the message I read in her eyes was more powerful than any words. At that moment, as clearly as in a relay race, I felt her pass the family stick. I nodded now, acknowledged it, accepted. Finally she said with authority, "Don't worry, Teri. We'll all help Jessie. We're a family."

Our family was the rich and fertile soil that nourished the individual saplings planted within it. Each of us took from it what we needed to survive and grow. Each was separate and unique, but together we became more than any of us alone. From those roots, each developed a sturdy trunk, then branched out in new directions, always understanding and trusting that we were deeply imbedded and strongly supported. The only threat that could cause real devastation and shake us to our roots was a natural disaster, an act of God. In that solid ground of family, the death of a child was a violent earthquake. Which of us would remain standing? Which of us would fall?

Each generation prepares the next, carries the heritage forward in time.

That day at the table, when my father had no words to give comfort or strength, Aunt Josie had looked to me. And I understood that my whole life had been lived in preparation for this time of family need.

For as long as I can remember, my father's wish was to be a beacon, a light to guide his family through the stormy seas of life. He brought from his Sardinian heritage a passionate vitality, an unending optimism and the ability to truly find joy in his world. He always acknowledged his Italian legacy, but thought of himself as an American, having arrived on Ellis Island when he was only two years old. He had a wonderful sense of humor and an insatiable curiosity. He valued intelligence and reasonableness above all else but goodness and, in his heart, I believe, he was more a philosopher than a religious man.

Each evening at the dinner table when I was growing up, as Mother served the meal she had spent the afternoon carefully preparing, my father would begin to quote or read from his gold-trimmed leather-bound Harvard Classics. Those books were a gift from a rich patron of a New York City hotel, where he worked as a bellboy when he was very young. It was at that same hotel, from their international clientele, that my father learned to speak six languages fluently. English, French, Italian (high Italian, not Sardinian), Greek, Portuguese, and Spanish. A parish priest from his neighborhood on the Lower East Side of New York taught him Latin when he was an altar boy.

From my father I inherited optimism and curiosity, his love of language, his competitive nature, his need for control, and his love of mastery. At nine years old I won a Catholic school contest by answering the question "Who is the wisest man you know?"

My answer, taken from a discussion on Plato we'd had at the table a few nights before, was "The wisest man knows enough to know he knows nothing." That was it. The whole paper.

When I told my father I'd won, he threw his head back and laughed with pure joy. I could feel his pride in me, his love for me. After we'd finished dinner and mother brought him his usual espresso coffee, he peeled the skin off an apple all in one piece, then sliced it, offering each of us a section before he ate his. For the next few hours he read Aristotle aloud while Mother and Barbara cleared off the table, washed the dishes, and cleaned the kitchen. Most of the time I sat rapt, listening. Occasionally I attempted to take the dish towel and dry a dish, but I never took my eyes off my father. Even then I was aware that my major contribution was to respond with interest and questions to any marvelous concept that sprang from those books through the lips of my father. It was an interesting and exciting time.

One evening, my father was telling me about the Talmud, how a Jewish father and his son could examine, interpret, and argue the meaning of the law, the rules for living, volleying ideas back and forth, analyzing, making hair-splitting distinctions over the text. I so loved that play of the mind that it was the only time I remember wanting with all my heart to be a boy, to be my father's son, not his daughter. It never occurred to me that even if I were a boy, we wouldn't argue the Talmud because we weren't Jewish.

I was only four when my father first took me fishing, over the tears and protestations of my worried mother. "She'll fall in the water," my mother cried.

My father reassured her. "I'll tie us together."

It was on those dim-lit mornings on a charter boat, with a rope around my waist and tied to his belt, that my father taught me how to bait a hook, catch a fish and kiss it, to thank it once I had pulled it in.

I practiced being brave and built up some of the emotional muscle that later helped me get through my clinical nursing training on those mornings as I learned to scale and clean a fish, and on other mornings, as I learned to gut freshly killed pheasant, squirrels, and rabbits.

My father also hunted deer. But part of his sacred contract with nature was that we would eat whatever he'd brought home. He felt that an animal who'd offered himself deserved at least that. Animals could not be killed for sport. Though my mother refused to eat small game and venison, in the spirit of camaraderie Barbara and I learned to eat it, thank it, and even enjoy it so my father could be forgiven for killing it.

But no picture of my relationship with my father would be complete without the precious memories filled with passionate opera music and dancing. Before I could even walk, he would place my small feet on his own and dance with me across the living room floor. Later, when I was older, and could move my own feet, we danced a mean polka. There was no car trip we took where we didn't sing, my father doing melody from the front seat, Barbara and I singing harmony from the back. We made some pretty good music together.

My mother was shyer, quieter, much more traditional. And she was goodness to the bone. She was a perfect wife for an extroverted Italian man of his generation. Most of what she did was to please him, to serve him, to nurture her children. She cooked delicious meals, was an immaculate housekeeper, and enjoyed her life within the family. She had a deeper sense of religion than he did, a stronger commitment to both conformity and Catholicism. She was dedicated to keeping us happy and together. Though she had loved and admired her own mother, she had suffered from her mother's independence and divorce. She didn't want a broken home for her own children. So she sacrificed herself . . . and often let me know it.

I loved her and depended on her tremendously, trusted her strong and steady support, but it didn't keep me from plaguing her with questions, competing for my father's attention, and pushing her limits while testing my own. I often drove her crazy. She was much less combative than I was, until I backed her into a corner. Then she threw whatever she held in her hand at me, whether it be a Melmac dish or a hard, shiny apple, and often hit her target. Still, she could never win, because whether she won or lost with me, she felt bad. I was her daughter, and she hated to hurt me. It was years later, after I had really grown up, that I began to understand what that poor woman had gone through having to deal with both my father and me.

But the universe is good. It balances. Her gift was my sister Barbara. Four years younger than me with lighter hair and a pleasant, easygoing disposition, Barbara was never a troublemaker. She required little attention, was loving and cheerful and content with life as it was. She was the good sister, the gentle sister, who kept my mother company. She loved to cook, to dress up, to help my mother in the kitchen. She loved my father with all her heart, but had no patience for Plato or Aristotle. She seldom asked the question "why?" She had no desire to be a boy, and would have hated to argue the Talmud.

Once my grandmother Catherine died, we moved from Queens to Long Island. Barbara and I shared an upstairs bedroom in our new house. At night before we fell asleep we also shared our secrets and whispered our different dreams into the dark.

On the nights that I'd done something wrong, committed some childish misdeed, I'd have to stay awake until my father got home to mete out my punishment. Then he'd come upstairs, kiss us both, and explain to me what I'd done, to make sure I understood. He never reproached me and he never insulted me. He simply explained. And he always took several minutes in which he sat in silence to consider fair punishment.

Sometimes the punishment was a strapping. I understood I was expected not to cry out. I was taught never to allow pain to weaken my resolve or break my spirit. I was reminded of the Spartan youths, trained to be outstanding warriors. When my father was sure he wasn't angry, because he felt emotion had no place in discipline, he took off his belt.

I never allowed myself my tears. Because Spartan youths didn't. But Barbara cried those tears I couldn't. She honored my pain in a way I didn't. And all my father's talks of Spartan courage couldn't sway my sister one little bit. She had her own strong and silent resolve.

Afterward, when my father had gone back downstairs to console my mother, now feeling terrible because I'd been hit, I'd walk the space between our beds and climb into bed with Barbara. "Why do you make him do that?" she'd ask in her small, hurt voice. "Why do you always fight with Mommy?"

I'd shrug into the night. "I don't know," I'd admit.

"I always say yes to both of them," she'd explain without excuse. "I always try to do what they want. But if I can't, I do what I want. I just don't tell them always."

"I can't sneak," I'd tell her. "There's no honor in it. And I have a right to say what I feel."

"Can't you just not answer back?" she'd whisper.

I'd answer fervently. "I can't give in. I'm fighting for our *rights!*"

"Not my rights. I don't feel like that," she'd say as she sighed. Then she'd put an arm around me in the dark. "I hate when you fight with them. When Mommy cries, and Daddy has to hit you. I hate when he hurts you."

"It didn't hurt that bad," I'd say. And after a while it didn't.

I never felt like a child; in fact, I felt old for as long as I could remember. But I believe Barbara enjoyed every minute of her childhood. All these years later, the picture that stays brightest in my mind is a day when she was six years old. I was taking care of her because my mother was at work.

I was sitting under a tree with my nose buried in a book, and I wouldn't play with her. She looked disappointed, but for only a minute, and then she wandered to the middle of the lawn to play by herself. After a few minutes sitting, studying the grass, she stood up and began to spin around and around. Her head was thrown back, her arms were outstretched, and the sun was making her blond hair sparkle. As I watched, she started to laugh, and it was such a joyful, happy sound, so full and so free that it made my heart soar. I could never let myself go with such joyful abandon. I could never play like that. But I knew she felt safe, I knew she felt loved, I knew she felt free and I believed all of it had something to do with me.

When I left home at seventeen to get married, it was Barbara I missed the most. As soon as possible after I married, I wanted to start a family and have a baby of my own. I wanted someone to take care of, to play with, to connect to. My pregnancy was wonderful and I felt more creative and alive than ever. I talked to the baby within me, reading her stories, telling her secrets and before she was even born, I knew her name was Teri. At night before I fell asleep, I'd share my hopes and tell her about all the possibilities for her life in the limitless world. When she was three months old, I'd sit her in an infant seat alongside me on the couch, and we'd sip tea together from our favorite cup. Even as a very small baby Teri looked bright and as interested as I was in the soap operas and documentaries that we watched religiously each day.

As I had grown, so had my curiosity about everything in the world. But the prince that I married never imagined a princess like me. Away from my family, far from the castle, whenever I tried to analyze, discuss, or interpret the things that he said, he thought I was fighting with him, thought I was challenging him, thought I didn't love him.

Thinking more children would make me less lonely, I decided to have another baby. This time I had a baby boy, Danny. Still, I couldn't find my place, I couldn't feel my passions. I wanted more. I needed more. It wasn't until many years later that I found out what my mother had known all along: that having my children and caring for them was one of the most important things I'd ever do.

When my marriage dissolved into nothing but tears, fury, and misery for all of us, I called my father collect and asked if we could come home. I needed to get back to safety, to regroup, to gather myself together. I had to reassess my strengths and my weaknesses in order to find a new direction.

It didn't take long before I knew I wanted to be a nurse. My grandmother was one of my inspirations, Florence Nightingale another, and from my own mother I'd inherited warmth, compassion, and the need to serve. Those tools and the sharper ones I'd gotten from my father prepared me for what would eventually be one of the greatest passions of my life. Nursing.

While I went to school, my mother cared for my children. And she prayed for them. She remembered her own childhood pain from her own broken home and she saw it for years in the eyes of my children. She was heartbroken over the breakup of my marriage.

My father, on the other hand, was not as heartbroken. He had new children to teach and read to, to play and explore with. More children to guide. He became Teri's father as much as mine, though he treated her more gently. He offered her the best of himself, leaving the discipline and limit setting to me. He took her for long walks through the woods, explaining to her the marvels of the animal kingdom and nature. She was a willing and enthusiastic student. My father and my daughter explored the world of nature with the same intensity that he and I had explored the world of ideas. Often he'd walked with her around the neighborhood, greeting his friends, engaging them in laughter and conversation. He made Teri's outer world as safe and exciting as he had made my inner worlds.

When I graduated and got my first job in a hospital, the kids and I moved out of my parents' house but stayed in the same town. And now my father loved having a son in my son. As soon as Danny was old enough, they went hunting and fishing. He taught Danny to clean a fish and gut small game, to find his way through the woods with the talent of an Indian scout. Over time, he helped my boy become a man. He was tougher on Danny than on Teri, but never as tough as he had been on me.

Barbara married a soldier and moved away, but when she had her first baby, Jennifer, her husband was sent overseas. She flew home to live with my parents. We were a whole family again. Later, when her husband was discharged, they bought a house near us and she had another baby, Christopher. So our kids grew up together and stayed very close.

When Teri married, she too moved back from California to Long Island, and my father and mother welcomed her husband, Gordon, as another son. Gordon, Danny, and my father began going hunting. Our family kept growing.

But it was with Jessie's birth that the cycle seemed to begin again. I don't know who knew it first, maybe my father, maybe Teri or my mother. Probably it was Barbara who noticed that Jessie was more like me than anyone else. She needed more attention than any of the other kids, was sharp and willful and loved words with a passion. She began to speak when she was only seven months old and later would look at pages of text in a book without any pictures for hours. She hated anyone telling her what to do and was always fighting for her rights. From the time Gregory was born, Jessica had helped feed him, dress him, thought of him as hers. She really loved her baby brother. What would she do without Greggy? What would I have done without Barbara?

That night after everyone left, Teri, Gordon, Jessie, and Danny grabbed some blankets and pillows and scattered themselves on my living room floor. I stood watch until they fell asleep.

Then I went into my study to call Mario. He was another man who valued intelligence and reasonableness above all else but goodness. And he understood that when he said something and I countered with hair-splitting distinctions, I was moving toward him, not competing with him. I'd finally met someone who could see that for me, mind play was a way of making love. The bonus was that he was also gentle and kind, and he had an Italian family of his own. It wasn't exactly a traditional fairy-tale ending, but we had been living happily ever after for years now, just in separate castles.

When Mario answered, the sound of his voice alone was a comfort to me. "How's Teri?" he asked. "And you?"

"She's better than I would be for now," I admitted. "And I don't know how I am because most of my energy is tied up worrying about everyone else."

"How's your father?" Mario asked then.

"I don't know that either," I answered. "He's not really talking."

"Honey, sometimes there are no words to say, especially for a man," he said. "Women are stronger in these situations. They understand life's mysteries better."

"I don't," I said. "I mean, my mind knows but my heart's having a real hard time catching up."

Mario sighed. "I wish I could help in some way," he said. "Is there anything you need?"

"Just say it will be all right. That's all I need to hear."

But he hesitated for too long and he didn't say it with conviction. "Do you want me to come back?" he asked then.

"No," I said. "Not yet."

Later, alone in my bedroom, I stood in front of my favorite statues, arranged in a semicircle on my black teak dresser. A beautiful bone china figurine of the Blessed Virgin draped in a light blue shawl stood at the center—a remnant of my Catholic childhood. She had been a mother in the best sense. I never could have stood aside as she did while fate crucified a child of mine.

Now I silently asked for her ability to surrender.

Next was a black obsidian mother goddess that I had bought from a Mexican holy man who stood between the sun and the moon pyramids. She held a child and was a reminder of an earlier time, when death brought blessings and birth brought tears.

I asked for her simple but profound acceptance of life.

Standing watch was the largest and most precious statue I owned. A graceful guardian angel with flowing pink porcelain robes, her outspread wings protecting one small child, her outstretched hands holding a small bird.

Suddenly my eyes filled and I began to cry. That little bird reminded me of Greggy. And the small child . . . Teri.

Please help me, I prayed now with all my heart, *I can't protect her any longer. I can't fly high enough to see the meaning in her pain. Please help her through the darkness that will follow, and, if possible, please help me to understand.*

The following morning Gordon's mother arrived from California. Dakin had been divorced for many years, and no one ever heard from Gordon's father. Gordon had two brothers with whom he was very close. The oldest, Chan, was away on business and couldn't return in time, and Doug was a soil scientist mapping unexplored territory in Nevada, so he couldn't be reached.

That morning, family and friends were again milling around my house, setting out food, sitting in clusters, speaking in whispers. Teri had gone into my room to talk to Gordon and I was sitting on my couch in the living room, watching Jessie. Barbara had dressed her in a short purple floral dress and had put a matching purple headband on her wispy blond hair. She was kneeling on the carpet, leaning forward on my coffee table, head bowed low, as she carefully colored a picture of Snow White.

When Dakin walked in, and Jessie first saw her, she frowned and asked, "Gramma Dakin, how come you're here?"

Dakin's short blond hair was messy, her blue eyes rimmed with red from crying. But her voice was controlled and falsely calm when she said, "I came to read you stories and to play with you."

Jessie stared at her in disbelief, then she looked at me. She shrugged her shoulders and asked Dakin, "Did you know that my brother baby got sick and died yesterday?"

Dakin began to cry.

Jessica lowered her eyes. Then she stood up, reached for Dakin's hand, and said, "You can read to me. I'll play with you."

Gregory's funeral service was planned for that afternoon. Danny had been glued to Gordon's side, but now that Dakin had come, Danny wanted to go home to shower and change his clothes.

"Pick up some cold cuts on the way back?" I asked him.

"Sure," Danny said. "Anything else?"

"Rolls," I said. Then I asked him, "Are you going to the service with Gram and Poppy?"

"Are you?" he asked me.

"No," I said. "Teri wants to go back to her house to pack away some of Greggy's things. She wants some time alone to stand in his room and just think about him. I want to go with her."

"Will Gordon be there?" Danny asked.

I shook my head. "No," I said. "They wanted to go separately. He's at the house now with Dakin. They're watching the video of Greggy that Gordon took last week." When he looked puzzled, I explained. "He needs to get the picture of the dead Gregory out of his head. Watching pictures of the live Gregory might help."

Gordon's last image of his baby, stiff, blue, and motionless, had embedded itself in his mind. He couldn't erase it. He needed another image, his pink, smiling, moving baby, to emblazon over the other.

Danny stood quietly a few minutes, then said, "If you're not going, then I better go to the funeral parlor with Gram and Poppy. In case they need me. What about Aunt Barbara, is she going?"

"I don't know," I said. "Maybe if she knows you'll be there, she will."

Danny walked over to talk to my sister, then left to get into his suit for the service.

Later, in the bathroom, when I was getting ready to go with Teri, I found myself wondering what comfort I could offer her as she went into her baby's room to face his empty crib, for the first time.

Stalling, I absently pulled up the blinds and stared out the small bathroom window. It had snowed hard again the night before, and drifts of snow had built bunkers around the bushes in my yard. A bitter winter wind still blew a powder of light snow. I watched as my nephew Christopher lifted his sled out of the shed and pulled it toward the street. The ground looked hard as ice. No place for a baby, I thought, and was glad that Greggy wouldn't be buried, grateful he would be cremated.

But suddenly my mind played a trick on me. In the hard bitter wind, the snow-covered branches of the tall trees came alive. They waved now like the bandaged limbs of all the children I'd cared for on the burn unit. Images of those children flooded my brain. The smell of their burned flesh sneaked up my nose, the sound of their screams echoed in my ears, the feel of their skin as it stuck to my fingers, took me right back.

Fear grabbed my thoughts and filled them with illusion. How could I let them cremate Greggy? How did I know he was really dead? I hadn't seen him dead. How could I be sure? My body began to shake uncontrollably.

"Mom," I heard Teri call through the closed bathroom door. "I'm ready."

"I'll be out in a minute," I told her through chattering teeth.

Frantically I looked around. I had to pull myself together. She couldn't see me like this. It would make her crazy.

I turned the shower on full blast and jumped in, clothes and all. The warm water pounded my face and my body. I told myself over and over again that Gregory was dead. And for the first time, I cried. Really cried.

Then I tried to pull myself together. I tried to reassure myself. Teri said she *knew*, even before she walked into his room, she *knew*. When she lifted that baby, stiff and cold, she finally understood that there was more to a person than just a body. Some unseen life-force: call it energy, call it soul, call it spirit. She said she could feel it was missing, that her baby was gone, only his body left behind. Now, I reasoned, even if I didn't trust hospitals, even if a doctor could make a mistake, even if I hadn't seen Greggy myself, I did trust Teri. She had never seen death before, but what she described was no impostor.

During all my years of nursing, I had studied the stages of dying and grieving. Those concepts had captured my attention from the very beginning of my career. Dr. Elisabeth Kübler-Ross, who first described them, was one of my heroines. I knew those five stages like I knew my five fingers: denial, bargaining, anger, depression, and, finally, acceptance. I recognized each stage my patients and their families were in, and that helped me to help them.

But though I knew what those stages looked like, until that day I never had a clue how they felt. Because if I had really accepted the fact that Gregory was dead, I would have known that nothing would happen to him that afternoon. I would have understood that later, a baby body would be cremated, but the essence of that baby we called Gregory was already safe somewhere else.

I drove. Outside their small house I hung back to let Teri walk ahead of me, to let her pace herself. At the front door she fumbled with the key, already seemed upset.

Inside, the door to the baby's room was shut. Gordon must have closed it. Teri walked past it into the living room. She sat in her favorite chair. The one in which she always used to rock Gregory. I sat across from her on the couch. She took a deep breath, seemed to be bracing herself against the emotions she knew would come. When she looked around, she shook her head. "You know, Mom, I was sure I'd hate this house now. But I don't."

She and Gordon had saved every cent they could in order to buy this house before Gregory was born. It was special to them. They had struggled hard and raced with time to have it ready when the baby came home. His room was the first one behind the front door. They had painted it robin's egg blue, put colorful stencils on the walls, and bought all new furniture.

After a few moments of sitting with neither of us saying a word, Teri announced, "I better go in now."

"Do you want to be alone?" I asked.

"No," she said. "Come with me."

Teri opened the door slowly, tentatively, as though she expected something to come flying out of the room. I stayed close behind her as we walked inside. There was a coffee cup still standing on Gregory's white diaper changer, coffee spilled down the side. Now Teri walked toward the far wall, past the crib, her eyes averted, and she stared at a silk screen of a colorful clown. He was holding red, blue, and yellow balloons in one hand and multicolored wildflowers in the other. "Greggy loved that picture," she said, smiling. "He used to goo at it for hours."

Teri began to cry as she walked across the room back to the wooden crib. She reached down to pick up the baby's soft yellow checkered quilt, still crumpled from being tossed aside that terrible morning. She held it to her face and took a deep breath. "Baby powder," she said. Then, looking at me she added softly, "Baby powder and death. It's a lousy combination."

Teri was still carrying the quilt as she walked back out into the living room. This time she sat in the chair with her back to Greggy's room, still holding his quilt against her cheek. She leaned back, rocking, and closed her eyes.

I sat and looked at her, the brave, gentle child of my heart, while a thousand thoughts raced through my mind and as many pictures appeared before my eyes. Teri wore the same expression of sadness now that I first saw on her face when she was only three. . . .

It was the morning her father left. I was very young and so was he when we had gotten married, with such big hopes and dreams for the "happily ever after." Four years later we were arguing constantly. I was tired of his drinking and he was tired of my nagging. No matter how hard we tried, there seemed to be no solution except to split.

So Teri woke up that morning and knew in her heart that her father had gone. As a baby she had always been more his child than mine. She looked more like him, was as gentle and as fiercely self-contained. She was daddy's little girl, and they were crazy about each other. But when he left, he moved to another state and there were no more of his strong hugs, his gentle laughs, or his funny stories. The relationship she'd had with him was lost. And for that child of three it was a devastating loss.

As I grew older and realized what our decision cost her, that cost multiplied my own. I had lost a husband, a lover, and a dream, but for Teri, the loss of her father was the loss of her smile. Every picture in my album, every picture in my head, was a testament to that loss. It seemed I never saw her smile again until she was a teenager, when she began to have some freedom, and feel the comfort of her many friends. She didn't begin to really laugh again until she took off for California, married Gordon, and brought Jessie home. Since then she smiled a lot; she laughed a lot. Until now.

Watching her sit there, hugging her baby's quilt, spun me back to another time. When she was six years old. I could almost hear our voices. . . .

Teri, dressed in her green and black plaid uniform, had just come running into my bedroom from school, cheeks red with excitement, dark hair in braids. "What's the best gift you can give someone?" she asked me.

I was still in bed, half asleep, having worked the night before, and without hesitation I told her, "The one you love the most."

"Okay," she said resolutely, "thanks, Mommy."

That night when Teri, Danny, and I were sitting at the table having dinner, I asked her, "Was that a trick question you asked me when you came home from school?"

She looked at me, her dark eyes fervent, and explained. "Sister Angela showed us pictures of poor kids in an orphanage. In Africa. They have no parents and no toys. We have to send them toys."

"Not my toys," Danny had said as fervently. "I like my toys."

Teri wrinkled her nose and made a face at him. "I wouldn't touch your toys. Those kids wouldn't even want them. I'm giving them one of mine."

Between cutting pot roast and spooning mashed potatoes, I asked, "Which toy are you going to bring in?"

"My favorite," she told me, looking thoughtful. "The one I love the most."

"Why don't you give them one you don't even like if they have no toys?" Danny said, with four-year-old practicality.

"Because," she said sincerely, "the best gift to give away is the one you love the most."

That night Teri and I were very excited about the idea of doing a good deed, making some poor children happy, and giving away something more. We were heady with purpose, warmed by our feelings of virtue. This stuff builds character, I thought.

But the following morning, when Teri came down the stairs for breakfast, I was stunned. Behind her she was dragging her big stuffed tiger, Stripes.

"I'm going to give them Stripes," she said simply.

Stripes was the tiger her father had given her the Christmas before he left. She loved that tiger. She slept with him, sat on him as she watched TV, talked to him.

"Are you sure that's what you want to do?" I asked, having second thoughts. I wasn't sure *I* could live without Stripes.

Danny looked up from the couch, eyes still clouded with sleep, and said, "Maybe we should keep Stripes and you could give them my new teddy bear. I don't love it that much yet."

Teri smiled at him and then shook her head. "I think Stripes will make them happy," she said.

I drove her to school that day. Within seconds the other kids were all over Stripes. Teri turned to me long enough to say, "You were right, Mommy. Stripes is the best gift of all."

Three weeks later we got the picture from Sister Angela. It was Stripes, surrounded by a crowd of small African children, their arms wrapped around him, big smiles on their faces. "Do you still feel okay about giving him away?" I asked Teri.

She shrugged and smiled wistfully. "They sure do look happy," she said, "I wanted them to be happy." But then she looked at me and added, "You know, Mommy, I really did love Stripes best in the world."

Now, watching Teri so many years later, I wondered, Why would I have taught that kind of sacrifice to such a small child? What could that sacrifice add to the gift? Suddenly I heard my father's voice, an old tape playing in my mind. Moses had stone tablets; my father's rules were etched in deerskin. This one was the Teaching of the Giveaway. A Native American ceremony, an ancient tradition that put the *sacred* into sacrifice: to give another something of value from the heart would bless the giver with a gift from the Great Spirit. My father looked Italian, could speak Italian, but when he wasn't being a Greek philosopher, he had the consciousness of an old Indian.

Now, sitting in Teri's living room, watching the pain and confusion drawn on her face, I asked myself, What happens to a heart that's been broken too often?

Teri's eyes were still closed as I got up quietly and walked back into Gregory's room. I stood next to his crib, both hands resting on the wooden rail. I stared down at the sheet, covered with happy scenes of small brown bears playing. Then I tried to *"see"* what had happened. I tried to *sense* any struggle. I had stood, over the years, just like this, at the bedsides of my patients who had just died, and had often been able to hear what they were saying, sense what they were feeling. It had always been a comfort.

Now I closed my eyes and silently asked, "Greggy, what happened?" but even before my question was completely formed, I *sensed* something. A soaring bird, a child laughing, small feet running fast and carefree through a flower-filled field. Then I heard a clear child's voice, a musical voice singing, "I'm *free*, Grandma, I'm *free.*"

And for just one moment I could feel that freedom like a warm wind blowing across my face. I opened my eyes slowly. No one else around. It had to be Greggy. No one else would call me Grandma.

How many years had I tried to deny that I could see and hear things others could not? Working as a nurse, in a system ruled by a medical model of mental health, I had bought the labels psychiatrists used to cage their patients, and tried to pin them on myself. Eventually my patients taught me better. Because they trusted me, I learned to trust myself.

They knew I loved to talk to them, and I loved to listen. I loved to lift their burdens and make them smile. Years of taking care of them, doing for them what they couldn't do themselves, gave me a new and different sense of myself, a sense of worth, of value.

Most of the time I worked at night. Days, I slept. In the beginning, surrounded by green walls, white uniforms, dimmed lights, and hushed voices, my senses starved. There were no sunny days, no music, no laughter.

As my skills improved, I cared for sicker patients. In time, my eyes began to burn with the sight of physical decay, my ears began to ring with the sound of people's suffering, and my hands grew numb from the touch of sore and rotting flesh. My heart grew heavy as my work grew more difficult. So with my physical senses gloved by my defenses, I had to touch them heart to heart, not always hand to hand.

Later, as I worked with those in coma, those dying, I spent my nights in the still, stark place of silence. I had to learn to talk a different language; I had to learn to listen deeper. While I washed and turned those bodies stiff as stone, I whispered comfort, told my stories, sang some lullabies. Eventually those I loved talked back to me. Not in words now, not with hearts now, but soul to soul. Finally I could see that there was a special kind of beauty in healing. Even when that healing was called death.

Knowing that, I wrapped the bodies of the newly dead with care, sang them traveling songs, and asked them to watch over me. Then I made them promise to come back and tell me what was up.

And some did.

The brilliant doctor who finally admitted that between the times we'd shocked his heart back to life, he'd been in a tunnel, gone to the Light, met people he knew who were dead.

The young engineer dying of cancer, who in the last days of his life comforted me and told me not to cry, "I saw God," he said. "It's all so simple."

"Mom," Teri called, and her voice brought me back. "Mom, come here." I walked back into the living room. New tears were streaming down her cheeks.

"What's wrong, honey?" I asked.

Teri shook her head. After a few minutes she blew her nose and cleared her throat. "I always thought that my intelligence was the thing that would help me survive. That, and my common sense. I thought I could control the direction of my life and protect myself from danger because I could always see it coming. I trusted myself. I trusted my mind."

"You'll learn to trust yourself again, honey," I told her. "And you have a fine mind. But you can control only so much of your life. The rest belongs to destiny. The Divine Plan includes so much more. And you can't pit your personal mind against the universal mind."

"I had no idea that life had a mind of its own," she said.

"And a heart," I added gently. "Even a soul."

"Mom," Teri said, confusion on her face. "Even though your life worked out for you, I have to admit, I always thought you were a little bit crazy, seeing things, hearing voices."

"Did you think all the stuff I told you when you were growing up was my imagination?"

Teri shook her head. "No," she said. "I just figured we were interested in different things. You liked to read about healing, death, and philosophy. I was interested in things I could see, and in living my life. I never thought death had anything to do with *my* life."

"Death has everything to do with everyone's life," I said gently. "It's only when we face death that we can learn to really live. And it's the *unseen* that gives purpose and meaning to our lives."

She hesitated for another moment, and when she spoke, she looked amazed. "I know this sounds crazy, but I think I just saw Gregory, and he talked to me," she said.

"Did it feel okay to you?" I asked. That was my litmus test for truth.

Teri smiled, and her face relaxed a little as she remembered. "It's funny," she said, "for someone who didn't believe there was anything else before yesterday, it felt good. It wasn't even scary. For the first time since Greggy died, I felt peaceful. And grateful. Really grateful to be able to touch that part of him that I thought was gone forever. Mom, when he spoke, I felt as close to him as I did when I was pregnant."

"What did he say, honey?" I asked gently, aware that if I wasn't careful, I would frighten her.

She said softly, "Greggy's little round face was glowing in front of me, and then I heard, 'I didn't mean to hurt you, Mommy. I love you.'" Teri's eyes were shiny with unspilled tears.

"Did he say anything else?" I asked, wanting to help her understand what was happening. I knew any reaction from me would affect her. What she needed now was reassurance.

Teri nodded, frowning. "He said, 'I didn't want to leave you, but I had to make room for my brother. He needs you more than I.'"

Suddenly Teri sat up straight. Something in her shifted, her expression changed, and she looked tense again. I could see she was trying to fit this new piece of experience into some logical place in her mind, but when she could find nowhere to put it, she started to cry. "Mom, Greggy doesn't have a brother. None of this makes any sense."

I put my arms around her and hugged her tight. I knew how hard this was for her. Yet some part of my heart soared. Greggy's soul had touched her own and she had been able to hear it.

Chapter Three

W inter. Ice-crystal branches, snow-covered earth, harsh wind. The end of the cycle of seasons. The end of a cycle for us.

It was bitter cold when Teri and I left her house to drive back to mine. Once in the car, we shivered. Gregory's death had chilled us to the bone.

Danny and Barbara had built a fire in my fireplace before they left for the service, so when we got home, it was cozy and warm.

Gordon was sitting alone, crowded into the corner of my couch, his head down in contemplation, when Teri and I walked in. Opposite him, Jessica was kneeling on the floor, at the coffee table, laboring over some pictures she was drawing.

"The medical examiner called," Gordon said softly. "He told me that Gregory was labeled a probable SIDS."

"What does that mean?" Teri asked.

"It means they won't know for sure until they get the results of the autopsy, which could take months," I said.

"Where *is* Gregory Thomas?" Jessica asked, looking up at Gordon. "And when is he coming back?"

Gordon said softly, "Jess, Gregory died of something called SIDS. It happens only to little babies, not big girls like you. But Greggy isn't in his body anymore, so he never can come back."

In front of Jessie was a huge pile of construction paper, and scattered all over the table were pictures she had drawn. Gordon said she'd been drawing since we left.

I moved over toward Jessica, but she intentionally moved away.

"What are you drawing?" Teri asked her now, leaning over her shoulder.

"I'll show you," she said. "I'll make you one."

Then, with black Magic Marker on yellow construction paper, she drew four circles, just like the others. They were all the same. Each had two eyes, a small nose and an upside-down smile. But on the smallest circle she colored one side of the face black.

"What's that?" I asked her, pointing at the black marks.

"That's my brother baby," she said, but her voice was cool, impersonal. "That's how he looked."

Teri explained. "That morning when we found him, he had a bruise on the side of his face. I don't know how he got it. He didn't have it when I put him to bed."

"It's called mottling," I explained. "When someone dies, the blood pools and settles at the lowest point."

"Oh," Teri said, "I was afraid someone would think I did it."

I wanted to reassure her, to tell her that no one would doubt her, but I knew that wasn't the truth. When it's hard to find a reason, it's often easier to blame. There were still too many times when parents whose babies died of SIDS were suspected and accused of child abuse.

Jessie had been acting strange since I'd come in. She hadn't run toward me as she usually did, and whenever I moved toward her, she deliberately moved away.

Now, suddenly, she was standing in the middle of the living room, her arms folded in front of her, facing me, frowning. "Are you mad, Jess?" I asked softly.

"Yes, I'm mad," she shouted, and before any of us could stop her, she began crying and screaming as she turned over my rocking chair, pulled the cushions off the couch and tossed them onto the floor. She began to run then, staggering and tripping, a small bird with a broken wing, out of the living room and into my kitchen. She kicked the cabinets only once before Teri grabbed her, picked her up, and hugged her tight.

I stood back, watching from the doorway as Teri asked her, "Why are you so mad, Jessie? Tell Mommy."

Jessie stopped crying and kicking long enough to stare at me with coal-black eyes. "I'm mad at Mama Carol," she said, pointing her small finger at me.

"Why, Jessie?" Teri asked.

Jessie's breath was still coming fast with fury. "Our baby died yesterday."

"I know you're angry, Jessie," Teri said, "but why are you so mad at Mama Carol?"

Jessie struggled out of Teri's arms to stand. Then she marched up in front of me, but when she spoke, she didn't look at me. "You're the nurse who helps sick children," she accused, "and you didn't help Gregory Thomas."

"I would have helped him if I could," I said, trying to talk past the lump in my throat. "But God must have wanted him in heaven."

Jessie stamped her foot. "Yucky God! Yucky heaven!" she shouted, looking straight at me now.

Teri was devastated. She put her hand over her face and walked over to Gordon, shaking her head.

I kneeled down in front of Jessie and looked deep into her eyes. "I'm so sorry your brother died, Jessie, I really am," I said. "I loved Greggy, honest. I would have done anything I could to help him. And I'm going to miss him too."

Jessie searched my face, and her expression softened. Then she walked closer and let me hug her, her little body shaking. When I whispered, "I love you, Jessie. I'm so happy you're here with us," I knew she had forgiven me, because she let me hold her while she cried.

Danny was the first one home from the service. "That white casket was so small and covered with so many flowers, it looked like a flowerpot," he said.

Gordon stood up to greet his mother as she walked in behind Danny. She held out a Polaroid picture of the casket to Gordon, one he'd asked her to take. When he looked at it, he said, "I thought seeing it would make me feel better, but it doesn't."

I walked over to look. "It does look like a flowerpot," I said.

Teri, looking at the picture over my shoulder, said simply, "Not to me."

My father and mother came in next, along with Aunt Josie. I saw my sister Barbara for only a minute.

After a death, rituals serve. As many people called and came the second day as the first. They set out the food, cleaned the house, and played with Jessie while they fed us.

My father, dressed in a brown sports jacket and slacks, carried his hat in his hand as he paced through the house. He, who was usually so gregarious and sociable, was now silent and, like my sister, stayed very private in his pain. He hated to see any of his kids suffer, but it was even worse for him when he could find no words of "wisdom" to offer consolation. Several times that day he walked over to Teri, then he just shook his head, and walked away.

The only thing I heard him say to her was "The good Lord never closes one door without opening another." Those words, though cliché, and not all he would have wished, offered a bridge. He finally hugged Teri and they cried.

Each time someone Teri hadn't seen before walked through the front door, there were more tears. The story was repeated a hundred times. The question they kept asking was, *"Why?"*

When friends and family attend a wake, they often tell tales of times shared with the person who has died. Recounting those experiences breathes life back into the loved one, resurrects them for the time. But Greggy was just a baby, there were not a lot of memories to decorate his wake.

So they told Death stories, stories of loss. And while they talked aloud, they traveled deep within themselves to unearth memories of their mournings.

My father, sitting next to my mother on the couch, admitted that he never felt such loss since his mother, Justine, had died. He was only twelve when she was very sick, and suffering at home. At the time, few people went to hospitals. He said he could still hear the sound of her screams, and he remembered there was no relief. That day, he hid in the movies to cry. He told us he knew the very moment his mother had died. His own breath almost stopped. When he got home, no one had to tell him she was already gone.

Aunt Josie spoke next. She said that when her baby died, her husband tore the house apart, broke every piece of furniture. Still, he couldn't speak his grief for years after.

My mother was thirty-three when her own mother, Catherine, died. She remembered how she locked herself away in a darkened room, hid behind a closed door for months.

That afternoon, Teri was raw. Neither she nor Gordon had ever been to a wake before. And though there was no body to view because Greggy's would be cremated, Teri could bear seeing only so many people, could stand only so much retelling before she had to withdraw to my study. I brought her tea, sat with her, and tried to give her what she needed.

Danny stayed close to Gordon. He tried to form a shield, to be the extra skin that Gordon didn't have. In that, Gordon seemed to find some comfort.

When Teri emerged from my study that day, after hiding for almost two hours, she sat on the couch next to my mother. But she talked directly to Aunt Josie when she said, "Years ago, before modern medicine, before hospitals, mothers expected some of their babies to die. Now we feel it shouldn't happen. We have so many cures."

A baby's death didn't interrupt the order of the Universe before we made technology our God. When people lived close to nature, they saw tiny leaves fallen to the ground, baby birds who never flew, small fish floating. They accepted Death as part of Life. It was the graven images of science and technology that now filled us with illusion. They made us feel our bodies were immortal.

That night we were exhausted. Dakin went to Gordon's house, and my mother and father went home. Gordon and Danny were watching TV, and Jessie had fallen asleep in Jennifer's bed. Barbara tucked them in together and was staying on her side of the house in case Jessie woke up. I was sitting at the dining room table, reading.

Teri walked past me on her way to my study. "I need a tape I can listen to that will make me feel a little better."

Shadows under her dark eyes made her face look ashen. "I'll come with you and we can check," I said.

In my study we scanned my tapes, but Teri couldn't decide. So I chose one for her, a soft, classical version of Pachelbel's Canon. I handed it to her. Then I walked back out and, not wanting to hover, picked up my book again.

"Do you have any Vitabath?" she asked. "The green kind?"

"Yes," I said, "it's under the sink in the bathroom." But I had a nagging feeling she needed more from me. "Honey," I asked as she walked past me on the way to the bathroom, "is there something else?"

She hesitated, shook her head, and said, "No, I've got to take a bath and try to relax."

"Sounds good," I said. "Holler if you need anything else."

I heard water running in the bathtub.

Baths, warm baths, water washing wounds. Back to womb, float-

ing free, tied to love's beginnings. Hearing Spirit, mother's heartbeat,
safe and warm, and new.

I picked up my book again and tried to read, but the words kept
swimming around the page, making no sense at all. I hadn't even
turned a page before the bathroom door opened and Teri was standing
in front of me.

"What's up?" I asked. "Forget a towel?"

She shook her head. "Could you come in and sit with me?" she
asked, embarrassed. "I feel weird, kind of scared. I'll feel better with
you there."

"Sure," I said. "No problem."

"You can bring your book," she said. "I don't need you to talk
to me; I just need you to be there."

I walked into the bathroom and sat on the tile floor in the corner
with my book. I wanted to be out of Teri's way. The bathtub was
already full, brimming with bubbles. There was a white bathmat on
the floor and a green towel thrown across the toilet bowl.

Now, as Teri stood in front of the large mirror that covered the
wall opposite the tub, she hesitated. I thought she was embarrassed,
so I said, "Go ahead. I won't look, my nose is in my book."

"I'm not worried about you seeing me," she said, "I'm just feeling
funny about taking my clothes off. It makes me feel more vulnerable."

Naked as a newborn baby. Exposed. Helpless.

Teri took her sneakers and socks off first, then she slowly pulled
her sweater over her head. When she finished undressing, she stared
into the mirror. "I hate looking at this scar from my C-section. It's
not even healed yet, and the reason for it is already gone."

An angry red slice crossed the soft creamy white skin of her lower
belly. Teri ran her finger carefully over the scar, her eyes searching
the reflection in the mirror. "I never noticed how ugly the battle scars
of birth are. I feel like those soldiers who fought in Vietnam, wounded
for a war without a purpose."

The battlefield of Motherhood and Soldiers . . .

Each soldier is almost a hero. When he enlists to fight a war, he
gives himself to destiny. On the road of Death's deep mystery, he
walks a path into the dark unknown. Alone. When a soldier takes
another's life, it joins them both together. Bound by Death. Who is
this soldier? Will he come home with two arms, two legs, a heart
that beats, a brain that thinks? Who is this enemy he must hate, fight,
capture, kill? Is he someone's brother, father, or friend? Each soldier

is almost a hero. Each mission's success, we reward. With ceremony. With medals. With music. With marching bands.

The call to war is a Rite of Passage; the boy becomes a man.

A mother is always a hero. When she consents to bear a child, she gives herself to destiny. On the road of Life's deep mystery she walks a path into the dark unknown. Alone. When a woman gives another life, that joins them both together. Bound by birth. Who is this child that she must love, feed, clothe, set free? Will he be born with two arms, two legs, a heart that beats, a brain that thinks? Will he be a scientist, a killer, or a king? Each mother is always a hero. Each mission's success, no reward. No ceremony. No music. No medals. No marching bands.

The call to motherhood is a Rite of Passage; the girl becomes a woman.

Teri explained. "I thought my sacrifice was worth it. When this scar was the cost of giving life, it seemed like such a small price."

Suddenly a look of complete revulsion crossed her face. "What's the matter?" I asked her. "What's going on?"

She started to cry and the words spilled out. "I feel like I let death into the family to hurt everyone I love. I hate this scar because no matter how long I live, it will always be evidence of the pain I felt and the pain I caused." Her eyes were wide and frightened. "Mom, I feel like instead of giving birth to Life, I've given birth to Death."

I stood up and put my arms around her. "Honey," I said, "you didn't hurt us, you didn't do any damage. It's just *Life*, Teri. People are born and people die." I stepped back, held her chin, and looked straight into her eyes. "Teri, only God can breathe life into a soul; only He takes life away."

"Then why do I feel like the Grim Reaper?" she asked, still in tears.

"Because in this death-denying society, we take the credit when someone lives, and we take the blame when someone dies. But Life's much bigger than just us. Gregory was a beautiful baby and I'm glad we got to meet him, if only for a little while. He was a gift, I know that, and so he broke our hearts with love. But *Life* did that, honey, not you."

It was four o'clock the next morning when I heard a knock on my bedroom door. "Carol," my sister called, "wake up."

I jumped out of bed and opened the door. "Jessie's sick. Very sick," she said. Standing behind her, Teri's eyes were wide with fear.

I ran to Jennifer's room on the other side of the house. Jessie was white as a sheet and listless as a rag doll. I touched her forehead.

"It's 102," Barbara said.

"She's had much higher than that and didn't act this way," Teri said in a monotone.

I reached down and tried to lift Jessie up. "Jessie," I said in a loud voice, "Mama Carol wants you to drink something." She drooped in my arms; she wouldn't wake up.

Standing in the doorway, Teri began to cry. "Oh, Mom," she said, "I couldn't stand it if anything else happened."

"Nothing's going to happen," I said with more conviction than I felt. I'd never seen Jessie like this. I called to her again, and this time she opened her eyes, but they quickly closed again. I shook her gently. "Jessie?" I repeated, but there was no response. I turned to my sister. "Do you have any pediatric Tylenol suppositories?"

She went to get one. But Teri said, "Jessie will never let you put a suppository in. She gets crazy."

"I'd like to see her get crazy right now," I said. "I'd like to see that kind of response." I bent and put my head on Jessie's small chest to hear her heart. It was galloping fast. But when I turned her over to insert the suppository, she never complained, she never even opened her eyes.

Now Teri grew frantic. She paced back and forth, shaking her head.

"Is Dr. Chen on?" I asked her. He was her pediatrician, a very good one.

"He's away for the holiday," she said.

"Call to see who's covering him," I suggested.

I wondered if this could be something simple like a virus and prayed it was nothing complicated like meningitis. I sat on the bed, rocking Jessie in my arms.

Dr. Chen's covering doctor was someone I didn't know, and therefore didn't trust. After two more hours, when Jessie's fever was down and I still couldn't wake her, I called two of my best friends. Both were nurses and had spent years working with children. I trusted them more than I did most doctors.

Maureen and Bridie were there in fifteen minutes, and even they thought Jessie was too drowsy. So against my better judgment I had Teri call the covering doctor.

Then I watched Teri's face as she listed Jessie's symptoms and listened to the doctor's response. Her eyes widened and she covered the phone. "He says there's a lot of meningitis around," she whispered. "He wants me to take her to an emergency room."

Maureen, Bridie, and I all shook our heads and said, "No."

When the doctor heard Gregory had just died and they hadn't gotten the full autopsy report yet, he flipped out. "You have to take her to an emergency room," I heard him scream as Teri held the phone away from her ear. "You don't know what killed him. You don't want the same thing to happen to her."

Teri was crying when she hung up.

I knew an emergency room would scare Jessie to death now. She'd see the same ambulances that had taken her brother away. Jessie's fear of separation and of a strange hospital would be overwhelming. Her little heart was already pounding with fear as well as fever.

Teri was too upset to think. Even I couldn't decide. Meningitis could be a killer.

Bridie said, "Keep her home unless her level of consciousness changes. All they'll do if they admit her are some tests she might not need."

Maureen reminded me, "Don't you remember how short-staffed hospitals are over the holidays? And don't you remember who they got to work? Forget it. We can watch her better here. If she gets worse, we'll take her."

Jessie's neck wasn't rigid—if it had been, that would have been a real sign of meningitis—and though she was still very groggy, she had opened her eyes a few times.

Bridie said then, "If you need someone to take responsibility for keeping Jessie home, I will. They'll have to do a spinal tap, and that can introduce infection. Especially on a holiday, when the staff is overworked, they can't take the time to be careful enough."

So we all agreed to wait. Hours passed while Jessie lay unmoving. She wouldn't drink her bottle. She stopped urinating and her fever began to rise again. Bridie, Maureen, and I took turns sitting on the bed wiping her down with cool water, while Teri and Barbara paced.

Jessie was so pale, her skin seemed translucent. When her arms and hands began to twitch from her fever, I gave her another Tylenol suppository.

I fluffed her pillow and tried to prop her up a little. "Jessie," I asked, "what's wrong? What hurts?"

She opened her eyes and looked at me, but only for a minute. Then she lay still as stone again. "Tell Mama Carol what you want, Jessie," I pleaded.

"I'm sick, Mama Carol," she said with a soft, sad voice.

"I know," I said gently.

"My brother baby was sick like me," she explained, her eyes still closed.

"Not like you, Jessie," I said firmly. "Daddy told you, what happened to Greggy happens only to little babies. This is a different kind of sick, like Jennifer and Chris had last week. And they got better."

"I want to be with Gregory Thomas," she said then, opening her eyes to look at me again. "I'm a sister."

We all froze with fear, as though her will alone could fly her to the heavens. Teri, who had been watching, came over now and sat where I had been. "Get Gordon," she said to Barbara. She lifted Jessie and held her like a baby. She was crying when she explained to Jessie, "Mommy needs you here with her and Daddy. She wants you here. We all miss Greggy, but now we have to stay together, to help each other." Her tears were falling on Jessie's face as she pleaded, "Help me, Jess? Please don't be sick anymore. Mommy and Daddy love you very much. Do you understand?"

Jessie looked at her mother and nodded.

Gordon had been standing, watching, from the foot of the bed. Now he put his hand on Teri's shoulder. He lifted Jessie out of her arms and laid her back down on the bed. Teri moved away, stood in the doorway. The rest of us were glued where we stood.

With Jessie on her back, Gordon lifted her pajama top. Then he put his hand on her chest over her heart. He looked right at Jessie when he said, "I think we need some special Daddy magic now." He gently turned Jessie's face toward his own. "Open your eyes, Jessie," he told her softly. "Daddy's going to concentrate real hard on making you better. Daddy's going to send his heart with yours to God and ask Him to make your sickness go away. And when Daddy stands up, you're going to start to feel better. You're going to drink your bottle because you love us as much as we love you." *Gordon, in his white pajamas, an ancient temple priest, carrying his daughter to the altar of a healing god.*

Jessie lay perfectly still as Gordon closed his eyes. He seemed to be praying, and willing her well. After a few minutes he got up without a word, walked over to the refrigerator, and filled one of her bottles with iced tea. But when he tried to give it to her, she pushed it away. "I can't drink a bottle," she said. "I'm not a baby."

"Just this once you can," he said. "Just till you get well."

"I can't," she said, her eyes open, her voice a little firmer. "Babies drink bottles. And babies die."

Gordon didn't argue. He got up and poured the tea from her bottle into a cup. He held the cup for a long time, telling her stories, giving her sips. Within three hours Jessie's fever was down, and she was sitting up.

This time Gordon's prayers were answered. This time his *Daddy magic* worked.

Still, that afternoon Teri stayed in my study, far away from Jessie, and let Barbara care for her. After a few hours I walked quietly in to see if she had fallen asleep. But she was sitting upright on my couch, wide awake.

"Jessie's feeling much better," I told her. "She's drinking fluids and Barbara said she had some soup."

Teri looked down. Didn't respond. Started to cry.

I walked over and sat down beside her.

"I'm really scared, Mom," she said. "And really mad at Jess. I can't trust her anymore if she's just going to slip away like Greggy."

"She's not going anywhere, Teri," I reassured. "She's just been under a lot of stress and she probably had a virus."

"I don't care, Mom," she said. "I don't care about reasons. I won't be able to stand another hurt. I know I'll just go crazy."

"You won't go crazy," I said. "It's not so easy to go crazy."

"It's a lot easier to lose a mind than I ever thought it was," she said. "I don't know what I'm doing, I don't know where I'm going or how to get there, I don't even want to be alive anymore. I feel dead inside, and each morning I wake up and find out I'm still here, I don't believe it. Until I remember Greggy and feel the pain again. Then I hate it."

Teri had never been as dramatic or emotional as Jessie or me, so I knew that even though she wasn't shouting or screaming, she was pretty furious.

"Sometimes, the only way to get past feelings is to go through them, honey. You've been through a terrible time," I said. "I can understand how you feel."

"You don't understand," she snapped back. "You can't understand. It didn't happen to you."

She was wrong. It did happen to me. Now I was watching my own child, the person she used to be, die slowly. I understood she could lose her mind and then be lost to me. She could stop the fight, and not want to live enough; she could hide from life and lose herself to drugs or alcohol. She could stanch the flood of love she felt for Gordon and for Jessie. She could wind up embittered and fearful for the rest of her life. She could possibly never feel joy again, or passion. There were thousands of traps in this tragedy. Each one left me feeling helpless and afraid.

Though I trusted my belief system, it didn't keep my heart from breaking as I watched my own child's struggle. I knew there was a universal script of higher purpose. I didn't doubt its justice or its thrust toward evolution, but I cringed at the very thought of another hard lesson. As I looked at Teri now, my own eyes filled, but all I said was "Aunt Barbara offered to take care of Jess tonight. Why don't you just try to relax, watch TV, and not think about anything?"

When I walked out of my study, Teri was lying down with her arm over her eyes. Crying again.

That night, Gordon, Teri, Danny, and I sat in my living room in front of the TV. It was good to see Teri leaning against Gordon on the couch, tucked under his arm. Danny was lying on the floor.

Gordon worked as a manager for a jewelry company. On the day Greggy died, his boss told him to take whatever time he needed. But now he said to Teri, "I want to go back to work. It will keep my mind off things. Without work I feel completely lost."

"Sure," Teri said, "you'll go back to work, Jessie will start nursery school, and I'll be left alone in an empty house with no baby and no life."

"Maybe you could keep Jessie home for a while," I suggested.

"Mom," Teri said, "that's not fair. She loves school. I can't stop her from living to give my life a purpose."

"Do *you* want to go back to school?" I asked. I knew she needed time to heal, but I wanted her to know she had a future to look forward to. She had always planned to finish her degree in social work.

"I'm not supposed to be going back to school yet," she said. "I wasn't planning to return until Greggy was in preschool."

The script she'd created for who she was and the part she was to play in her world had been destroyed. Without the script she felt lost. I wondered what could help her create a new one? Gordon must have been thinking the same thing, because he said softly, "We could have another baby."

Teri sat up and glared at him. "Are you crazy?" she asked. "That's like asking me to commit suicide. What guarantee do we have that another baby wouldn't die?" Her voice was very low when she added, "I couldn't live through it."

"I'm sorry, honey," Gordon said. "I was just trying to make you feel better. But I guess it's too soon."

Teri shook her head and said firmly, *"Never* is too soon, Gord. I never again want to walk into a room and find a dead baby."

Teri, Gordon, and Jessie moved back home early in the morning on New Year's Eve. They thought Jessie would feel better sleeping in her own bed, feel safer surrounded by her toys and other familiar things. Dakin had flown back to California the day before. The rest of the family was going over to spend New Year's Eve at their house so Teri and Gordon didn't have to spend it by themselves.

But I stayed home alone. After days of being surrounded by people, I needed to be by myself. Whenever there was a crisis, something within me shifted, and I automatically began to pick up the pieces and comfort others. My own emotions had to wait until I could afford to feel them.

Teri and Gordon wanted to move the furniture out of Greggy's room before they brought Jessie home, and I had asked if I could have it. I wasn't ready to let it go. So Danny and Gordon brought over Greggy's crib, his dresser, and bright red and blue diaper changer, and placed them in my spare room.

Several times during the day, as I walked around my house straightening up, I wandered into that room. It was warm and homey with crisp white curtains, and it was comforting for me to still see baby furniture.

Late that afternoon Teri called me. "Guess what?" she said, excited. "Danny bought Greggy a star. It's registered with the International Star Registry."

"What's the Star Registry?" I asked.

I could hear the pleasure in her voice. "There's an agency in London that charts the position of the stars. They assign a star for each special person. Then they register it under the name you choose, in England, Switzerland, and here, in the U.S. Then they send you a constellation map that shows exactly where the star is. Cool, huh?"

"Where's Greggy's?" I asked.

"Just a little north of the Big Dipper," Teri said. "I love it, Mom. The night sky will take on a whole new meaning for me now that Gregory's up there."

By the time the sun went down, my house was quiet and the phone had stopped ringing. I put on some soft music and went to spend some time with Greggy's things. Danny had thrown all the baby's toys and clothes into large brown plastic bags. Now I opened one, filled with clothes, took out some small things, and began to fold them carefully. I put them neatly in the dresser drawers. It was peaceful. In my mind, memories began to form. . . .

The first one took me back to the night Greggy was born. Gordon had been in the labor room all night with Teri. Finally he had called and asked me to come. He told me the doctor had to do a cesarean section because the baby was refusing to be born. Teri's contractions had stopped and the baby had turned around and was moving back up. I thought it odd at the time, but now it seemed to be foreshadowing. The nurses who were working that night wouldn't let me into the delivery room to see Teri until the doctor came. Only a minute later she was wheeled into the delivery room. All I had time to say was "It will be okay, honey. You'll be okay."

Afterward, Greggy did well but Teri was very sick. She couldn't move for days, couldn't walk, could hardly speak. The peristalsis in her intestines slowed to a stop because of the medication, so she couldn't eat a thing. Her sutures got infected and she had to be put on IV antibiotics.

Gordon stayed most days and nights, and when he wasn't there, I was. Teri hadn't been prepared for this. With Jessie she'd had an easy natural delivery in a California birthing center.

The next memory that floated to the surface was the night of Teri's twenty-fourth birthday. Gordon took her out for dinner and then, to celebrate, they were spending the night alone. Jessie stayed with Barbara, but Greggy stayed with me. I laughed just thinking about that night. I never let him out of my sight.

We sat on the couch and I read aloud from Jean Houston's *The Possible Human*. She was a philosopher, mythologist, and a real humanist. She inspired me with a vision of a kind and gentle future world, one where anything was possible. Greggy sat, watching every move my lips made, smiling when something I read tickled him, and finally fell asleep to the sound of my voice.

When he awakened, I sat in my rocking chair and held him, gave him a bottle, let the starlight in his eyes touch me. I rode that feeling of loving back through the time tunnel to my own babies. Afterward, we lay on the floor and listened to soft music.

When we finally went into my room that night, I pulled Greggy's portable crib right against the side of my bed. But after an hour of tossing and turning, I couldn't fall asleep. Greggy was being his usual perfect baby self, sleeping comfortably, breathing easily, but I felt uneasy. I moved his crib even closer, but couldn't get it close enough. Finally, we were almost nose to nose, separated only by the netting of the crib.

In spite of that, I was still restless, prodded by a vague uneasiness. So I finally gave up, propped myself up on the pillows, lifted Greggy out of his crib, and placed him on my chest. He woke long enough to smile, then we both closed our eyes. But now I couldn't sleep because I couldn't *feel* him on my chest. I kept having to open my eyes to make sure he was there. I was feeling crazy again, my perceptions playing tricks on me. Greggy weighed much more than Jessie when she'd first come home, but I could always feel her on my chest. I always knew where she began and ended. Her tiny fingers dug into my neck and her climbing tiny toes pushed into my stomach. Jessie's heart beat in rhythm with my own, her hot, sweet baby breath flew up my nose.

But not Greggy. He seemed to have no edges, no boundaries. He was weightless as a cloud, no probing fingers, no digging toes. No heat, no sweat, no baby smell.

That night I got out of bed and examined him completely. I even listened to his heart and lungs with my stethoscope. Perfect. I laid him on my bed and checked every inch of him. Beautiful, with two big dimples in his cheeks. Sparkling light blue eyes. Finally I kissed him all over with relief, and with a little too much enthusiasm. When he began to cry, I felt better. The sound of his voice was real.

Real? I mean concrete, dense, not light pretending form.

The next memory sneaked up on me. I had almost forgotten Christmas Eve, three days before he died. . . .

I had walked into my bedroom to change into something more festive before everyone arrived. I had opened my door and turned on the light. Then I glanced over at the playpen, worrying that the light would wake the baby. I lifted the blanket to check on him, and I was surprised when he wasn't there.

When I came out of my room I asked Teri, "Where's the baby?"

She stared at me. "Mom," she said with an expression of amusement, "he's asleep in your room."

"Wrong," I said. "Someone must have picked him up."

"Mom," she insisted then, "I put him down myself, in the playpen in your room."

She got up and followed me back into my bedroom. She turned on the light, and there, clear as a bright new day, was Gregory, sleeping peacefully. Teri made a face at me and shook her head.

"Teri," I said, "I really didn't see him before. I spent at least fifteen minutes in this room, changing my clothes. He really wasn't there."

"Mom," Teri said, laughing, "I don't know how you could have missed him with that red sleeper he's wearing."

"I see it now," I said, confused. "I'm just saying I didn't see him before."

"You need cement boots, Mom," Teri teased. "You need to be able to see what's on earth, in the here and now. And you need to be able to identify an object like your grandson when he's asleep in your room. Otherwise you're in very big trouble."

"Don't be such a smartass," I said, shutting off the light and carefully closing the door. "That never happens to me. I know when I see something if it's real or not."

"Apparently not with Greggy," Teri had said, laughing again.

That night I also remembered that the photographer who came to take pictures of Jessie and Greggy returned with several of her and none of him. When Teri asked what had happened, the photographer was puzzled. He didn't know why Greggy's pictures didn't come out. There was nothing wrong with the film and Teri had watched him take the pictures. The images just weren't there when the film was developed. In fact, the only pictures we had of the baby were on the video Gordon had taken.

I'd spent hours in the spare room with Greggy's furniture, just puttering around. Those memories of him seemed to come from lifetimes ago. I ran my hands over the crib rails again, then I picked up the red sleeper he had worn on Christmas Day and held it to my nose. I smelled it. Still holding it, I lay down on the carpet, thinking.

Gregory would never have a first day of school, a first class trip, or a visit to the planetarium. He was my grandson and I loved him. But I would never have the chance to show him how much. That made me incredibly sad. I missed Greggy, but even more, I missed all we could have done together, all he could have been.

That night, when I stood in front of my dresser before I tucked myself into bed, I asked Mother Mary, the beautiful porcelain angel, and my Spirit friends to watch over my grandson. As I slid under the covers, I looked up to the heavens and asked all my patients who had died to keep an eye on him and to see that he did well. I said a special prayer to my grandmothers.

I fell asleep almost immediately, the only thought in my mind a kind of wondering. Not why Greggy. Not why us. Just *why.*

That night I had a strange dream, a haunting dream. . . .

Sounds of drumming, and ceremonial cries. Then the flying feathered bodies of Native American warriors dancing around a bright orange campfire. From that fire, as though rising from the flames, there appeared a tall, handsome warrior. His thick black hair hung in one long braid, his shiny red chest was bare. Deerskin trousers and light leather boots tied high around his ankles. When he kneeled, he bowed his head as though in prayer. Then he raised his upper body, threw back his handsome head, and stretched his arms out to the skies in a gesture of surrender. The sound of chanting intensified and the rhythm of the drumbeat quickened.

After a time the Indian stood up slowly. Now, cradled in his arms, he held a small bundle, swaddled in rough cloth.

The drumbeat grew more urgent, more insistent. But the chanting now came from a distance.

The handsome Indian then raised the small wrapped bundle to the Heavens. Not an offering. An accusation. His lips were tight, his jaw was set.

Then he kneeled and laid the bundle on the ground, and lifted up another. Just the same. He held that up as well.

The drumming surged, demanded, until it was deafening.

I watched the Indian carefully lay those bundles down, one beside the other.

Then I heard a baby cry. I didn't know it was a grave, that tiny hole, until I saw him cover it with earth. In that instant the drumming and the chanting stopped.

An eerie silence fell.

I saw the Indian stand again. Circled by darkness, I watched him break a stick, put it between his teeth. And then he took an antler, a sharp-pointed bone, and dug it deep and hard across his chest diagonally. First from right to left, then again from left to right. He made no sound as his blood fell to the ground below, raining on the dark brown earth over the small bundles he had buried there.

When he reached inside his freshly opened chest and ripped out his heart, still beating, I began to wake. And in the twilight between sleeping and waking, in that space between dream and reality, he held it out to me, his bursting heart, still dripping with his pain, his guilt, his sadness, and his shame.

Transfixed by both my horror and compassion, I watched myself hold out my hand, and take the heavy heart to hold against my own.

In that moment the warrior threw his head back and from his lips escaped a cry—a cry of such grief, such agony, such torture, it echoed through time to pierce my ears.

In my bed I was crying too, my arms wrapped around myself, moaning with his grief and mine.

Now the tall handsome Indian stood opposite me, his head bowed.

Who are you? I asked, my mind reaching toward his.

He didn't answer. But when he lifted his head, what I saw almost stopped my breath.

His eyes, those dark brown, almost black eyes, were the same eyes I'd seen in the mirror every day of my life. His eyes were my eyes.

I blinked then, and tried to bring myself back. The Indian was gone, the sound was gone. I was alone again, back in my bed in my own room.

That night I didn't understand it. I knew I'd had a vision, but I couldn't make the jump. I should have recognized the chanting. I should have known my soul was stretching, that damn drumming should have warned me. I was really waking up. . . .

Chapter Four

When a hole has been torn in the tapestry of a family, it takes time to reweave it. It needs a new backing of love and it has to be reinforced again with trust. The weavers must lace in the new experience with stronger and more resilient threads, and once completed, though it will never look or feel like the original, it may be more intricate, more colorful, and possibly even richer.

We could all see that Teri was in the impossible position of having to be a mother to Jessica while she was more vulnerable and more frightened than ever before. She had lost her baby, her life as she knew it, her belief system, and her role in society. She had, as far as she was concerned, lost herself. In order to finally be able to nurture Jessie again, she herself would have to be nurtured.

Each of us had a place in Teri's healing. Along with our family, Teri and Gordon had lots of good friends. She had enough support in the outer world, but that wasn't where I saw the danger. It was in restructuring the inner worlds. That's where I hoped I could help.

Teri called early the following morning, and she sounded upset. Gordon had gone back to work. For the first time, she was home alone with Jessie, and she was afraid.

"Come over?" she asked.

When I walked into her living room, Teri was lying on the couch.

"What's up?" I asked. But before she could answer, Jessie heard my voice and came running in from her bedroom.

"Hi, Mama Carol," she said, jumping up to kiss me.

"What's that?" I asked, pointing to the construction paper she held in her hand.

"More pictures," she said. "Look."

They were dark and angry. But one picture had a small yellow sun. It gave me hope.

"They're heart pictures," Jessie said as she pointed to a big black flower.

"They look sad," I said, kneeling next to her.

She shook her head. "Nope. Mostly they're still mad," she said, showing me one with red crayon scribbled all over it.

"About Gregory?" I asked.

Jessie lifted her face to look at me. "Did you know, Mama Carol, that we are *never* going to see our baby Gregory Thomas *ever* again?"

I nodded.

She stamped her foot. "I *hate* that," she said, her voice impassioned.

"Me too, honey," I said, and I kissed her forehead.

Jessie ran back in to color.

I went to sit on the couch with Teri. She had thrown on a long T-shirt over a pair of loose jeans. Without her makeup she looked like a teenager. Except for her expression.

"Mom, a baby shadow or ghost is awful," she said sadly. "The house is a mess, but I'm afraid to clean up. I keep finding things of Gregory's everywhere: bottles that slipped behind the cushions in the couch, cloth diapers, toys. I found formula cans in the back of the refrigerator this morning, and I didn't even know what to do with them. I'm walking around picking up the remnants of a life that never really was."

I said, "Can I make you a cup of tea?" Italian mothers offer food or drink when they can offer nothing else.

Teri got off the couch and followed me into her kitchen.

Sitting at the table, her head leaning on her hand, she said, "I miss him so much, Mom. For the first time, I hate being home, but I don't want to leave. It's crazy. I love finding pieces of Greggy's life, but I really hate being haunted by a life that took so much of mine." Then she shook her head and began to cry softly. "I want him never to have been born. . . . And yet I thank God for those three precious months."

"Honey," I said, "I know it seems impossible to imagine, but this will become bearable. This pain and confusion won't last forever."

"Mom," she said with complete innocence, "nothing seems clear anymore. This wasn't how it was supposed to be. I know I'm losing my mind."

"Teri, listen to me," I said. "I want you to remember that losing your mind isn't losing yourself. There's more to you. A deep strong core that will survive this. A mind is only a place that holds who we *think* we are. It's not all we are."

She shook her head again. "I really feel like I'm dying."

The phone rang and I picked it up.

It was the public health nurse. She said she had been assigned the case and she wanted to stop by. But Teri seemed too fragile. I knew that any insensitive remark, wrong information, or negative judgment could cause a setback in her healing. Still, it was Teri's choice to make, not mine. I held my hand over the phone as I told her.

"Let her come," Teri said. "Lois said someone would call. It's part of the SIDS program."

Lois had lost a baby several years before, and now she was *Parent Contact Director* for the Sudden Infant Death Syndrome Foundation. She called Teri on the day that Gregory had died and talked to her every day since. Teri liked her. Lois offered support, they shared experiences, and Lois gave Teri all the information that was available about SIDS. But more important, she was a mother who had managed to stay alive after the death of her child. She had said whoever came was not coming to check on Teri, just to offer help and bring her information. Teri was anxious for some answers.

As soon as I opened the front door, I knew we were in trouble.

It wasn't only that she was a rigid stick of a woman with tight, thin lips, she seemed cold and distant. I knew the one thing Teri needed now was someone warm and compassionate.

"I'm Sadie Malaenka," she said as she walked past me into the house. "I'm a registered nurse."

"I'm Teri's mom," I said. I didn't tell her I was a nurse.

She repeated her name and rank to Teri when she reached the kitchen, but when I offered her a cup of tea, she ignored me. Instead, she sat opposite Teri and plopped her attaché case down on the table. Without even looking at Teri, she began to fill out a questionnaire, asking questions like a drill sergeant.

I began to pace, trying to restrain myself as Teri answered one question after another. As soon as she was finished, Sadie got up without a word, and, without permission, began to walk around the house. Investigating. She walked into Jessie's room and began to speak to her, to ask her questions. But Jessie wouldn't play her game. She ran into the living room and lay on the couch.

I was going to say something to her, but Teri touched my arm and whispered, "Mom, please. Just let her be. I don't want any trouble."

I didn't want to cause Teri any more distress, so I went inside and sat on the couch with Jessie. Now Sadie was wandering through Gregory's empty room. As she passed us on her way back to the kitchen, she stared at Jessie.

"She's pale," Sadie announced. "Is she sick?"

"She was," Teri said, "but she's better now."

"Have you taken her to the doctor?" Sadie asked.

"Her pediatrician's away till the end of the week," Teri explained. "As soon as he comes back, I'll take her."

"Don't wait too long," the nurse warned.

Teri was nervous, so she lit a cigarette. Sadie frowned, looked as though she was going to say something, then looked at me and thought better of it.

She reached into her attaché case, took out some pamphlets and a brochure, and handed them to Teri. "Here's some information. I haven't had a chance to look at it yet, but it's probably helpful."

Teri frowned. I was furious. "Mom," Teri said, afraid what I would say, "make me some tea?"

I turned the gas on under the kettle. "What do you do when you're not helping the public?" I asked Sadie, and even I could hear the chill in my voice.

Sadie sat straight, preening. "I'm a thanatology clinician."

Teri and I just looked at each other. Both of us had noticed anytime we used the word "dead," Sadie almost fell off her chair.

"Did your girl go to the funeral?" she asked, pointing to Jessie.

"We had the baby cremated. We're going to scatter his ashes at the beach," Teri said.

Sadie lowered her voice. "Is she going to go?" she asked.

"No," I said testily, "it doesn't seem appropriate."

Teri lit another cigarette, and Sadie reached out to stop her. "Have you always smoked this much?" she asked. This time she didn't try to keep the judgment from her voice. Smoking had been identified as a risk factor in all infant deaths as well as in SIDS, but Sadie made it sound like a cause.

Now Teri's eyes flashed. "I used to smoke more," she snapped. Then she lost it. She stood, and with her voice raised, said, "It's really none of your business whether I sit here with a bottle of scotch in one hand and a cigarette in the other. I'm trying to deal with my son's death the only way I can."

Impervious, Sadie stood up and handed Teri her business card. "Call me if you need anything."

I walked Sadie to the front door, out of Teri's earshot, before I said, "Do you have any idea how important the first response of a professional is to a grieving parent? You had an opportunity to help here, to heal, but you didn't do it. Remember when you took that nursing oath? Didn't you swear if you couldn't help, you wouldn't harm. . . ."

She looked confused.

By the time I got back to the kitchen, Teri was crying. "It hasn't even been a week," she said. "What the hell does she expect of me?"

I put my arm around her. "Honey," I said, "it doesn't matter what she expects. Or what she says. Death scares people. They'd rather blame someone than believe that death can happen to anyone at any time. It's dumb. But dumbness wears a lot of different uniforms."

"I thought she was supposed to help," Teri said.

"She hasn't the faintest idea how," I said.

When I got home, Barbara had already made dinner. We always ate together, but since Greggy died, we were both so involved with others, we hadn't had time to really talk.

Barbara's brown hair was tied back at the nape of her neck and her heavy turtleneck sweater brought a warm blush to her face.

"Thanks," I said, pointing to the food on the table.

Her eyes filled and the tears got stuck on her long lashes. "Is there anything else I can do?" she asked.

"No," I said. "Is there something I can do for you?"

She just shook her head. She was just picking at her food.

"It might make you feel better to talk," I suggested.

She began to cry. "It doesn't," she said with more certainty than I expected. "Nothing will make me feel better. It's always worse for me to try to put it into words."

"Why?" I asked her.

"I have only my pain when I keep it inside," she said. "But if I talk, I have to listen. And hearing other people's pain makes it more painful for me."

"It doesn't help you to share what you're feeling?" I asked.

"Not at all," she said. "I don't want to hear that death's not the end. I don't want to know that there's a bigger purpose. I don't care what gifts follow. Nothing will ever make up for this."

"So how will you get through it?" I asked her.

"Just let me handle it the way I have to," she said. "Don't ask me to be different. And try not to judge. Let me hide when I have to. Let me watch Jessie, hold her and love her. But don't ever ask me to accept this, Carol, because I never will. Never."

From that day on, I tried not to burden my sister with my vision of life.

That night, when I told her I would respect her wishes, she asked me, "Don't you remember when we were little, Carol? Don't you remember our different prayers?"

I shook my head.

Barbara smiled when she reminded me. "At night, kneeling by the side of our bed, you always used to pray, 'God, if Bernadette had a vision, why can't I?' At the same time, I was praying, 'God? I know my sister wants a vision. But when you show her one, please, God, don't let me see it.'"

I hugged her then. "No more vision talk," I promised.

Barbara really didn't need it. My sister didn't examine her spirituality, didn't talk her beliefs, but she did love, live, and give.

Later that night my mother and father stopped by, as they always did after dinner.

"Do you think Teri will be all right?" my mother asked, concerned.

"I hope so," I said. "I think so."

"Well, let everything else go," she said. "I'll do whatever I can for you. I'll shop, I'll cook. Anything. You be with Teri when she needs you. Help her with Jessie."

I nodded and looked toward my father. He was sitting, his head leaning on his hand. Quiet again.

"Daddy, are you okay?" I asked.

He shook his head no.

My mother went inside to Barbara so my father and I could talk.

"Is there something I can say to help?" I asked.

When he looked up, I could see his pain. I wondered how he was feeling physically. He had been healthy his whole life, was still active and in amazingly good shape. In fact, he had just gone hunting with the boys and he was the one who tracked for them. Then, without warning, three nights before Greggy died, my father had passed out in the middle of the night and landed hard on the bathroom floor.

An ambulance had rushed him to the emergency room. The doctors did tests and found nothing. But now I suspected that some part of my father had glimpsed what was coming, and that *knowing* had knocked him out cold.

"Carol," he said, "I've had a good, full life. That baby's life was just beginning. He had his whole life ahead of him. It should have been me, not him."

I put my hand on his shoulder. "Daddy," I said, "apparently that wasn't the plan."

"But I would have *offered* myself, Carol," he said, tears falling. "Gladly."

"I know that, Daddy," I told him. "And whoever's running things knows that too."

He looked at me now, searching my eyes. "You really believe this is not a random thing?" he asked.

I knew my father respected my analytical ability, but now I felt him asking something more. "Don't you believe in a Compassionate Intelligence that runs an ordered Universe? Something that we call *God* for want of a better word? Something that represents the Mystery?" I asked him. All our lives we had discussed concepts of Life and Death in abstract terms. But a belief has to have meaning for the heart, not only for the mind.

"I don't know, baby," he said. "Faith is a gift. You either have it or you don't. It would be so much easier if I could be *sure.*"

"Faith isn't what I'm talking about," I explained. "I've had too many experiences in my life and in my work that have pushed me past the limits of my mind. Even if I don't understand it completely, I know there is an Unseen Force that clearly has a place in, and an effect on, my life."

"I hope you're right, baby," he said, trying to smile. "That would be a comfort. To believe something like this tragedy has meaning."

"I'm sure it does, Daddy," I said. "We just can't see it yet."

He was quiet for a moment. Then he said, "I just wish it had been me instead."

I reached for his hand. "Don't be offering to go anywhere, Dad," I told him. "We need you now more than ever."

The following day, when Teri called me, she said she spent the morning walking past Gregory's hamper, wanting to hold his clothes. She didn't want to wash them. They were all she had left. She said her neck hurt the way it used to when she sat in the rocking chair holding Greggy, looking down at him, hugging him and loving him. *The body, too, holds memories.*

"Why don't we go to the mall?" I asked her. "Maybe you'll feel better if you get out of the house."

"Okay," she said. "I guess we could buy something to put in Gregory's empty room, something to make it a playroom for Jess."

"Sounds fine," I said. "I'll pick you up in an hour."

When I got to their house, Jessie told me, "Mama Carol, I want a Sesame Street table to draw on."

"Got it," I told her.

On the way to the car, Teri was wearing a jacket that was too thin, but when I offered to run in and get her another, she said, "I don't feel cold. Actually, I don't feel anything."

Jessie was jumping around the backseat of my car. "Toys 'Я' Us, Mama Carol," she said. "Get my table?"

"I need to put some child life back in that room," Teri said, her voice flat.

Toys 'Я' Us. I held Jessie's hand as we wandered around. But the whole time, I kept my eye on Teri. For someone who'd lost a baby, walking up and down those aisles was like walking through an emotional mine field. Formula, baby clothes, high chairs, and playpens threatened to blow up and blind us.

Everywhere we looked, there were mothers carrying babies.

While we were standing on line to pay for the green and white Sesame Street table and chairs Jessie had chosen, there was a cute little baby boy sitting in a stroller behind us. He wanted to see Teri and Jessie. So he kept moving his head from side to side to try to see around me. He even giggled to try to get Teri's attention. Finally, hanging over the side of his stroller, he waved and smiled at her. I was surprised when she smiled back.

Then, before I could stop her, Jessie wiggled around me and walked right over to his stroller. She smiled at the woman holding it. "Is this your baby?" she asked.

And the woman smiled proudly.

"What a cute brother baby you have," Jessie said, touching his hand. "We had a baby just like him. His name was Gregory Thomas Griswold."

Teri and I held our breath. But it was too late.

The woman was smiling at Jessie, completely unprepared, when

Jessie, with an expression of complete innocence on her small, upturned face, added, "He got sick and died."

Teri looked at the stricken mother and reached for Jessie's hand. "I'm sorry," Teri said. And she quickly took Jessie out of the store.

As soon as Dr. Chen returned from his vacation two days later, Teri, Barbara, and I took Jessie to see him. Dr. Chen's eyes were soft with compassion, and when he examined Jessie, he was particularly gentle.

Afterward, while Barbara took Jessie into the waiting room, Teri and I went with Dr. Chen down to his office. We assumed he wanted to talk about Jess.

Now, as he sat behind his large paper-covered desk, he said, "I'm so sorry about your problem." Teri hadn't spoken to him since Gregory had died, but the medical examiner had notified his office.

He studied the medical chart in front of him and quietly asked if Teri would take Jessie to a lab to have some blood drawn. He said he understood it was difficult, but because of what had happened, it would ease everyone's mind, including his.

Then he took another chart and walked over to where Teri sat. He bent down to show her Gregory's medical history. He pointed to a line on his record: weight at birth; 5 lbs. 14 oz. He showed her where he had recorded that the baby had nursed well from the beginning, and traced, with his finger, the findings of each visit until the last. Two days before he died.

"See," Dr. Chen said, "he was perfectly healthy. Thirteen pounds. Good weight gain. Lungs clear, heart sounds good, abdomen soft." Teri nodded each time he pointed out a written word, proof that they had both done their best. "He had no periods of apnea in the hospital nursery," Dr. Chen added. "I don't know why this happened. SIDS is not predictable. We cannot prevent it. I'm sorry." Dr. Chen's voice was compassionate but firm when he said to Teri, "There is no blame here."

Early the following week, the funeral director called to tell me that Gregory's ashes had been delivered. Teri wanted to come with me to pick them up. She left Jessie with Jenny and Christopher and then we drove to the funeral parlor.

It was a large white colonial house, warm and cozy-looking. I could imagine it filled with the happy sounds of children playing, running up and down the stairs, women cooking in the kitchen, men chopping wood in back. Only the sign on the front porch, DUDLEN'S FUNERAL HOME, suggested something different.

It was still very cold, so I left the engine running. Teri decided to wait in the car. I felt better about that; I needed a few minutes to get myself together.

Inside, the heavy smell of flowers mixed with death almost knocked me over. Flowers don't smell like that when they're growing in the sun.

I walked quickly past the two front viewing rooms and couldn't help looking in. In one casket there rested a man, and in the other a woman, twins now. Each wore the yellow powdered mask of death, eyes closed, rosary beads strung across rigid fingers on hands posed for eternal prayer.

A housekeeper was vacuuming the long, dark hall. "Hi," I said as I passed her, but she kept her head down. Except for the vacuum, there was an eerie silence.

Once I reached the thick oaken door of the business office, I knocked. "Come in," a male voice answered.

Inside, the funeral director sat behind a large wooden desk, dressed in a dark gray suit and a thin silk tie. His face was expressionless.

"I came for my grandson," I said. "Gregory Griswold."

He stood up and held out his hand. "I'm sorry," he said.

I just nodded and waited. I had ordered a pretty brass container to hold Greggy's ashes.

The funeral director walked over to a long metal cabinet and looked through the shelves, tapping his pen against the labels as though he were checking inventory. He pulled a small brown cardboard box from the bottom shelf, but when he tried to hand it to me, I refused. "I don't want to take a cardboard box out to his mother," I explained. "Please take him out of there."

He shrugged, put the box on his empty desk, and slit the masking tape with a silver letter opener. Then he carefully pulled out a shiny quart-size paint can and held it toward me.

I frowned, puzzled. "Where's the brass container?"

"The brass containers have to be ordered," he explained.

"I *did* order one," I told him. "I spent an hour telling Mr. Dudlen what I wanted."

"Well, I'm sorry," he said nervously. "He never mentioned it and I can't reach him. I have nothing on file here." The small tin can was between us, both of us holding it, neither letting go. "Do you want to wait until tomorrow, when he comes back?" he asked.

"No, I don't," I said, snatching the can from him. The kids had already made plans. On the can was a plain white paper label: CONTENTS: 1 GREGORY GRISWOLD. I looked at the funeral director. "What am I going to do?" I asked him. "I can't show his parents this paint can. What can I say? Here, this is your baby."

He looked at me but no longer seemed able to speak.

I had nothing else to say. I walked out of the office.

In the hall I hugged the can to my chest, hid it under my coat. I wondered what I could say to Teri. How could I show her?

Outside, I was freezing. The cold and my misery were making my eyes water. I ran across the front porch, walked fast across the parking lot to the car door, and slid into the front seat.

"Where are the ashes?" Teri asked.

I couldn't say anything. I was crying.

"Mom," Teri asked, worried, "what's wrong?"

I slowly unbuttoned my coat and pulled out the can. I held it in front of me. Teri reached for it and the can seemed to float into her hands. Gently, silently, she hugged it against her heart as tears ran down her cheeks.

"We have to go to the store and buy a brass container," I said quickly.

Teri frowned. "Mom, what are you talking about?"

"We can't show this to Gordon," I said. "We have to find a pretty container."

"Don't be crazy," Teri said. "What are you going to do, transfer Greggy with a spoon?"

"Yes," I said. "Or we could just pour him out into something else."

Teri shook her head. "Mom, that's disgusting," she said. "I don't want death disguised in a pretty container. This way it will be easier to set Greggy free."

I looked at the small can and started to cry. "I can't show this to Gordon."

"Then I will," she said. "If I can handle it, he can. Let's just go."

As we drove, Teri asked, "What did you expect?"

What did I expect?

I expected a tall, regal funeral bier built out in the open under the sun. His body anointed with special oils, shrouded in sacred cloths. Ceremony, incense, and loads of colorful flower petals scattered over him. And all around, crowds of people, voices chanting, raised in celebration and in prayer. I expected raging flames that would inciner-ate his body, would lift his spirit, and soar high enough to reach the sky. Then I expected it to rain. To pour. With a pounding, cleansing rain that would wash away his ashes and wash away our pain. That's what I expected.

Gordon and Danny were waiting outside the house, leaning on the fence as we drove up. Teri got out of the car and I watched through my closed window as she handed Gordon the tin can. He looked puzzled as she spoke to him. Then he turned away, and when he turned back again I could see he was crying.

I drove us all to the beach. Danny sat in the front seat and Teri and Gordon huddled together in the back. As we sped across the almost empty parkway to the beach, I was constantly checking them. In the rearview mirror I could see Gordon hugging the tin can, crying. Teri reached over, wiped his cheek, touched his hair. The radio was off, no one spoke, and the only thing I could hear was his crying.

It was late afternoon, and the day was clear and sunny. During the drive to Tobay Beach, the sun burned my eyes; they kept tearing, and there was no visor big enough to block it. The ride there seemed to take forever and I remembered. . . .

Ashes. Kneeling at the altar on Ash Wednesday when I was a kid. A white-robed priest drew a cross of blessed ashes on each forehead. Ashes to remind us, *From dust we come; to dust we shall return.* But that day I didn't want a small smudged cross on my forehead. I wanted heavy black war paint, the long, dark lines of a warrior across my cheeks, hard, burnt slashes of Greggy drawn across my lips and forehead. Primitive marks for primitive pain. I said it aloud. No one replied. But in the backseat, Gordon stopped crying.

The parking lot was empty, but I parked on the far side, almost in the dunes. I got out of the car and Gordon, protecting his precious metal can, climbed out behind me. The wind was fierce and cold. He began to struggle with his coat, to try to slip it on, but the can was in his way. "I'll hold Greggy," I said, but he shook his head.

Then, the next moment, he stopped and looked directly at me. "Here," he said, holding the can toward me. "I'm sorry."

I smiled and carefully took the can, held it close.

"Carol," Gordon said, his voice thick with sadness, "I don't mind if you want to draw lines of Greggy on your face."

I thanked him. "With this wind," I said, "I think we'll all be wearing Greggy."

Gordon smiled. "That would be nice."

On the walk to the beach, Danny was carrying the big black boom box. In it, a cassette of Teri's song to Greggy. A passionate song, a lover's song. Teri had asked us to park on the bay side, she said that Greggy was too little to scatter across the ocean. Now short rushes, scrub weeds, and sand led us to the calm waters of the bay. All of us just stood.

"Did anyone remember a can opener?" Danny asked Gordon, who was clutching the tin can tight. And it was suddenly so absurd that we all laughed.

Gordon used his Swiss Army knife to pry off the cover. When it fell to the ground, only cotton batting showed, a soft white blanket over Greggy's ashes.

The whistling wind blew our hair into our faces; it stung our ears and burned our eyes. Gordon looked at me, holding the can toward me, and I slowly pulled the cotton out. One piece, then another. Finally we reached Greggy's ashes. Rough, chunky gravel. Thick black charred pieces and some fine gray dust. I had never seen cremation ashes before, yet they were familiar, somehow remembered. I reached inside. I took a handful and threw it. Then Gordon reached in. He took a handful and threw it. He offered it to Danny, but Danny drew back, put his hands in his pockets and turned away.

"Put the music on," Teri said to Danny, "I don't want it done that way." Then she quickly took the can.

The music played above the sound of the wind as she began to run. Running fast across the sand. Suddenly she turned, twirled in a circle, once, twice, three times. And with one swift motion, an Olympian discus thrower now, she flung Greggy's ashes.

They danced downwind to where we stood and fell on us like dark confetti. Danny, with tears running down his face, held his collar up, tried to turn away again, but Gordon stood tall, let the ashes hit. Now Teri's song was barely audible over the sound of the wind. And she was standing upwind, eyes alight, no tears.

It was too cold to stand outside for long. We walked quickly toward the parking lot. Teri held Gordon's hand. I tried to catch up with Danny, who was walking fast, alone. I reached him, but he wouldn't look at me.

When we got back to the car, I kissed Teri.

"You were right, Carol," Gordon said. "We are all covered in Greggy." He sounded pleased and somehow proud.

"Not me," Teri said, but when she smiled, on her front tooth was one small piece of black ash. A sign, a symbol, a small private jewel.

The sun was going down as we all climbed back into the car.

I placed a cassette of "Path of Joy," a gentle spiritual rendition of Bach's "Jesu, Joy of Man's Desire," into the tape deck. As it played softly in the background, we all sat together silently, each of us lost in our own thoughts.

The tall, wheat-colored rushes danced against a backdrop of the orange twilight as two snow-white sea gulls, soaring and diving in perfect harmony, flew across the winter sky. Then, as the fiery sun began its slow descent into the horizon, those gracefully dancing rushes seemed to form a final curtain, and a large full moon appeared. In the dusk, before the close of day, for just a moment, the bright, shining sun and the full, smiling moon shone side by side: two beacons in the clear evening sky.

There's an Indian myth which tells of the freeing of the soul. In that story the keeper of the soul must release it on either a red or a blue day.

A red day is a clear day lit by a brilliant sun; a blue day is when in the light of day a full moon appears.

For Greggy, God gave us both. A red and a blue day.

Chapter Five

*I*n hidden chambers of our hearts, we stash all the terrifying secrets we believe will cause our annihilation. For most of us the death of a child is one of those secrets. From our child's first breath our own breath either hesitates in fear or hands itself over in tentative trust and innocent hope. Unconscious bargains are struck, unspoken sacrifices offered, as well as promises of gold and goodness to the Great Power of the universe. So it's understandable that we cower in pain and crouch in panic when faced with the death of a baby. Written on our cells, as primitive as the fear of the dark, is this fear of and for our children.

When that fear forces our normal five senses to shut down to protect us, I believe another sense, a sixth sense, emerges and we experience ourselves as we never have before. It is then we have the opportunity to reach our own heights, to touch that seed within ourselves where the human soul grows to meet the heart of God.

But when it happened to Teri, she didn't exactly see it as an opportunity. It just threw her into more of a spin. . . .

The following week, one morning after she dropped Jessie off at nursery school, she stopped by to see me. She sat at the dining room table as I made pancakes for breakfast, and she told me she still couldn't get her mind to do what she wanted it to. She couldn't follow her own thoughts long enough to complete even the simplest of tasks.

"It's the mind's way of protecting you," I explained again. "Grief and shock allow only small amounts of information in at a time, until your full experience is integrated."

"Mom," Teri said, "there's something else." She hesitated. "Something strange happened as I was falling asleep last night. Something I don't understand."

"Tell me about it," I said as I sat across from her with a cup of tea.

"When I climbed into bed last night, I was so exhausted I was sure I would fall right to sleep. But instead I heard a name over and over. At first I thought it was *Maureen,* but then I realized it was *Moira, Moira . . . Moira.*"

"Do you know any Moiras?" I asked.

"Never even heard the name before," Teri said. She took a small bite of a pancake and chewed it a long time. "I'm crazy, right? I've gone over the edge."

"Stop," I said. "Just because you don't recognize a name doesn't mean anything."

"I'm not talking about not recognizing a name," she said, making a face. "I'm talking about hearing voices."

"Who was it?" I asked then. "Did you recognize the voice?"

"Mom," Teri said, exasperated, "why do you sound like this makes sense? It doesn't. I'm just cracking up!" Teri shook her head and took a deep breath. "It was a male voice. He said his name was Hopkins."

I got up to get more tea and asked, "Did he say anything else?"

"I don't know what's real and what's not real anymore," Teri said impatiently. "I feel like I'm in a nut house already when you act like this. Mom, I'm scared."

I walked over and put my arms around her. "What's real is what you're experiencing now," I said. "Don't try so hard to put it in a slot. It will fall into place. Give yourself some room."

She rummaged through her pocket to get a tissue to blow her nose, then she said, "He said I was his wife in England in 1743. He said it was cold and foggy and we were walking holding hands when a man came from behind and grabbed me. He said he ran. He thought he was running for help, but really, he ran because he was afraid."

"So you think he's from a past life of yours?" I said.

Teri stood up and began to pace. "I'm not even sure I believe in past lives."

"I thought that was the one place we didn't disagree," I said. "I thought you believed in more than one lifetime."

"As philosophy and as a possibility," she said. "But believe in it?

I don't know. But it sure as hell doesn't allow for past lives slipping into my present life. For what possible reason? I hate this."

This was tricky territory, and I knew it. It could be a path to enlightenment or a descent into the darkness where Teri could be lost. Over the years I'd struggled with my own beliefs, and had found that while experience could be a brutal teacher, if we allowed it, it could take us through the Gates of Knowledge into realms of Higher Truth. It could wake us up. I knew that once something beat the hell out of us, and we felt our life was over, then it could really begin. If we survived with our mind and heart intact, we could arrive someplace new, different, more hopeful, and more true. That's the breakup, breakdown, breakthrough that Jean Houston and other philosophers talk about.

But that breakthrough can fling us into realms of consciousness we never even imagined. Here we can touch Archetypes, Angels, Gargoyles, and Demons. Darkness and Light, Truth and Illusion. It's timeless, with no past, present, or future. It's not only an altered state of consciousness, it's a place our consciousness goes. And in this place, real dangers lie. These realms can be the realms of enlightenment, but they can also trap the unprepared in a state of psychosis.

The level of the soul's development, as well as the soul's intention, affects the outcome, but once a person arrives in this territory, only the grace of God offers true protection.

"Maybe Hopkins is just trying to help," I suggested. "Let's just give it a little time. I don't feel any danger now."

"Earth to Mom," Teri called, cupping her hands over her mouth. "There is danger. I'm hearing voices. I'm losing it. I'm trying to hang on, but it's all slipping away."

I was determined to watch her carefully. I knew that fear itself could make her more vulnerable, so I tried to reassure her by sharing some of my own experiences. "There were times I'd be sitting at the nurses' station and I'd hear a soft voice say, *There's trouble in Room 322.* The first couple of times I ignored it, but after a few times when I didn't trust my intuition, and something did happen, I began to listen."

"We're not talking intuition, Mom," Teri said. "We're talking about *me* hearing voices."

"That's what I call intuition," I told her. "That's something other people can understand. It doesn't frighten them. The voice that I now know as Eva is a Spirit who has guided me through some of the biggest changes in my life."

"Like what?" Teri asked.

"When your father and I split up, my whole world fell apart," I explained. "Everything I believed had been built on a foundation of Greek Myth, Grimms' Fairy Tales, Disney movies, and the American Dream. Well, when I couldn't have the 'happily ever after,' I had no script to follow. So I was terrified. Remember when I told you about seeing the vision of Florence Nightingale? Well, I thought I was crazy too. I went to therapists. Searched for someone who could explain, but it seemed no one knew any more about it than I did. Teri, I just had to accept that there were some things I'd never really understand. Still, that vision spun me headlong into nursing. And nursing saved my life. After a few of those visions, I learned to trust my experience."

"Just because you weren't crazy doesn't mean I'm not," she said.

"Do you recognize your refrigerator and your dishwasher?" I asked her, trying to lighten her mood. "Do you know your husband and your child?"

Teri nodded.

"Then you're okay for now," I told her. "Sanity is just knowing your priorities, just understanding what the rest of society agrees is real. Next time he comes, just ask if Hopkins is from God, the Light." Discrimination is a necessity once we've reached these realms. One must navigate on wings of prayer.

Teri was horrified. "Next time? Next time?" she said. "You're not taking me seriously. I don't know whether you're not listening or you can't hear me."

I pulled my chair right in front of her and looked straight into her eyes when I said, "Teri, I've worked in hospitals and crazy houses, as you call them, for years. The one thing I've learned for sure is that the definition of sanity is much too narrow and the definition of insanity is much too wide." I touched her cheek. "Honey, this is a very hard time for you. But you will be okay, honest."

She began moving her pancakes around her plate like a little kid who doesn't want to eat. "Mom," she said, "I don't like voices in my head. I'd rather believe it's my own subconscious mind doing this."

"Fine," I said, "maybe it is. But any mind is limited—so sooner or later you'll start getting a lot of repetition. If the information you get is new, then you'll have to rethink your premise. Maybe you're tapping into something larger."

I believe that everything ever thought becomes part of the universal mind, which continues to exist and transmit throughout time. Like a really good radio with a sensitive fine-tuning knob and a terrific antenna, the evolving human brain can act as a receiver for an endless number of stations. But only if we're tuned in.

Still, I knew it had to be very frightening for Teri to have thoughts in her head that didn't seem to be her own. Whether it was her own subconscious mind or a Spirit from another plane of consciousness didn't concern me. But Teri feeling she was crazy did.

"Would you like to go into my study and try to relax?" I asked. "I could put on some soft music . . . or better yet, maybe we could meditate. That always makes me feel better."

"I don't know how to meditate," she said. "Any time I've tried, all I do is fall asleep."

Teri still looked drawn and pale. "You look like you could use some rest," I suggested.

She nodded. "Let's try the meditation. I'm willing to try anything that you think might help."

The morning light had not yet entered my study. My shades were still drawn and the room was dim. Teri walked over and immediately lay down on the sofa. After I covered her with the patchwork quilt, as it was still a little chilly in the house, I put some soft music on. I sat opposite Teri in my leather armchair. Her eyes were already shut. I closed my eyes also and began to breathe deeply.

"What are you doing?" she asked.

"Following my breath," I explained. "I just focus on my breath as I inhale, and then follow it as I exhale. I try to empty my mind of all thoughts. If a stray thought comes in, I just gently let it go and focus on my breathing again . . ."

"Okay," she said, sounding very young, "I'll try that."

My breathing had slowed, my heart rate was regular, and I was on my way to total relaxation and peace, when I heard Teri say, "Stop it!"

"Stop what?" I asked.

"My mind won't stop," she explained. "It keeps saying, 'Get a pencil and paper.'"

"Try not to get stuck on it. Just notice it and gently let it go," I suggested.

"Okay," Teri said.

I was almost completely relaxed again, almost into peace, nothing in my mind, when I heard Teri's voice. "It's happening again."

The music was soft and lilting in the background and I myself was in a warm, comfortable place, so I repeated, "Don't hold on to it. Just notice it and let it go. If you don't get stuck on it, it will pass."

I heard Teri take a deep breath. I heard her try again. But a short time later I heard her say with irritation, "This is just like Gram nagging me to write thank-you notes. I feel like screaming. 'Get a pencil and paper. Get a pencil and paper,' " she mimicked. "I don't want a pencil and paper. I don't have anything to say."

I opened my eyes. "You could get a pencil and paper. . . ."

Annoyed, Teri sat up, threw off the quilt, and stormed across the room to my desk. "This is dumb," she said as she grabbed a pencil from the drawer and a large yellow legal pad from underneath the piles of paper on the desktop. "This is really dumb. And it certainly isn't relaxing!" She sat on the couch again and looked hard at me, "Now what do I do? Just sit here and wait? What am I waiting for?"

I shrugged. "I don't know," I said. "I'm open. Let's just see what happens."

Teri sat with her eyes closed, her pencil poised above the yellow pad. "Mom?" Teri said, "My arm feels weird. It's warm and all tingly." She sounded frightened.

I said a prayer.

At that moment it was as though I'd been swimming underwater my whole life. I needed air; every cell in my body trembled. I began to struggle, to kick my feet, to rise to reach the surface. A warm glow had filled my study, turning everything in the room pink.

Suddenly I was flying upward, flying free . . . I hit the surface just in time, broke through. My head thrown back, I took a breath, a deep full breath. . . . I felt such relief, my whole body relaxed.

I blinked my eyes and tried to focus my attention. Behind Teri, over her right shoulder, I saw a radiant figure, male and tall. A blond mustache was apparent on his young and handsome face. The clothes he wore issued from a different time, a time long past. From his vest, on a thick gold chain, hung an old-fashioned pocket watch.

I felt my senses waken. I smelled the clean air of a cold winter night as well as the flowery perfume of a warm summer day. I heard music . . . a Christmas choir at midnight mass. My senses reached a peak of perception they had never reached before.

It was then I saw the angel. She seemed to float into the room. Majestic as a snow-capped mountain, magnificent as a glowing sunset. More beautiful than I could ever have imagined. Instead of staying my breath, I became the breath I breathed. My heart seemed to beat in time with the universe while the hands of time stood still. At that moment I felt as great a peace as I have ever known.

It was the sound of Teri's pencil scratching on the paper as her hand took off like the wind across the page that brought me back. I watched, unbelieving, as she turned one sheet after another until ten pages had been written. All with her eyes closed.

"Whew!" Teri said, opening her eyes and smiling. "That felt strange. It was as though someone else was pulling my hand across the pages."

The vision of the Spirit and the Angel had disappeared and my study was no longer pink.

Teri looked at the pages incredulously. Then she frowned. "How could this be happening?" she asked. "There wasn't a thought in my mind, and yet my hand was writing."

I tried to view it with some rationality. I tried to put my vision in perspective. "I don't know," I said. "What does it say?"

I moved over onto the couch next to Teri and looked at the pages. The writing was big and scrawling, not at all like her own. And the sentences ran on in a funny way, not punctuated. Yet they made sense. Both Teri and I began to read it together. . . .

This is to be the first communication of many. We welcome Teri to the Light of understanding and we wish to introduce ourselves as guides. Those of Light are to be with you in this changing, growing reality you are experiencing at this time. We wish to say your son is with us and is beautiful, kind, and a very high Spirit. We will write each day, if you allow, and will sign our names after each contact so your awareness grows each time we meet.

Love & Light,
All

Quite a nice day, I must say. This is Hopkins and I am here as your guide of protection, for you are quite vulnerable at this time, my dear. Do not fear, we are all of love and wish only to aid you in this saddened time of life.

I wish for you to know that I never forgave myself for running away. Can you forgive me? I chose this mission this time because I saw you needed guides. It's like roll call for duty except no one calls, one just knows. When I heard it was you, I had to come.

Hopkins

Teri, welcome child. This is Janith, your angel and higher under-standing of self. This will all take some time to fall into the place it is meant to. We have come to help you heal through this time in order for you to become all you can be. We are here to offer love, peace, and insight. Allow this for your highest good.

Be with the Light,
We will come again

I felt enormous relief and a deep sense of something sacred.
The Hand of God reaches out, the Heart of Compassion unfolds, and the Voice of Comfort speaks. . . .

But Teri put her hands over her face and began to cry. "Oh, Mommy," she said, "I'm like Sybil. I have different personalities in my head."

"This is not the same thing as multiple personality," I said, trying to comfort. "Even in this time of grief you know who you are, you know this is something else."

Teri waved the papers in front of me. "Look at this, Mom. I'm writing stuff that I don't even believe. That's not crazy?"

I took a deep breath. "I saw them," I said.

Teri's brown eyes widened with fear. She didn't give me a chance to explain, she just stood up and said, "If you're going to lose it too, I can't stay here."

"Okay, okay," I said, pulling back, trying hard to ground myself in ordinary consciousness so I could talk to her in terms that might help her. "All I'm saying is, it is *possible* that you're *not* writing it. It is *possible* that some kind of energy is just borrowing your arm to communicate information. You know, just like a newscaster bor-rows a TV to broadcast the news. He's not *in* the TV. He's just using it as a vehicle to communicate. When Spirits do that, it's called automatic writing."

Teri sat down again, frowning at me. "Are you going to try to tell me that babies who die for no reason and Spirits who borrow people's bodies are normal?" she asked.

"Honey, I don't mean to sound flippant, but 'normal' is a judgment call," I said. "And it's not the same in all times and all places. Different cultures have very different ideas of what's normal. Some cultures do accept Spirit voices as normal. This society doesn't."

"But I'm not able to *function*," Teri said. "I spilled a can of coffee this morning and I couldn't even figure out what to do about it. Nothing seems right or real to me now."

I didn't want to confuse her, but I did need to keep her from flailing around. I was counting on her trust in me. On an emotional tightrope, I tried to talk slowly, calmly. "Honey, there are things in this world both seen and unseen. That's the first thing you have to accept. I had to learn to discriminate between the voices of my own mind and the guide I call Eva. But she seemed to know things I didn't. I know you worry about being crazy. And it's true that psychosis impairs your ability to function in society—but so does grief. Psychotic voices often berate, undermine confidence, are insulting, and tell people to do things that are against their values and good common sense. These pages don't do that."

Teri sat watching me warily. She didn't say a word. "Look," I said as I picked up the papers and pointed to some words. "Here are some clues that make me feel better. Whoever this is is giving you a choice. They're using words like 'offer' and 'allow.' There's nothing about 'force' or 'power.' They're promising help, insight, and understanding. Not material gifts."

In Eastern religions this period between Death and Rebirth is called Transition. It's a very difficult and sometimes dangerous period, because though one is still living in the same world, one's perceptions of that world have changed. In any great grief, the same thing happens. But, still, that's not psychosis.

Teri looked unconvinced. "What am I going to tell Gordon?" she asked. "I always told him that I'd lose my mind if anything happened to one of my kids. Now he'll be sure I've gone crazy."

"I don't think so," I said softly. "I think he'll understand. Gordon's always been sensitive to other realities and visions. Show him those writings." I added, "I know this is scary for you. But any time any one of us takes a step into the unknown, it is frightening. I'm sure your great-grandmother Justine was scared to death to bring three little kids to a strange new country. My grandmother was undoubtedly scared to learn to drive, shoot a gun, and get divorced. Some journeys are taken into the outer worlds, some into the inner worlds. But in reality, it's all about overcoming our fears and becoming all we can be."

"I get it," Teri said then, and she didn't look happy about it. "Assuming I'm not crazy, I'm just going to wind up being one of those spacey spirit people."

"Like me, you mean, honey?" I asked her.

"No," she said, "you have enough emotional stuff, and your nursing, to keep you grounded. I mean like all those spirit people I met wandering around California."

"Don't be such a harsh judge," I teased. "I'll love you anyway. Please believe me, things will change."

"Mom?" Teri said, looking at me with deep sadness. "I still don't want to get up in the mornings. I still don't feel alive. How far out can I go before I can't get back again?"

"Honey," I told her, "you're not as far out as you believe, honest."

Teri paused. "Maybe I should call Gerty," she said. "Maybe I should make an appointment and get a second opinion."

Dr. Gertrud Ujhely was a gifted Jungian therapist. Teri and I had both seen her over time whenever we had "growing pains" and needed help. Aside from keen insight, Gerty also had great credentials and a lot of common sense, which in a therapist is an unbeatable combination. I hoped Teri would be reassured by seeing her.

"Maybe she'll give me medication or something," Teri said.

"I don't think so," I said, laughing.

Teri took out a pencil and paper and copied down Gerty's number. "Sure—*you* can afford to laugh," she said. "It's not your mind that's going."

That evening, after Barbara and I had supper, I was in my study trying to reach the Society for Physical Research in New York City. I knew Teri would need any of the hard facts available to help her find a meaningful context for her experience, in the "real" world. I heard my mother call me as she walked over from Barbara's side of the house.

When I stepped out of my study, I met my father in the hall. His hat was on but his head was no longer bowed. He kissed me hello. "Hi, baby," he said. "Mother wanted to come over to see how everyone was doing."

"I'm okay," I said, walking past him to kiss my mother.

She sat at the dining room table while my father walked over to the couch and sat in the living room. "We just came from Teri's," my mother announced, and shook her head. "She's upset. Gordon's upset. Jessie was playing with one of the baby's toys." Her eyes filled. "I don't understand," she said. "I just don't understand how this could have happened."

"Ma," I said, putting my hand on her shoulder, "what are you saying? You never knew babies died? You never knew about sudden infant death?"

She blew her nose into a wrinkled tissue she had taken out of her pocketbook. She just kept shaking her head. "I don't understand how this could have happened. . . ."

I felt helpless, so I sounded irritated. "I don't get what you mean," I said. My mother loved me even when I was snappy, depressed, or angry. She loved me however I was, so I was always my worst with her.

She finally hollered at me. "What I'm saying is I don't understand how this could have happened to *our* family. That's what I'm saying. I don't understand why it happened to *us.*"

"Mother," I said. "Be real. This kind of horrible stuff should only happen to other people?"

"It shouldn't happen to *anybody*," she said, eyes rimmed with red. "But even more, it shouldn't happen to *us.*"

Trying to soften my voice, I said, "You're not making sense. I know you're upset and I can understand you're angry—"

She cut me right off. "You and your father make *sense*," she said with disdain. "Go ahead. But that precious baby was my great-grandson. I go to church every Sunday, I do good whenever I can . . . I *don't* understand and nothing you say will change that."

"Okay," I said. "Be mad."

Her expression changed. Now she looked concerned. "Are you feeling all right? How are you?"

"I'm fine," I said to her. "Don't worry about me."

"I'm going to light a candle to the Blessed Mother tomorrow," she said. "I'm going to church." It sounded like a threat. If I knew my mother, she was going right in there to ask Mary what her Son was thinking about when He took Gregory back.

Now I heard my father's voice. "Baby, when you have a minute . . ."

As though on cue, my mother got up to visit Barbara again so my father and I could talk. I walked into the living room and sat on the couch next to him. "Yes, Dad?"

"Your sister mentioned something about Teri hearing voices. Something about writing messages," he said. "Can you explain it to me?"

"Not yet, Daddy," I said, "I'm not quite sure. It could be just the shock and loss, or it could be something else. Some special compensatory healing mechanism that we don't know about yet."

He nodded thoughtfully. "And of course you're interested in human potential? You're curious about healing capacities."

"Of course I am," I said. "Our technology isn't sophisticated enough just yet to track everything about us. In some situations our own consciousness is the only tool we have."

He nodded thoughtfully. "You'll watch your step?"

"In what way?" I asked.

"Teri is your child," he reminded me. "You have a responsibility to guide with care. And because you're also her mother, you have a responsibility to protect her. Don't let your curiosity lead Teri into places she won't be able to handle."

"Dad," I said, "what do you think can happen?"

"When you play around in arenas that you shouldn't, there's sometimes unexpected danger. I just want you to be careful. I don't want you to take any unnecessary chances." His eyes began to fill again. He took his handkerchief out and wiped them, then carefully folded it and put it back in his pocket.

"Dad, I wish I could reassure you completely. I wish I could tell you I know exactly what's happening, but the fact is, I don't," I explained. "I'm just giving it my best. I'll follow to see where it takes us. And I promise I won't be reckless."

"You're a smart girl, Carol," he said. "Fools rush in where angels fear to tread."

"Dad?" I asked. "Do you believe in angels?"

"I'm prone to dismiss them as wishful thinking," he said. "But I've lived long enough to understand that anything is possible. My mind resists the existence of anything I can't see. Still, great philosophers have gone round and round that very question for centuries. I wish it were different, baby, but you can't reach faith through reason."

"Why do you go to church every Sunday, then?" I asked.

"To make your mother happy," he said, smiling at what he knew

I saw as hypocrisy. "But it's a small thing and what harm can it do? They preach kindness, goodness, love."

"So you don't believe in angels," I said, wishing he could have seen the one I saw.

"I believe in the forces of good and evil in the world. Call them what you will."

"Dad," I said with more confidence than I felt, "most minds are not as fragile as we think. I'm sure Teri will be fine. It's at times like these that we can explore who we really are. It's in crisis and tragedy that each of us can take a hero's journey to find our real self. What is it exactly that worries you?"

"If you remember, baby, in all those Greek myths, the gods punished mortals for 'thinking thoughts too great for men.'" He stopped and thought before he added, "Every hero has a tragic flaw, one character flaw that is the seed of his own eventual destruction."

"Dad, what are you trying to tell me? Do you see something that I can't see?"

"I don't know, Carol. I don't want Teri to have to suffer any more than she has. Arrogance was a pretty common tragic flaw. . . ."

I was stunned. "Daddy," I asked, "you think I'm being arrogant? In what way?"

"*Hubris,*" my father said, giving arrogance its Greek name. "Having too much confidence in your own ability and power."

"It's not my own power that I have confidence in, Dad. Not at all. I feel quite humbled by all of this. It's the power of God I trust, the power of good in the universe. That's what gives me courage to try to expand our limits; I see it as an opportunity to grow. And a way to honor our Creator."

He shook his head. "I'm not criticizing you," he said softly, "I'm trying to help you avoid the pitfalls. I'm asking that you tread gently, as gently as I do when I explore an unfamiliar woods. There may be hidden traps. I want you to be on the lookout for them. I want you to stay alert."

Chapter Six

T here are healing covenants throughout the planet where clusters of individuals are growing toward their full humanity,
small groups of people who have experienced deep woundings but,
in spite of their own vulnerability, have the courage to reach out to
others.

These people, from all walks of life, all economic levels, all races,
religions, and ethnic backgrounds have broken through the barriers
that have kept them prisoners of separateness. They are bound
together by a wound that seems too deep to heal. But if they *can*
heal themselves, they become true healers of others. They touch each
other soul to soul, and in so doing they bring some of heaven to
earth.

The Sudden Infant Death Syndrome Support group was one of
these small healing clusters. Lois Caprioti, from the Long Island
chapter was one of those true healers.

One night, when the whole family was over at my house for dinner,
she called to ask Teri and Gordon to attend a meeting. I encouraged
them to go.

"How about coming with us, Carol?" Gordon asked. "Lois said
family members could come."

I turned to my mother and father, who were sitting on the couch,
and asked, "Would you like to go?"

My mother shook her head and my father said, "You can tell us
about it."

"Dan?" Gordon asked. But Danny shook his head too.

Then Jessie said, "I could come, Daddy."

Teri kneeled down in front of her and explained. "Not this first time, honey. Let Daddy and me go and see how it is. Maybe next time you can come."

Jennifer, my niece, said softly, "I think I'd like to come."

But Jessie reached for her hand and insisted, "You come next time, with me."

Jennifer picked her up and smiled. "Okay," she said.

"Bibs?" I said, turning to my sister, who had just walked into the living room. "Do you want to go to a SIDS support group meeting with Teri and Gordon tomorrow night?"

Barbara's eyes widened as she said softly, "I can't. I'll do anything else you need me to do, but I can't go."

"Okay," I said, turning to Gordon. "I'll go with you and Teri."

Later that night, after everyone went home, I walked into my sister's room to talk to her. Though it was still early, she was already tucked into her bed, hidden under loads of covers.

"Are you asleep?" I whispered.

She pulled the covers down and hoisted herself up in bed so she was now leaning against the headboard. But before I could even say anything she blurted out, "I'm sorry. I'll sharpen pencils for Teri's Spirit writing, I'll sit with her when she does it, I'll read those communications and tell you what I feel. I'll cook and clean and take care of Jessie for as long as you need me to. But please don't ask me again to go to that meeting."

Her eyes were already filled with tears by the time I said, "I wasn't going to, I just wanted to see how you were."

"I'm terrible," she said. "I can't stop crying. I don't know how Teri can keep breathing. I wouldn't be able to. I can't think of anything more terrifying."

I sat down on her bed. "It's scarier than Spirits?" I asked, teasing.

"Much scarier to me," she said.

"Why?"

"When Teri's doing the Spirit stuff, I can believe it's real or not," she said. "But whatever it is, if it helps, I'm okay with it. To sit with other couples and listen to them talking about losing their babies kills me. I can't pretend that isn't real, and I can't pretend they're not like me. Being in the middle of all that pain is like falling into quicksand. I'll never get out. I'm not like you."

"What makes you think *I* can do it?" I asked.

"You've been around death for years, Carol," she said. "You've been with parents of dying children before, that's what you do. Your mind can defend you with things you believe. And you have the right words. You can help. So your heart doesn't keep breaking."

"You're wrong," I told her, and I felt my own eyes fill. "My heart does keep breaking over and over again. I can't be a nurse in that support group. There, I'm Teri's mom and Greggy's gram."

Barbara sighed and leaned back in bed. "Do you think we'll ever be okay?" she asked. "You, Teri, me . . . all of us?"

I took a deep breath. "I know we will. We'll just take it one day at a time, and we'll help each other. We'll be okay."

"What did Daddy say about the writings?" Barbara asked me.

"He told me to be careful," I said. "Do you think it's dangerous?"

"No, I think it's fine as long as we don't lose Teri," she said. "It would be strange if our little rebel got holy."

"Not much chance of that. She's not at all happy about it," I said.

"Are you?" Barbara asked.

"I'm relieved and I'm grateful. I like that they sent in some troops to help."

"How do you know they can help?" she asked.

"Do you believe in angels?" I asked her.

"Of course," she said. "What kind of question is that?"

"I saw the angel Janith today," I said. "And Hopkins, that past-life lover of Teri's who says he's here to protect her? I think I saw him too."

She sat up straight again. "What do you mean, *you think?*"

"Well, my study got pink and I saw this Spirit and this huge angel," I admitted.

"Well, who else could they be?" she asked.

"I don't know. I keep going over and over it in my head," I said. "You wouldn't believe what that angel looked like. I mean she wasn't only big, she was magnificent. Skyscrapers are big, but mountains have something extra. Well, this angel was like the Himalayas, she was like the Grand Canyon, she was like—"

Barbara laughed. "I get it. Like God created her, not man."

"Right," I said. "I keep going over it in my head to try to analyze it. But before Teri even started to write, I saw them. So how could I have imagined them?"

"Have you ever seen them before?" she asked. "Are they familiar?"

"They didn't seem strange," I said, thinking about it. "They didn't frighten me at all."

Familiar? Remembered? From where? When?

The doors of my memory flew open. . . .

I was seven years old. It was a rainy day and I was looking out my grandmother's bedroom window, trying hard not to blink at the huge drops crashing on the foggy pane in front of my eyes. My grandmother Catherine's voice broke my concentration when she said, "Carol, I have to go away."

I turned around to look at her; I searched her face. I could see she wasn't angry. She was sitting on her bed, thick orange cotton stockings half pulled up.

"Why?" I asked.

"Because I'm sick," she answered softly.

I walked over to the bed and stood right in front of her. "I could get you an aspirin," I said.

"I have a lump," she explained as she took my hand and ran it across her breast over her ivory satin slip. Something hard pressed back against my fingers. I got a sick feeling in my stomach and my head started to go funny. "I have to have an operation," she said, and then she added more gently, "And I won't be able to come back."

My heart was beating so fast in my chest that it made my body tremble. I was more frightened than I had ever been. I threw my arms around her neck, crying as I hugged her. "Don't go away, Gram. I'll be good. And if you're sick, I'll take care of you."

My grandmother gently peeled my small arms from around her neck. She kissed me. She kissed my hair, my face, my nose, my lips. Then she took one of her lemon-scented handkerchiefs, put it to my nose, and ordered, "Blow." When she put her fingers under my chin and lifted my face to look into my eyes, she said, "Now, remember I love you and I'll miss you as much as you miss me." She began to say something about a secret, but I didn't hear her clearly. Her voice sounded as though it was coming from very far away.

Suddenly a warm glow filled the room, turning everything pink. And I was staring over my grandmother's shoulder straight at an angel. . . . Her head seemed to go through the ceiling, her wings seemed to push through the walls. I blinked my eyes. But she was still there.

"Carol, are you listening?" my grandmother was saying. But I just smiled back at the angel, whose eyes were smiling at me. "Carol," my grandmother repeated, "trust yourself and try to do what makes you happy." Then she gave me another quick hug, slapped me affectionately on the butt, and said, "Go play."

* * *

The following afternoon, on his way home from work, Danny stopped by to see me. His light hair was almost shoulder-length and his uniform smelled like printer's ink.

From the time Danny first walked into shop class in ninth grade and saw a printing press, his life's direction was set. He loved printing the way I'd loved nursing. There was nothing else he ever wanted to do.

"How's everybody?" he asked. "How's Teri?"

"She's still feeling pretty crazy," I said. "But she's trying to work through it. The SIDS meeting is in a couple of days, so maybe that will help."

He said, "Whatever works."

"You're sure you don't want to go, even to keep Gordon company?" I asked.

He just shook his head. "It's not where I need to be, Mom," he said. "Gordon and Teri need to go together."

"But usually you're good at feelings and stuff," I told him. "Maybe this will help you too."

"Feelings and *family*, Mom," he said patiently. "Not feelings and strangers."

The night of the first SIDS support group meeting was crisp, cold, and beautiful as Gordon drove through the narrow tree-lined streets of the North Shore of Long Island. The sky glittered with stars.

"I hope their stories make us feel better," Teri said.

I sat in the backseat, trying to cover the dread I felt by holding my coat tight around me. What was the matter with me? I wondered, why didn't I want to be going no matter how much I knew those groups helped? I tried to think about it.

Somehow I needed to feel that even my pain was special. In some crazy way, it was a tribute to Greggy. Nobody, nowhere, at no time, felt like I did about him. It was a flaw, of course, I knew that. Still, I didn't want my tears washed away in the rivers of other human tears. I wanted my tears to be one drop of dew on a single rose.

Through the dark night inside the car, Gordon's voice cut a path like a sharp knife. "I wonder how many fathers feel like I do? Like they failed their families?"

Teri didn't respond, she was struggling in the dim light of the street lamps to read the directions she had jotted down. "Look for number thirty-six."

The brown-shingled house was so well cared for that it was impressive. The sculptured driveway carved a path through a large front yard that was neatly landscaped with tall, manicured evergreens.

"They don't look poor," Teri said.

"Are they?" I asked.

Teri shrugged and said, "I had some picture in my head that most SIDS babies came from poor families."

The front door was ajar. Inside, the house was warm and inviting. A tall, good-looking gray-haired man introduced himself as Mr. Landell, our host and the grandfather of one of the SIDS babies. He led us into the dining room, where several young couples were milling around the buffet table. There were carafes of coffee and tea, small sandwiches, and trays of cookies. It was completely disarming.

A woman with fair skin, a motherly bearing, and short blond hair wore a bright smile as she walked toward us. "Hi," she said, "I'm Lois." She turned. "Teri?" she asked. Teri nodded and they hugged. "You must be Gordon," she said then, moving toward him. "Welcome."

Teri introduced me. "I'm glad you came," Lois said.

Later, sitting around in a circle of chairs in the living room, all of us made a living mandala. A circle of pain, a circle of healing, a circle of love. They began by telling about themselves.

There were the Landells, and their daughter, Louise. Her baby, Tory, had died while his grandparents were baby-sitting for him. Their son-in-law had never attended a SIDS meeting.

There was Rita, a pediatric ICU nurse, whose husband, Bill, was also a nurse. She had tried to resuscitate their baby, Claire, and then went through four agonizing days waiting for the doctors to take Claire off the respirator. Bill didn't come to the meetings either.

Lois's baby, Sean, was almost a year old when he had died seven years before. Her husband Ted, a policeman, also found it too difficult to attend.

Paul and Linda, a sweet-looking Jamaican couple, had lost their baby after Linda had seven miscarriages. They adopted a little girl, Bonnie, then Linda got pregnant. She was finally able to carry the baby to term. Their daughter, Cheryl, was born eight pounds and healthy. At three months that baby died of SIDS.

Pam was pregnant again. She had stopped teaching when she had her Willie, but her husband, Johnny, a social worker, was the one who found him dead in bed at six months old. He had been sleeping with Johnny.

Pete and Maria's baby died on the same day he was born. Pete had just enough time to put an announcement on his answering machine so that anyone who called would know he had a son, before the doctor called to tell him to come back to the hospital. Pete said that was the best and the worst day of his life.

Gordon told about Gregory then. And I could hear for the first time how many of his hopes and dreams had died with that baby. The hope for a son to take fishing, to play ball with, to teach how to be a good man in a changing world. Gordon had missed having a relationship with his own father and had sworn he'd be the best father any son had ever had.

Teri reached for his hand to comfort him as he confessed feeling guilty about not changing the batteries in the intercom because maybe he would have been able to hear the baby cry or struggle. He also shared his feelings of helplessness over not being able to do anything once they had found Greggy. But Gordon, like me, had already begun to look for meaning in his tragedy. "I think this has something to do with knowing real sadness in order to be able to experience real joy," he said.

The expression on Teri's face told me she wasn't buying it. She looked straight at Gordon and said, "I think that's bullshit. I don't care about having real joy. I was happy just as we were. I loved having my house, my girl and my boy, my husband, and my picket fence. It was enough for me. I didn't want any more."

Lois smiled gently at Teri. "Given a choice, none of us would have paid the price of admission to be part of this group."

Back at my house, my mother and father were waiting for us. They were sitting together on the couch in my living room, watching TV, and Barbara was on her side with Jessie, Jennifer, and Chris.

After we took off our coats, my mother offered us some food, but none of us were hungry. We sat at the dining room table and settled for a cup of coffee and some cake my father had baked.

"How did it go, baby?" my father asked Teri.

"I found out a lot I didn't know, Poppy," she explained. "I found out that a baby dies every hour in the United States. SIDS is the leading cause of death in infants from one month to one year old. And most of the babies who die of SIDS are just like Greggy. Typical SIDS babies are healthy babies, with nothing wrong with them that we can see. Most of them come from middle-class families, like us, who ate well and whose mothers had good prenatal care."

Without judgment, my mother asked, "Do they smother?"

"No," Teri said, "I thought about that too. But Lois said they've even done studies where they tucked the blankets in on all sides of the crib, covering the babies, and their oxygen levels didn't go down. It's not smothering."

"The researchers have no idea what causes it?" my father asked.

"Lois said they keep coming up with studies every month that show different risk factors and research makes it sound like the cause. But each study winds up being discounted by another. She said not to pay too much attention to the media coverage. It would just make us crazy."

My father turned to Gordon. "Did you find it helpful, son?" he asked, his voice soft.

Gordon looked pensive. "A lot of good guys, Poppy," he said, "who loved their kids and did their best. They talked about their feelings. It did help."

After my parents left, Teri and Gordon walked over to Barbara's side of the house to pick up Jessie. But she had fallen asleep in Jennifer's bed. Teri tried to wake her, then Gordon tried, but she stubbornly refused to open her eyes. When Gordon tried to lift her in his arms, she kicked her feet and began to cry. "I don't want to go home," she screamed. Neither of them could stand to cause her any more pain, so they just laid her down again.

Finally I went into the bedroom to talk to her. She was lying in bed, still as a statue.

I closed the door behind me and sat down carefully next to her. In a teasing voice I called to her. "Jessie, my girl, tell Mama Carol what's going on behind your sleepy eyes?"

I could see Jessie's eyelids flutter, but she kept them shut.

"I know you're hiding in there," I whispered. "And I bet I know why."

I was going to bluff. I was counting on her need to prove me wrong to make her talk to me.

"Bet you don't," she whispered back right away.

"I can see everything," I told her in a slow voice. "And I know why little girls don't want to go home."

Jessie made a face and opened her eyes. "About the baby ghost and the white horse?" she said then with her eyes narrowed. "Mommy told you!"

I was surprised. I didn't have a clue what she was talking about.

"I can't believe it," I said, my eyes wide. "I can't believe you saw the baby ghost too! Did it scare you?"

She sat up now and in the half-dark she rubbed her sleepy eyes. "No, the baby ghost isn't scary. But the white horse scares me. He hides in my closet and then he flies around my room. He wants to take me with him."

"Don't go," I said. "Tell him you belong to Mommy and Daddy and you have to stay in your house."

Jessie started to cry. "I don't want to go home, Mama Carol! I don't want to see the white horse."

"Okay," I said. "Let's see if we can make some ordinary magic. Let's see if we can get Mommy and Daddy to let you stay here tonight."

Jessie clapped her hands and laid down. I tucked her under the covers and kissed her.

When I walked back over to my living room, I told Teri, "She wants to stay because of the white horse."

Teri and Gordon both looked concerned. "She's been having that nightmare for over a week now," Teri said. "Last night she made me turn on all the lights and search her closet. Then she made Gordon double-check. She told us it was like her Rainbow Bright horse without the colors. She was afraid it would take her away. Finally she fell asleep in our bed with us. But we were all up for hours."

"Then let her stay," I said to both of them. "Get some sleep and come pick her up in the morning. It will give you two a chance to spend the night alone."

They looked at each other. Gordon deferred to Teri for the decision. "Tomorrow's our anniversary," she said. "Maybe . . ."

Barbara came over then. "Jessie's already asleep," she said. "I don't mind her staying here. You can leave her for as many nights as you want. Get some rest. Spend some time together."

After Teri and Gordon left, Barbara and I sat and had a cup of cocoa together before we went to bed.

Barbara asked me, "What's going on with Jessie?"

"I'm not sure," I said. "She's either following everyone else's lead or leading us to a place we'll have to follow."

That day seemed endless. As I undressed to go to bed, my body felt as bruised as my emotions. I quickly said my prayers. But it wasn't until I was tucked in bed that I could even try to process all that was happening. The tears came silently, without any thought.

Finally, after lying awake a long time, tossing and turning, a truth seemed to surface that had been hiding in my heart. And I knew why I couldn't bear going to support groups.

Without my nurse's uniform, dressed only in my humanness, I slipped into the skins of the others and lost myself without half trying. My boundaries blurred so quickly that I saw my face in everyone else's. I *was* like my sister. Because I *knew* we were all a part of God's one heart, it wasn't possible for me to stand apart. How could I have imagined that I loved Greggy any more than those parents or grandparents loved their babies? And I wondered: *Is it possible that the tears we all shed can be so much the same that they're all part of the great river—and yet so very special that each is one drop of dew on a single rose?*

Chapter Seven

T eri's favorite story from the time she was a child now seemed
to offer her some comfort:

Once upon a time in the Land of Magical Dreams Come True
there lived two children who loved each other very much. One was
a beautiful blond-haired girl and the other a handsome dark-haired
boy. Each day they played, wild and wonderful, in the grass and the
trees of the thick wooded forest. As they grew, they learned, and
each day they found they loved each other more.

But in this Magic Land there was a Wisdom Council. That council
called the children to them. They told those two free spirits it was
time to spread their joy and love throughout the world.

When the children found that the girl must go west and the boy
must go east, they were in deep despair.

"How will I live without you?" she asked.

"And how can I live without you?" he asked.

They sat on the forest floor, crying.

It was then that Owl came. Fair and funny white owl, an odd and
creative owl. "Have the birds weave your hair together," he suggested.
"Then no one can ever separate you."

"Together?" the boy said, his eyes radiant with joy.

"Together," the girl vowed, her lips tight with resolve.

All their forest friends came to help. Birds sang happily while they
wove the children's hair into one long braid. When they were finished,
the children could not move, one without the other.

The council came again. "You must obey," they demanded.

"We cannot," the boy insisted. "We are joined together from now until forever."

The Wise Ones shook their heads. "The world needs Love in Life," they said. "You must leave this place of magical dreams and roam among the peoples of the land."

"But we cannot," they exclaimed again in one voice.

"Enough of this," the wise one said.

Thunder clapped and lightning flashed as his sharp silver sword chopped the braid from their heads.

They were separate again. They were two. But still not free.

It was the girl who reached down for the woven tresses. With tears in her eyes she cut the braid in two. Then she threw the boy one half. "Tie this on your wrist," she called as she was pulled away. "And I will tie it onto mine. Then, from this day until forever, a piece of me will be with you, a piece of you with me."

Lifetime after lifetime, these two children roamed the land. Everywhere they went they searched for their missing piece—and each told everyone they met the story of their love.

Teri had been looking for weeks to find something that she could wear that would represent her connection to Greggy. But no matter how hard we looked, we couldn't find anything. Nothing seemed right.

It was Jennifer who found the solution, and she hadn't even heard the story of the children.

One day when Teri and I came back from the mall, Jennifer was waiting for us. With her dark hair pulled back, she looked very much like Teri had when she was twelve. She talked as little, and smiled as seldom. She had loved Greggy with all her heart and, in the vacuum created by his leaving, Jennifer had not only grown closer to Jessie, but to Teri too.

Secretly, for the past week, Jennifer had spent hours each day weaving a macramé band, a thick white cotton bracelet that Teri could wear on her wrist. It had no clasp. It had to be slipped over her hand. Once Teri had showered, the macramé shrunk.

"How will you get it off?" I asked her.

"I won't," she said simply.

"You'll wear it forever?" I asked, smiling at her.

"No," she said. "Just until I'm whole again. Just until I can find that piece of me that's been missing since Greggy died."

* * *

The night Teri and Gordon went home without Jessie had been very uncomfortable for them. Without her in the house, it seemed too empty. Teri didn't know whether to celebrate their anniversary or not. She didn't even know how she felt about it. The sacred part of it, the union that helped create Greggy, had also caused each of them the deepest pain of their lives.

As soon as she got home, Teri got on the phone. She called Lois to try to stop the loneliness. Only talking with someone who had been through it seemed to help. They talked about SIDS studies, research, tried to share their feelings. Teri was writing down another list of articles that she could search through, more information she could send for, when she heard crying coming from somewhere. When she hung up with Lois, she tiptoed toward her bedroom.

Gordon was lying on the bed, holding Gregory's music box, the one my mother and father had given him for Christmas. That music box, a small caged bird played, "The Impossible Dream." When my mother had chosen it, she didn't recognize the music, she just fell in love with the delicate porcelain bird in the gilded cage.

Now Teri walked over to the bed and sat down. She put her hand on Gordon's shoulder to comfort him, but he cried even harder. His whole body shook. "Gord," Teri asked, "do you want to talk?"

He turned over, tears streaking his face. His green eyes looked hurt but his voice was angry when he said, "At least God knew why they took His only Son."

Teri, caught off guard because it was so unlike him, began to laugh. "Gord," she said, "of course God knew—but I'm sure St. Joseph didn't have a clue."

She lay down next to him, took him in her arms. When he kissed her, it was with both longing and pain. They tried to make love, they tried to climb inside each other's skin and prayed for the obliteration that had always come from losing themselves in each other. But this time it didn't happen. When they sat up, they felt more lonely than before.

They came back to my house then. And the first thing they did was go inside to check on Jessie. That night they fell asleep in my living room, on the floor. When I found them in the morning, they were still holding hands.

In nursery school that week, two-and-a-half-year-old Jessie was having her own struggles. Outside in the playground she had a fight with one of the little boys. He said she was lying, she didn't really have a brother.

Jessie told him, "I do too have a brother. He's a *dead* brother, but he's still my brother."

When the little boy still didn't believe her and kept tormenting her, she punched him and knocked him down.

The teacher called and Teri went to pick Jessie up. But Jessie refused to talk about it.

It was days later, when she and Jennifer were playing house, that she was willing to explain what had happened—and only because she wanted to know from Jennifer, "It's the truth I still have a brother, right?"

Jennifer told Jessie, "Of course you still have a brother. He just lives somewhere else."

The fall off the cliff of the known world into the dark void of the unknown happens in an instant. But the death of the old self doesn't happen all at once. It takes time. To try to break the fall we keep trying to grab onto some familiar concepts and fit them into the belief system that once supported us. But one by one those old beliefs crack like dry brittle crags. Then, with no known ground in sight and no hope for a safe landing, we flap our wings and try to fly. Only then can we begin to soar toward our potential.

Two months after Greggy died, Teri was still in free fall. She had been keeping herself busy by doing all the household chores she could manage, and she had begun trying to take care of Jessie again without the family's help. But she still wanted to find answers for what happened. When the preliminary autopsy report came back with the definitive diagnosis of SIDS, she felt a little better. She knew at least she hadn't missed anything. But she still didn't believe there were no answers. She thought she just hadn't found them. So she spent hours going to libraries, looking up data on Sudden Infant Death Syndrome. She made hundreds of calls to try to find the answers. And she talked to Lois every day.

Teri continued to do her automatic writing with Gordon's help or mine, but she said it was only to take up the time that was left empty by having no baby to care for. Her heart wasn't in it.

The Spirit writings themselves were always reassuring and supportive. Teri's guides always asked how she was doing, and in each session there was something that helped take her farther into trusting not only them, but also herself. They seemed to be able to monitor how she was feeling, and they often answered her questions before she asked.

One day she was sitting in my study, and she had been feeling particularly crazy and worried over Jessie. Nothing anyone said seemed to help. But her guides explained,

Crazy is quite a different sight than yours. Do not be alarmed. Love will guide you with a strong hand if you let it. Be patient. Your daughter, Jessica, is fine. Do not question your gift but accept and use it. Your eyes are open.

Love & Light,
All

Teri was furious. "They make it sound like it's easy to accept all this stuff, as though it's just an ordinary event and I'm being thickheaded."

"Is there anything they could say that would make you feel better," I asked, "anything you don't understand?"

"Look, Mom," Teri said, "all they're telling me sounds like the same things you say when you're trying to reassure me. I still don't understand why Greggy died, or why a good, kind, loving God would allow a baby to die."

Almost before the words passed Teri's lips, she felt the urge to write again. She frowned, but reluctantly picked up her pencil.

This one, this special baby, gave you a gift like no other. Janith may tell you that the God of kind, loving presence has not allowed or disallowed this. It is something that you came in to do with the consent of your spirit as well as the consent of the baby's spirit and the rest of the family members involved.

Be with the Light,
Janith

* * *

When Teri read that she was furious. "I don't believe for a minute that I had anything to do with this," she said. "I can't believe I would set this up."

I looked at her. "Do you still think it's your subconscious mind?" I asked. "Because you seem to disagree with what's being said."

Teri began to cry. "I don't know what this is. It sounds like blaming the victim. I know I wouldn't do this to myself . . . or to anyone else I loved! I know it's not me!"

Teri kept doing the writings because now that she allowed for the possibility that this might not be her own subconscious mind, she was afraid not to.

Teri finally got an appointment to see Dr. Gertrude Ujhely and she was eager to go. Since all her research on SIDS had left her with more questions than answers about the reasons for Gregory's death, she was looking forward to a concrete explanation for her "voices." She didn't care anymore what that explanation was.

But I did. I trusted Gerty as much as I trusted any other human being. She was honest, bright, and creative in her therapeutic approach to problems. Still, Teri was *my* child and I felt very protective toward her. I knew that a diagnosis of pathology could cause as much damage as real pathology. A diagnosis that makes someone afraid could become a self-fulfilling prophecy. On the other hand, interpreting symptoms in a positive way could give someone hope. If Gerty told Teri she was psychotic, she could fall toward that darkness. If Gerty told her it was healing, she could climb toward that truth.

I waited in Dr. Ujhely's office, holding my breath and praying, while Teri was inside, talking to her. When Teri came out of the room, my heart skipped a few beats because she looked so disappointed. "She says I'm not crazy," Teri told me. "She said there was no medication she could give me for what was happening. She just read the stuff, shook her head, and said, 'This isn't crazy. I'm not sure what it is, but I'd recognize crazy.'"

Teri told Gerty that I thought they were Spirit communications, and she had warned, "Then be careful of the quacks and the kooks while you try to find someone who knows more about this than I do."

"Did she tell you where to look for help?" I asked Teri, enormously relieved.

Teri just made a face and said, "Mom, it's not the kind of thing you find in the yellow pages."

"So where will you begin?" I asked her.

She smiled in resignation. "With you. With Gordon. With the angel Janith. As long as I can't find any answers in the 'real' world, I'll try your world for now. But I'm not making any promises that I'll keep going with it. I just have some questions I want to ask."

I felt elated as we walked outside into the crisp, cold day. The sky was blue and the frost on the trees made them glisten like crystal. As we rounded the corner of the building into the parking lot, the sun was shining down bright as gold. And as I opened the car door to get in, Teri stopped, closed her eyes, and turned her face up toward the sky in an expression of childlike innocence and surrender. For the first time since Gregory died, I felt warm again in the "real" world.

Each day after Teri dropped Jessie off at school, she'd stop by, and we'd have breakfast and spend time together. She'd talk about her frustrations, her feelings, and whatever was going on at home.

Janith had told Teri that she could ask any questions that caused "earth point problems." So one day, Teri came equipped with a list. I was surprised.

We went into my study and began to meditate, Teri on the couch, me across from her in my leather chair. Most often when she did her writings I could see a halo of pink light, but not since the first time had I so clearly seen Hopkins and Janith. After that they were just impressions.

So after I put music on, sat in my chair, and began to follow my breath again, I wasn't expecting anything. But on this day, instead of the usual pink light, the room glowed again. I tried to focus my attention, I tried to keep my breathing even, and then I saw her. As majestic, as beautiful, as breath-giving. My heart again became a drum that beat in time with the music of the universe. And this time I saw her eyes, those same smiling eyes I had seen as a child. . . .

"Teri?" I whispered, "Teri, turn around. . . ."

"Why?" she said, and her voice was wary.

"She's behind you," I said, smiling. "Just look. . . ."

But Teri wouldn't turn around. "I can't, Mom," she said. "I really can't. If I see her, it will scare me to death, and if I don't, I'll think I'm crazy again."

I was disappointed. The angel stood with smiling eyes, bigger than life, wings now a jet stream of glistening energy. "Okay," I said. "Let's just ask the questions, then."

It took Teri a little while to relax again, but soon her hand was flying.

"How do I stop being afraid of everything now that I don't understand the reason for anything?" she asked.

Janith wrote:

You do not stop being afraid. You "be" with your fear. Try to understand your fear. Take your fear to the worst end and then come back again. You must go on a journey before you can come home.

Teri asked then, "Why do people say time heals?"

On earth time heals, for process is continuing. It is process that heals.

Teri had objected the first time Janith implied there were plans we make before birth, and I knew it still bothered her to think she had any part in this tragedy. So I wasn't surprised when she asked, "If I can't accept that I have responsibility for plans once made, will it affect my healing?"

Of course not. For your accepting or not accepting responsibility has nothing whatever to do with what is.

Teri's voice cracked when she asked, "Why do I feel like such a failure because my son died?"

Because at this time in your belief system and in your society, death is seen as failure. Lack of doing something that you should have done to prevent the inevitable is quite a silly concept. Would we look at a pregnant woman who says I will not give birth when it is time, and think her a failure when a child is born? Trying to stop a death is like trying to stop a birth. Let us not separate birth and death the way we do and we will not have the same fear of failure reaction.

Teri had only one more question, but it was an important one. I could hear it in her voice. "Why is life so unfair?" she asked.

It is not unfair. Please remember all is just from which comes learning. Life only "seems" unfair to those with a negative outlook on life's growth experiences.

Then, while I was trying to think of what I wanted to ask Janith, she wrote:

Teri, there is something you must do with your gift, your open soul. That is to help others to know themselves. This can be done in a number of ways. You can tell them of your own experience. You can help them experience their own understanding. You can combine both. Please let us know of your decision.

Be with the Light,
Janith

Teri opened her eyes and asked me, "Is she gone?"
The light had faded. "I don't see her anymore," I said.
"Good," Teri said. "Let's see her answers."
When Teri finished reading them, she was quiet.
"What do you think?" I asked.
"I wouldn't lay all this stuff on some innocent human being. I'd be a lot more sympathetic about their suffering. And I wouldn't be telling them they had more to do."
"Janith doesn't sound unsympathetic to me," I said. "She sounds sort of sensible, if you buy her premise."
"Mom," Teri said, testily, "she already said it doesn't matter whether I buy it or not. I made some sort of plans and now we have to live them out. What is that anyway?"
"What?" I asked.
"Making plans before you're born so you don't know what it feels like when you have to deal with it? And if it were true, how could I forgive myself for doing it? This is all too complicated."
"It's not really complicated if you've read anything about the Buddhist Wheel of Life. It's like karma. You keep coming back until you get it right."
Teri made a face. "It doesn't look like we have a choice, no matter what anyone says about free will. If I don't do it this time, I'll have to do it later. And I don't care how many lives I live, I never want to find a baby of mine dead again."

Mario still called at least once or twice every day from the house he'd rented in Malibu. The weather was beautiful, the food was great, and with the waves crashing on the beach, the house was just perfect for writing.
"But even Paradise isn't heaven when you're alone," he said one day, teasing me.

"I'm sorry," I said, feeling guilty. "I still think the kids need me here."

He was taken aback. I could hear it in his voice. "I didn't mean you should do anything differently," he said. "I know the family needs you. I just want you to know that when you're ready to come out, I'll be waiting."

"I know that," I told him. "How's the writing going?"

"Slowly," he answered. "I can't seem to concentrate enough. Same struggle as always. Have you been able to do any writing?"

"I'm taking some notes," I said. "Just the important things. I can't really work on my manuscript."

"How are the kids doing?" he asked.

I hesitated, realizing that as long as we'd been together, we hadn't talked about our spiritual beliefs. I'd talked about them. He hadn't.

"Do you believe in Spirits?" I finally asked.

"No," he said quickly.

"You don't believe in God either?" I asked. "I mean, you don't believe in any intelligent force that runs the universe?"

"No," he said. "I think this is it."

"How can you believe that?" I asked. "It doesn't make sense."

"There *may* be Spirits. You may be right," Mario said. "But I've built my life on a certain foundation, and if I had to change that now, I'd go crazy."

"I don't get it," I said. "Don't you ever revamp your thinking?"

"Not as far as my vision of my world," he said. "This one is hard enough."

Mario is a good man. He's kind and generous and compassionate as well. But he doesn't believe in Spirits. I wondered what motivated him if he had no belief in an overriding justice or an afterlife. I asked, "So what keeps you in line? What makes you try to live an honest, authentic good life?"

"Guilt," he said. "I can't stand the thought of living with a monster."

"Mario," I said, taking a deep breath, "I saw an angel the other day."

"You're a funny girl," he said.

"I'm serious."

"I know," he said. "That's why you're funny."

"You don't believe me?"

"Of course I believe you," he said. "Just because I don't believe in angels doesn't mean *you* can't see them."

"Doesn't that mean they're not real for you?" I asked.

"But they're real for *you*," he said. And then he sounded puzzled when he asked, "How can I say what's real for you?"

"I guess you can't," I said.

"Look, Carol," he said. "You handle life better than anyone else I know except maybe your father, so even if this is a quirk of yours—and I'm not saying it is—it works for you. That's all that's important."

"No, that's not all that's important," I said. "I wanted you to believe me."

"I do," he repeated.

"I mean I wanted you to believe in angels," I said.

"That's different," he said.

"Teri's got an angel writing through her," I explained. "Teri writes stuff and she doesn't know what it's going to be until she reads it. They write their names, these Spirits, in each paragraph."

"That's too bad," he said, and his voice was filled with compassion.

"You're not hearing me," I said, frustrated. "I believe it's a good thing. I believe they've come to help."

"Yes, I know," he said. "But does Teri?"

I tried to stop pushing so hard. I tried to watch my step. I tried to honor Teri's truth and not mix it up with mine. She was getting more comfortable with her voices. And it was she, not I, who decided to continue the writings each day. One day Janith wrote,

Once I was told a story of Divine Peace, of a dove called Whisper Wind. This dove was beautiful inside and out. One day the dove fell upon a beach that was deserted in nature but in reality there were many other doves with her. Still, she could not see them or hear their laughter. Yet for some reason unknown to Whisper Wind she returned to that silent place day after day. Until one day, as she landed, she knew enough not to land on any of the other birds who occupied this beach. This is silly, thought the beautiful white dove, I am here alone. But somehow she could not believe this notion any longer and never again did Whisper Wind feel lonely.

Teri shrugged her shoulders. "Why is Janith telling me stories instead of saying what she means straight out?" she asked.

"Lots of prophets talked in parables or told stories," I reminded her. "Jesus, Moses, Rumi, Buddha. So do many Zen and Sufi masters. Native Americans teach by storytelling. You're supposed to get the message from listening to the story."

"The only message I'm getting is that my mind is gone," Teri said. But she wrinkled her nose and made such a funny face that she made me laugh. She didn't look as angry as she had. She looked less frightened when she admitted, "But I am starting to feel when they're around. Something inside me shifts in a funny way."

"Like Whisper Wind?" I asked, laughing. "You can feel them even though you can't yet see them?"

Teri bristled. *"Yet* see them? I'm telling you, Mom, if I ever see anything that isn't there, I'm finished with all of this. Hearing things is one thing. Seeing things is even more horrifying."

"I don't think so," I said. "We don't know how our inner healer works. Do you even give a thought to how a cut heals? You've learned to trust your body's healing ability. But what about the healing mechanisms that have been built into our minds, emotions, and souls? At least eighty percent of our brain is unmapped territory. The only shot we have to map it is to use ourselves as tools. Who knows? Maybe this is a compensatory mechanism. Maybe you'll come out of this a better person. Maybe you'll be more whole."

Teri put her hands up over her ears and wailed. "Mom, I don't want to be a guinea pig for science or an example of an evolutionary woman! I just want to be like I was before, when my life seemed certain and I knew what to expect when I woke up in the morning."

I reached over to kiss her on the forehead. "Going back to the way it was doesn't seem to be one of the options right now. It looks like you're moving forward toward tomorrow . . . and the most important thing you're going to need on your trip is trust."

Teri looked at me and her expression was one of complete disbelief. "You want me to trust a God or a Universe that just took my baby?"

Chapter Eight

G ordon and Teri were snuggled together on the couch in their living room. Jessie was asleep. They were silent, mesmerized by the small, bright-colored fish swimming slowly back and forth across their large aquarium. Gordon had finally relaxed, freed from the responsibilities of work and the probing questions of those around him. He and Teri had spent the last hour sharing what they were feeling and now found comfort in just being together. They were both grateful no ties had been severed between them by Gregory's death, no breech had been made.

It came suddenly. Teri's heart began to flutter, at first a tiny stop, start, thump: a small bat, wings extended, hitting against the inner walls of her chest, trying to escape some unseen terror. Warned, alert, she sat up on the edge of the couch. But now she couldn't catch her breath. She stood and started to pace as though trying to outrun the fast-beating clamor of her own heart. But then her heart itself became the terror.

"What is it?" Gordon asked.

Teri's voice was scared silent, halted in her stopped breath, quiet as the night. *It might be Jessie,* her terror cried, and so she ran into the bedroom. Fear clouded her eyes and Jessie, her treasure, seemed gone. Frantically, with groping hands, she searched the bed. *Ah, found.* Jessie was fine.

It was the smell of fire next. Thick smoke burned her nostrils and loud crackling exploded in her ears. *The back room,* she thought, *the oil burner,* and so she ran again. Gordon, who had been sitting still as stone, seemed to come alive then and will himself to act.

"What is it?" he asked again, his voice high and thin. Contagious—her terror.

Teri's voice was still hiding. The cotton of fear filled her ears and she didn't hear his question. But she saw his face, she saw his eyes, searching. Her voice, in small, constricted sounds, tried to surface, she tried to tell him. But now the words wouldn't come.

Gordon grabbed her by the shoulders, tried to pull her back to him with words. "Tell me," he shouted, "tell me what's wrong."

She shrugged. No matter how hard she tried, she couldn't fit it into words, she couldn't make a bridge between them.

Softly now, Gordon heard her unspoken plea, he felt her spinning backward, falling away from him. He touched her face. Looked into her eyes. Deeply, lovingly, insistently. "Teri," he called, his voice a hand to reach through time, "ask Janith! Call for Janith! But only Janith!"

The bat in her chest stopped, and she began to cry.

Gordon sat her on the couch and ran for a pencil and paper. He sat close to her, his arm around her, and placed the pad on her lap. Then he bowed his head and said a prayer before he handed her the pencil.

Her hand flew like wind across the page . . .

This is Janith. Please take heed. You know there is something to be wary of. Leave tonight. You will be able to return tomorrow. But go! Go to solace! Then the feeling will subside—not before.

Gordon grabbed their coats and then ran in to rescue Jessie.

Outside, the night seemed black and quiet, too quiet, as though the wind in the starless sky had halted.

It was three A.M. when I awakened to the pounding at my front door. I jumped out of bed. Before I opened it, I asked, "Who is it?"

Gordon was holding Jessie wrapped in a blanket. She was still asleep. "Is she all right?" I asked. He nodded and I asked, "Where's Teri?"

"She's in the car," he said. Then he walked past me into the house and laid Jessie on the couch. Before I had a chance to ask anything else, Gordon was out the door again.

Teri was pale and shaking as he led her into my living room, but her eyes were wide with fear. "What happened, honey?" I asked, "What's wrong?"

Teri just shook her head and crawled onto the corner of my couch opposite Jessie. She sat with her legs bent, pulled up tight against her chest. Instinctively I walked over to her, kneeled down, and put my hands on her knees. "It's okay, Teri," I said. I had never seen her look so frightened. "You're safe, honey. It's okay."

She nodded her head. And then she looked at me. But her eyes weren't really seeing me. "Gordon," I said, "talk to me."

When Gordon finished, Teri had stopped shaking but she still looked scared to death. "It's okay, honey," I repeated. "Nothing can bother you here."

She looked at me. "You're sure?" she asked.

"I'm sure," I said. "I'm here. And this house is protected." In my head, I heard my father's voice warn of *hubris,* so I quickly added, "By God, the Light."

That night Gordon, Teri, and Jessie slept together in my bed, in front of my altar, watched over by all my symbols of protection. I slept on the couch.

The following morning, strengthened by a good night's sleep, Teri seemed to feel better. After breakfast Gordon kissed her good-bye and reluctantly left to drop Jessie off at nursery school. He had to go to work.

As soon as Teri and I were left alone, she asked, "Mom, what was that last night? What happened to me?"

Suddenly I was on unfamiliar ground. I believed in Spirits, but only good ones. That had been my experience. Though I had heard about it and read about it, I didn't really believe in evil. For me, it was only hearsay.

Even as a small child in Catholic school, I thought the priest was just trying to scare us when he told us about possession. *My* God would never let a silly devil torment a child, or any good human being. Guardian angels would always protect us. Good was always stronger than evil.

Back then, and I was no more than seven, I decided that people didn't always tell the truth. Even priests and nuns. A priest warning about the dangers of possession by the devil made me doubt religion. It was the wedge that separated me from the Catholic Church.

Later, when I began to study Eastern religions, and they warned of getting caught in states of consciousness filled with illusion, again I believed that evil was just a trick of the mind. I knew the mind was much more susceptible to illusion when we were afraid. So I vowed now not to be afraid.

But because I refused to see a truth, and didn't allow for Teri's reality, I almost made her stop trusting herself.

"Maybe it was just your fear," I said. "After all, your baby died in that house, it has to be scary. Maybe it's just a projection of that fear." Those words were like a grenade. They almost blew us apart.

I saw the confusion in Teri's eyes, I saw her suck in her breath. She recoiled from me as though she'd been struck. "You mean the feeling I had last night isn't real? You mean I just made up the voices?"

Open your eyes . . . Eva said.

I pulled us both back just in time by saying, "Honey, trust yourself. I don't know about this. I haven't had an experience like it. It makes more sense to get information from Janith."

Just my allowance of her reality, just the possibility that she could trust herself, helped. This many years later, I know that as there's a collective consciousness of all mankind, there's also a collective unconscious. A dark shadow that exists within the greater mind of all of humankind. I hadn't figured that out yet at the time, and so I didn't know that there was a big difference between projecting your own individual shadow into the ordinary world or finding yourself in the lower world of the great shadow.

When we went into the study to meditate, I took my phones off the hook so we wouldn't be disturbed. Then I put on the music and sat in my chair. Teri got herself some paper and pencils and asked Janith to explain what had happened.

This time, even more quickly than usual, Teri's hand began to move.

This is Janith. You are wary and that is wise. Good must never confront bad but instead try to overtake it and consume it with Light. God is with you and you must know this.

This entity is angry, jealous, and vindictive. You felt him arrive and knew nothing of the power he has drawn to him. With some guidance you may be rid of him, but nothing is absolute on your plane. Thus we cannot be sure of his departure.

Quite clever is he. Take heed at all times when dealing with this force. He is not kind and entities from the shadow side of the Light never are. I suggest you leave that place. He is strong and we are not able to help much. Another place will become available.

* * *

When Teri read what she had written, she said, "I don't understand why, if he's an evil spirit, they can't help much."

"It's like in the story of Sleeping Beauty," I said, still trying to process the information and find a bridge.

"Mom," she said, exasperated with me again, "fairy tales?"

"It's not as big a jump as you think," I explained. "In that fairy tale, the good fairies weren't able to reverse the spell that the evil witch had cast, but they were able to temper its effects. So that when Sleeping Beauty pricked her finger on the spinning wheel, instead of dying, she just fell asleep until true love found her."

Teri shook her head. "This is much more like a nightmare than a fairy tale," she said, and then she asked, "What on earth has that got to do with me?"

"Maybe fear can prick you like that spinning wheel and play tricks with your mind. Maybe there is something in that house to be afraid of, I don't know. I figure that Hopkins and Janith can't protect you from illusion if you stay there, but they can help wake you up to a bigger truth in another place," I said.

In a hero's journey, right after the call to adventure, a fairy god-mother, an angel, or a good Spirit shows up. There's a reason. It's for the battle with the dragons of darkness that guard the entrance into the unknown worlds. Aesop knew it, the Grimms knew it, even Disney knew it. But at the time I didn't.

Teri asked Janith then if he was, as I had suggested earlier, a negative projected part of her own psyche.

He was no more a part of you than of anyone else. He is a spirit entity not aware of his position or surroundings and not of your business anymore. Please listen to that voice of Light within you. This entity will make you fight hard for your life in that place is not easy. It has served its purpose. This force is strong and will divert your energies away from the Light. Feel free with the Light and move on. It is time. He will remain but he may not choose another as he has chosen you. Find home from within and go make your house somewhere else.

"Mom," Teri asked, "what should I do about the house?"

Gordon had put all his money into a down payment for that house. My mother and father had bought them a new kitchen. Walls had been torn down, put up, and painted. New carpeting and flooring had been installed. If they let the house go, it would be years before they could afford another.

"I need more information before I could even attempt to give any advice," I told her, shaken by her reaction to what I had said before. "And I need to meditate to try to find out what's really going on."

There are different kinds of meditation. I used both passive and active to accomplish different things. To relax myself, I followed my breath. But whenever I had an important decision to make, I did an active meditation. Then, I could see truths that I couldn't with my eyes open. I could tap into memories that I thought I'd forgotten, find creative solutions and new information that weren't accessible in ordinary consciousness.

Now, back in my study listening to my music, I said a very fervent prayer. To *"them"* who had always guided me and to my own guardian angel. For protection and for truth. Then I tried to clear my mind of all thought for a few minutes to center myself. I was in a state of such peacefulness, no sadness, no worry that I had to intentionally drag myself back in order to remember that I wanted to know about the energy in the house. I made my intention clear and asked to "see."

It happened in a split second.

I descended quickly, plunging downward, downward, downward, until I found myself in dark and murky waters. Thick mud forced my eyes shut, its weight pushed me deeper and deeper into the darkness below. Slimy water, like seaweed, grazed my skin, filled my nose with the smell of rotting fish. Then fear, like an octopus, engulfed me, tightening tentacles squeezing away my breath. . . . Spinning, spinning, spinning, and still spiraling downward, I tried to stop what was happening. I struggled to turn around, I struggled to come back up. But I was helpless! It was then, like the sound of a shark slicing through the water, I heard the echo of a laugh. A harsh, eerie laugh.

"Stop!" I said, terrified but angry now. I prayed. I tried to hold the Light in my mind. "Stop!" I shouted again. More forceful than before. "I will not accept evil. I am from the Light. God is my protector. . . ."

I swirled around so quickly that my neck almost snapped. It was as though I'd been ejected. Before I knew it, I was flying upward, flying fast, flying free through clear, clean waters. When I surfaced, this time, I was really shaken.

I would never again open myself to that kind of energy. I would never enter that place again. Or doubt that there was evil. I had never before had an experience like it. And if it was up to me, I never would again.

When I went back to talk to Teri, she looked at me, concerned. "What happened?" she asked. "You look pale as a ghost."

"I don't give a shit what anybody says," I told her then. "If I were you, I wouldn't live in that house again. Houses can be replaced."

Teri picked up Jessie and brought her back to my house after nursery school that day. Teri had been in school for a month now and she had gotten home from her own classes early. She didn't want to go back to her house alone after she saw my reaction. Instead, she decided to cook dinner at my house while Jessie played with Christopher.

After Gordon got home from work that night and we were all sitting around the table eating dinner, he asked Teri what Janith had said that day.

She got up from the table, walked into my study to get her pages, and then handed him the writings. When Gordon had finished reading them he said, "He's probably just a poor earthbound soul stuck between planes of consciousness. I know what I have to do, I have to help him through to the Light."

An earthbound soul is one who has died but refuses or is unable to get to the higher realms of consciousness. Some attachment to earth keeps the soul stuck in a kind of Limbo. Prayer helps those souls, as does the intention of loved ones who help release a soul from his connections to earth and help direct it to the Light.

Teri told us she felt Janith's presence around very strongly at that moment, but she couldn't sit to write until after she put Jessie to bed.

Later, as Teri and I sat in my study with Gordon, even before Teri asked a question, Hopkins wrote with otherworldly panic.

Do not enter the house with intent to help. This is dangerous. Then he reassured. There is a beautiful day ahead of you, my love. After this passes, you will be free to use the gifts allowed you. I am deep in thoughts of protection. I will not allow harm to come to you. Not again. I must do this for my own karma and lessons of the world. Once this is accomplished, I may move on, and so may you. . . .

Hopkins

* * *

Teri's hand raced across the page again.

*Gordon, listen with your Indian heart. There is no helping this
entity through. He does not wish to go. This force may enter your
mind but he may not enter your heart. You will not be able to remove
him. If such a thing is done, he will follow. Leave him where he lies.
Time and knowledge of the Light is important. Human domain must
be maintained from within, not without.*

> *Be with the Light,*
> *Janith*

That night, for the first time, I heard Teri and Gordon fighting.
Gordon was very unhappy. They had taken his son, now he had to
leave his house. But Teri stood firm and refused to return to her
house.

Teri insisted, "Gord, Jessie doesn't even want to be there because
of the white horse, and I don't want to be there. If there's anything
negative in that house, I'm not willing to take a chance with Jessie.
I don't know how this stuff works!"

"We can't run away whenever something frightens us," Gordon
fought back. "Love will keep us safe. Jessica needs to be with her
toys and other familiar things. Too much in her world is changing
too quickly. She'll lose all sense of security."

But Teri was so upset, Gordon finally agreed that they could all
stay at my house for the rest of the week. Gordon called Danny that
night and they went to the house together to gather some clothes
and toys for Jessie.

When things had quieted down, I stayed in my study, thinking. I
picked up the pages Teri had written and reread her writings. Something nagged at me and made me uncomfortable. What was it? There
was the Indian in the dream I'd had, and now Janith's reference to
the Indian heart. My mind, a tracker now, looked around. On the
unknown path before me, I saw some broken twigs and heard the
sound of crackling leaves. *A war cry? A raid? An eagle feather?*

During that week, Gordon kept returning to their house after
work to feed his parakeets and his fish and pick up more of their
things. Each time he went there, he was gone long into the night.

"Time just seems to fly while I'm there," he explained when he
got back, but Teri was furious.

"Every time you go over there you forget to come back," she said. "You get sucked right back in. I don't understand why you keep doing it."

"I can't just forget I live there," Gordon insisted. "It's my house."

Teri began to cry. "You said you believe in spirits. You told me to trust myself and to trust there was a bigger plan. But then even when Janith says that we should only make short visits to the house, you ignore her. How am I supposed to know what to do?"

Gordon tried to soothe her, but he stood his ground. "I'm still having a rough time letting go. I keep trying to figure out what else I can do to stop everything from falling apart."

"There's nothing you can do, Gord," Teri said. "You can't control this any more than you could control Greggy's death."

"I don't want to fight with you," Gordon told her. "I'll try harder. I won't go as often."

Another week passed, and Gordon and Teri tried again to decide what to do. Teri felt guilty about getting rid of the house, but she was too frightened to keep it. Gordon wanted to keep it for practical as well as sentimental reasons. It was the only house that Greggy had been in.

So Teri got up her courage and tried to go back. But she was so uncomfortable the one time she tried to return that she came running back to my house almost immediately. "I can't stand it there," she told me. "It plays with my head. It sucks me right in too."

The following Friday night, when Gordon returned from the house Teri was working on a report for school and I was lying on the rug, editing some manuscript. When Gordon sat down on the couch next to Teri, she moved away.

I had noticed that on the days that Gordon stayed away from the house, they got along just fine. They were as affectionate as always, they could talk and even laugh sometimes. But on the days he stopped by the house, when he came home she recoiled from him. I had asked her about it.

"Mom," she had said, "he feels different to me when he comes home after he's been there. It's a funny feeling. Not fear but something else, just a weird feeling."

I wondered if negativity could cling to an energy field in some subtle way, and now that Teri was sensitive to subtle energies, maybe she could feel that negativity. I wondered if it could somehow sneak into Gordon's pores, hide in his hair, and reach her on his lips.

That night when Gordon tried to put his arm around Teri to hug her, she jumped off the couch again. "This has to stop!" Gordon said in a voice filled with both sorrow and anger.

Teri was crying. "I know," she said, "but how? Am I supposed to trust myself only when it's convenient? When it doesn't go against what we want for ourselves? I don't know what you expect."

Gordon sat by himself for the rest of the night. And before he went to sleep, he came into my study to ask me, "Would it be okay if we slept over here awhile longer? Just till Teri feels safe or we decide what to do?"

"Of course," I said. "That way you'll all have some time to heal and I can be there for her."

But the universe and my family had very different plans.

The children in an Italian family don't belong only to their parents, they belong to the family. No matter how old they are. Every decision had to be a communal one. Everything had to be done for the good of the family.

My mother and father came over as usual, but this time they brought Aunt Josie. I should have known what was coming. When Barbara walked in and Danny came over from his apartment, it should have occurred to me. A family council meeting had been called. But not by me.

My father looked very serious. "Baby, you know we're all concerned about Teri," he said, talking to me. "And we all want what's best for her."

"Daddy," I said, sitting on the rug next to the coffee table, "what's this about?"

Aunt Josie spoke next. "It's a better idea for you, Carol, to go back to Mario. It will do you good."

No one ever questioned Aunt Josie, so I turned to my father.

"What are you saying?" I asked.

"I think it's important that Teri and Gordon are able to resume some kind of a normal life," he said.

"How am I stopping that?" I asked. "And how will it help if I go away?"

My mother spoke next. I could always count on her to tell it straight. When she had something to say, I didn't have to wade through a marsh of words. My mother never threatened with a dagger, she hit right away with a hammer. "Carol, what your father means is that you're encouraging Teri. Those voices. You let them talk to her. She wants your approval so she does what you want."

"Ma," I said, "that's nuts! I didn't start with the voices. I didn't make them up. And I'm not encouraging anything. I want her to honor her own truth. I'm supporting her. Don't make it sound like I'm an accomplice in some hideous crime."

My mother shot back, "If she wants to talk to angels, she should go to church."

"You're gonna drive me crazy, Ma," I said. "What are you trying to do?"

Aunt Josie tried to placate me. "Carol, a little rest will do you good. Mario needs you. And you always go away in the winter. It's cold here, the sunshine will make you feel better. It's been hard for you."

I stood up. I was furious now. "Daddy," I said, "how can you think you can just ship me off to Malibu to keep me away from Teri. She's my daughter."

My father's eyes narrowed and he licked the side of his lip. A dead giveaway that he was controlling himself. He hated emotional outbursts. "Calm down, buddy," he said sternly.

"Why?" I asked. "Why, with all that's happened, should I calm down? Especially now when you're trying to accuse me of doing something I don't even understand."

"No one is accusing you of anything," he said, his voice softer now. "We're trying to see what's best. Raising your voice about it won't accomplish anything."

"You're not *accusing* me of anything?" I asked him, and then I looked at my mother. "Do you agree with Mommy?"

"I think she has a point," he admitted. "I think that your inquisitiveness may cause danger . . . I mentioned that."

I felt completely betrayed. "Wasn't it you who also mentioned human potential? Wasn't it you who told me about the value of adaptive behavior?" I didn't wait for him to answer. "I don't get it," I said.

My father looked down at his hat in his lap. He ran his fingers around the edge of the rim. "Carol," he said, looking up at me then, "we're just ordinary people. And we just want to do the right thing for Teri. Not all of us want a vision. . . ."

I started to cry with frustration. "Daddy, we're just ordinary people? Now you tell me that? My whole life you told me we were pioneer stock. My whole life you trained me like a Spartan youth for something. What was that? You told me to believe in myself, that I could be anything I wanted to be. And now?"

My mother cut me off. "We're not talking about *you* now," she said. "We're talking about Teri, Gordon, and Jessie. We're talking about selling a house they just bought. A house we paid a lot of money to put new cabinets in."

"Forget that, Wheezy," my father ordered, calling her by her pet name. "That's not important." Then he turned to me. "I want you to give Teri some time to get her footing. Go to Malibu so they can stay here. Your sister can help take care of them, and it will give them time alone."

I just looked around the room at them. All of them. Barbara wasn't looking back, and Danny said nothing. "I'm her mother!" I hollered.

"You remember the story of King Solomon," my father said sternly. "Remember it was the real mother who let the baby go rather than have the child cut in half?"

"This is crazy," I shouted. "This is *really* crazy. . . ."

I ran into my bedroom and slammed the door. And then I sat on the bed feeling sorry for myself. How could they do this to me? I asked myself, outraged. How could they do this to Teri? Didn't they know I wouldn't take chances with my own child? But then through the cracks in my certainty, some small doubts creeped in. Was I sure enough of my vision that I was willing to gamble Teri? I had always been willing to throw myself into the fire, but was I courageous enough to surrender my own child to my truth?

I knew by the sound of the knock on the door that it was my son, Danny. If it had been anyone else, I wouldn't have opened the door.

He sat at the foot of the bed and he smiled. "Mom," he said softly, "why are you letting them get to you?"

"They're acting like I'm making Teri do something she doesn't want to," I said.

"Is that true?" he asked.

"I couldn't make her finish high school when she didn't want to," I said. "I couldn't make her stay in New York when she wanted to go to California. I didn't make up the voices. I just tried to help her explore them."

"Okay," he said. "And do you think they're real?"

"What do you mean?" I asked.

"Do you think those voices are Teri's guides?" he asked. "Do you think that they're here to help her?"

"Yes, of course I do," I said. "Otherwise I wouldn't have *encouraged* her, as your grandmother says."

"Then why don't you just trust yourself. What difference does it make if you go to Malibu? If they're really here to help her, you might as well go."

"I feel terrible leaving her alone at a time like this," I said.

Danny shook his head and smiled. "She's obviously not alone," he said. "She's got an angel, a Spirit, a husband, a brother, and Jessie . . . not to speak of a grandmother, a grandfather, and a couple of aunts."

"True," I said.

He laughed when he teased, "And they're nice to her even if they're mean to you."

"I didn't say they were mean. Just misguided."

Danny's eyes twinkled. "Mom? Give yourself a break. Being with Mario will help you feel better. You should go."

"Traitor," I said. But for the moment I had begun to feel a little better.

He laughed again. "Mom, you're going to Malibu, not Siberia."

Before the family left, I did the right thing, though not with much grace.

I went back into the living room, where they were waiting patiently, and told them I'd think about what they had suggested. I'd talk to Teri and Gordon, I'd talk to Barbara, and I'd decide. Then I offered them coffee and cake. Before they left I kissed them all good-bye. But my fury was still fermenting and my heart was closed.

My sister Barbara loved harmony. Once she left the living room, I knew I'd never see her until my emotional thermostat reached normal again. And even then she wouldn't come to talk to me.

So after everyone had gone, and Teri and Gordon were watching TV in my living room, I went into her side to talk to her. We sat on her couch.

"Are you okay?" she asked me.

"I'm still a little pissed," I told her, adding, "I'm not mad at Mommy, she's just her. But Daddy and Aunt Josie . . ."

"They really do want to help," she said.

"Do you think they're right?" I asked her.

"I'm not telling you if you're going to get mad again or have hurt feelings," she said.

"Terrific," I said. "That allows me a full range of expression."

"I don't want to hurt you," she said.

"Then tell me you understand. Tell me that I'm perfectly right. And then tell me they had no right to say the things they did," I teased.

She looked down and played with the ring on her finger. "I can't do that," she said.

I took a deep breath. "Okay, I promise I'll understand that you want to help and that everything you say is really for my own good. And I won't hate you and I won't have hurt feelings. I won't even change the expression on my face, no matter what."

"Okay," Barbara said, looking at me. "I do believe you can see and hear things that the rest of us can't. I do believe that you have a vision of what human beings can be, that the rest of us can't imagine," she said, wrinkling her nose. "But I'm not sure that's what Teri needs right now."

I was trying to remain expressionless, but a slight frown must have shown on my face. She didn't say anything else until I said, "Explain it to me."

"I think things are changing too fast for Teri," she said. "Maybe she needs to be with ordinary people who are living ordinary lives. Maybe expanded vision is coming too fast and maybe without you around she can find some solid ground."

"What about her writings?"

"I told you I'd help her with them," she said. "I'll do whatever you would except go to SIDS meetings."

"What about evil spirits?" I asked. "Do you believe in haunted houses?"

"Yes," she said simply. "I do. I think there are evil forces, or evil energies. . . ."

"What will Teri do then?"

Barbara shook her head. "I think they can attach or attack only if you're not leading a good life and doing good things and thinking good thoughts. I think it's dangerous for Teri only because she's vulnerable right now, and confused."

"So I just abandon her?" I said.

Barbara looked thoughtful. "Leave the house to Mom and Aunt Josie," she said, "I heard them talking today. Something about *malocchio,* the evil eye. Aunt Josie was talking about making red ribbons and then Mommy said she would pour salt around and sweep the evil out the window. The Italian culture has superstitions . . . and rituals for dealing with evil. If I were an evil entity, I sure wouldn't want to tangle with those two."

"You believe that will do it?" I asked.

"I believe it will help," she explained. "They do want to help Teri. And love is a great weapon."

"I know it's irrational," I said. "But I feel I'm leaving her unprotected in some funny way."

Barbara raised her eyebrows. "Are you taking the angel with you?" she asked.

"Of course not," I said. "Angels don't go anywhere, they're everywhere. So I'm sure they can cover both coasts."

"Love, angels, good deeds . . ." Barbara said thoughtfully. "We have all of them. I think you can safely go away. And later, if Gordon can get off work, they can get away from here and visit you. By then they'll need a change of scenery."

As I stood up to walk back to my side of the house, Barbara added, "You can reach out and touch someone . . . even in Malibu there are telephones."

I impulsively bent down to kiss her. "Thanks, Bibs," I said.

But I still had to talk to Teri.

Believing in something isn't enough. The test of real spirituality is that we have to learn how to apply it in very difficult situations. And this sure as hell was one of those times. I had to trust that if I left, Spirit would take care of everything. It terrified me now. It forced me to see how deeply embedded my beliefs were and where I wavered.

That night when Mario called I was still a mess. I was sitting on my bed alone in my darkened room, still unable to shake my confusion and hurt feelings enough to make an intelligent decision about what to do.

When I answered the phone, I said, "Hi," and nothing else.

Mario, alert, asked, "What's wrong, honey? What happened?"

"My family thinks it's my fault that Teri's hearing voices," I said, crying into the phone. "They think I'm hurting her by being here. They want to send me away."

"Where to?" he asked.

"To Malibu," I said.

"That's terrible, honey," he said, and I could hear the smile in his voice. "Is that why you're crying? Because you're being banished to Malibu?"

"It's not that I don't want to see you," I said. "I even miss you."

"What is it, then?"

"I don't know," I said, trying to clear away the cobwebs. "It's just that while there's still some danger, I shouldn't be going away to Malibu to have a good time."

"It's doesn't sound like you're going to have a good time," he said.

"You don't understand," I accused him.

"Try me again?"

"I don't feel right leaving Teri yet, and I'm not sure why," I admitted.

Mario sounded serious when he said, "Carol, if you believe as you say you do, there can't be any danger. Come out here. If you can't stand it, or if Teri needs you, you can fly back home anytime."

I felt better having a choice. "Do you think the kids could come out and spend a few days? Maybe that would help."

"We could set them up for Disneyland," he offered.

"Okay," I said. "But I haven't talked to Teri yet."

The following morning after everyone left, Teri and I were sitting in my living room. She was looking through some of the textbooks that she had picked up for her courses and I was proofreading some of my old manuscript pages. But I couldn't keep my mind on them, I couldn't really concentrate. Finally I whipped up my courage and asked her, "How do you feel about me going back to Malibu?"

"Sounds okay," Teri said. I was watching her expression carefully for any telltale clues, but she was just taking some notes and marking some page numbers.

"I'll be happy to stay home if you need me," I told her.

Teri looked up at me, then she shook her head. "Gregory is going to be dead for a long time," she said softly. "And the healing I have to do, you really can't help me with."

"What about your Spirits?" I asked. "Are you okay with them now?"

"I'm getting more comfortable," she said. "Janith and Hopkins are a help. And you can't wait around for me to decide what to do with the house. Grandma, Aunt Josie, and Aunt Barbara can help me with that."

"Did Poppy tell you he thought it would be better for you if I went?" I asked.

She nodded. "He did. But I don't think it matters much whether you stay or go. I have to find my own way now. And maybe us being apart will help. I don't know."

I was crushed. Now it was unanimous. "I can call you every day," I said.

"I know," Teri said, "and I can call you. School will keep me busy and I'll keep doing my writings to show you when I see you."

"When you have a school break, maybe you all can come to California," I said.

"It's okay, Mom, really," Teri said, forcing a smile. "Go, have a good time. If I could get away from this myself, I would."

That night over dinner, Teri and Gordon agreed it would be a good idea to stay at my house while I was gone. That would give them until spring. By then they'd all be stronger.

Gordon came into my study to talk to me. "I'm sorry about all of this, Carol," he said.

I turned my chair away from my desk and computer to face him. "None of it is your fault," I said. "In fact, it's probably nobody's fault. It's one of those life situations. . . ."

"I don't know what else to do," he explained, running his fingers through his hair. "I tried to reassure Teri, I tried to make her feel safe, but I can't."

It was for Gordon that my heart broke most. "I don't think any of us can do that right now," I said. "I think it will take time for her to heal."

Gordon sat on the couch.

I asked him, "Do you really believe in evil spirits?"

"Yes" he said, his eyes intent, "I do. I just don't believe that they're as powerful as Teri does."

"And Hopkins and Janith?" I asked.

Gordon sat up straight again and looked directly at me. His green eyes shone with light. "I have no doubt at all, I never did, that Teri is tapping into some kind of pure spiritual energy. But whether it's a deep core of herself that we all are capable of reaching or something else, I don't know."

"Do you feel better about me going away too?" I asked then.

"No," he said, "but I do feel it's safe for you to go now." He shook his head. "I know it must feel like we're throwing you out of your house. That makes me feel guilty."

"Gord, it's not you," I said. "My own tribe has banished me to the wilderness."

He smiled. "I'm sure eventually it will all work out."

"How can you be so sure?" I asked. "Everyone else is positive that I'm taking Teri someplace she shouldn't be."

Gordon looked thoughtful and then he smiled. "You couldn't take her into the places she's going now," he said. "Nobody could. It's just her karma. And ours."

"You believe in karma?" I asked. "And past lives?"

Gordon looked down, took a breath, and looked at me again. "I *remember* past lives of mine," he admitted. "I had dreams about Teri's room in this house long before I ever met her in California. When I found myself standing in your house, in New York, in that room, I knew it was exactly where I was supposed to be."

"So you think this is all some kind of plan?" I asked.

"Yes," he said. "I'm sure it is. From the time I met Teri, something in me knew that we were together for some special reason. I knew it would be a hard thing. And I knew we had to help each other with it."

"Destiny, you mean?"

"Yes," he said. "I believe there's a bigger plan for all of us. I think Greggy was part of it, and so is this. I'm just not sure what the plan is or how much our own free will plays a part in our fate."

"Maybe Janith can tell us the bigger plan," I said. "Maybe she'd be willing to."

"I think that's why she's here," Gordon said.

Chapter Nine

*M*alibu seemed such an unlikely place to go in the time of my greatest grief. New York had been stark and cold, a winter skeleton of itself, but it was a world that matched what I was feeling.

At the airport in Los Angeles, Mario, dressed in one of his favorite white silk jogging suits, had been waiting anxiously for me to arrive. As I walked through the gate, I saw him. He looked healthy, with skin tanned from playing tennis, his hair a little longer and a little grayer than when I'd left just two months before. His large, dark eyes registered his concern for me.

"How was the flight?" he asked, putting his arm around me.

"Smooth in reality, rough in my mind," I said. The last flight I had taken was the one right after Greggy died. That flight kept replaying itself in my memory.

"Being on the beach will help," he said. "The sun will make you feel better."

Riding along the coast highway, on our way to the beach house, I didn't say a word. Mario never talked much. But that day his silence was a comfort. Just being with him seemed to help.

Through the car window I watched energetic runners jogging with dogs, healthy, tan couples galloping on sleek, well-groomed horses, and beautiful young people talking and laughing as they carried their tennis rackets. I wondered if any of them had ever been touched by death. If any of them had ever experienced suffering. My mind knew that a whole population of people couldn't have been spared the pain of being human just because of geography, but that day my heart didn't know it.

I had been surprised when I first saw them, that the houses were not as glamorous as I'd expected. Most were modest-looking, regular stucco or cedar, and were built so close together that they were almost attached. But they were right on the Pacific Ocean. I'd traveled enough to know that that stretch of beach and sky was one of the most beautiful in the world.

The house Mario had rented this time was nice, simple white clapboard, not fancy. Downstairs there were three bedrooms and a huge living/dining room that led to a deck on the beach.

The master bedroom, a large all-white room with French doors that led to a balcony that also overlooked the beach, was the only room on the second floor. On either side of that room against the wall was a long white table. One held Mario's typewriter and all his books and papers; on the other stood my computer and all my books and papers. Through an arch there were two large walk-in closets, a dressing room, and two full-sized bathrooms, one for each of us. In my bathroom there was a Jacuzzi.

"It's nice," I said to Mario as I looked around the bedroom, and then I walked out onto the balcony. The sun was shining hot and bright on the silver sand below. The constant sound of the waves as they washed ashore was comforting.

Mario walked up next to me and put an arm around my shoulders. "You can rest here," he said. "Take a nap and come downstairs whenever you feel like it."

Back inside, by myself, I aimlessly walked around the bedroom, then I began slowly to unpack. But by the time I had put three things away, I was already exhausted. I flopped onto the bed, and before I knew it, tears were streaming down my face. I turned on my side and curled myself up. Downstairs I could hear the chatter of other people, and I got up to close the door. I was terrified that someone would come up to offer their condolences and I would fall apart. At home I'd been able to be strong because my family needed me, but in Malibu, where I was free to be myself, where no one was in crisis, I finally felt again my own devastation. I wondered now, as I lay on the big down-covered bed, whether my being here at this point in my life was a reward for all my years of suffering or a down payment for all the things that were to come.

Rewards? Punishments? I had done nothing to manifest this kind of life consciously, I knew that. I had gotten here by inexorably following the iridescent arrows of Fate. Karma? I didn't know enough about it. But by trusting myself even when I was completely out of step with the rest of the world, it had somehow worked out well for me.

Now, I hoped with all my heart, that Teri's life, that all her suffering, would one day make sense, would lead to a place where she could see the gifts. But what kind of a gift could make up for the loss of a child?

I got up and walked out onto the deck. I stood silently staring, hands on the wooden railing, watching the blue waves ride onto the shore. The ocean's music soothed me. I studied the waves with the same fascination as I'd always watched new babies. What was so riveting about oceans and babies, I wondered. Was it that they were both completely true to their nature, or was it something more?

I stood for a long time, staring. I tried to understand what had happened. And again I asked, not why Greggy or why Teri. Why *us*. Why *now*. I wasn't asking for the reason, I was looking for the plan.

The sun was shining clear and bright over the shimmering blue water, and I felt it pierce my skin. A blanket of nourishing, penetrating heat warmed my bones. The mountains to the left, tall and majestic, comforted me. The sand below sparkled and glistened with light. No matter how much the structures of our inner world shift and change, nature remains remarkably constant. And now that constancy reassured me. *Mother Nature heals. Nurtured by her mountains, cradled in her valleys, rocked gently by the ocean's lullaby . . .*

That night, lying in bed next to Mario, I apologized. "I'm sorry I'm such a drip," I said. "It's just that I don't really feel great being here."

He patted my head. "Don't worry about it," he said. "You're not that much different than you usually are out here. . . ."

"Really?" I said. "I'm usually this out of it?"

He looked over at me, and by the light of the moon shining through the skylight, I could see his eyes both compassionate and smiling. "You only really come alive when you talk about ideas, sickness, death, spirits. Those are the subjects that interest you."

"You don't think it has to do with Greggy's dying?" I asked.

"You were always more comfortable with the stars in the heavens than the stars on earth. That hasn't changed," he said.

"Do you think I'll ever get better?" I asked.

"Better than what?" he asked.

"I mean, do you think I'll ever stop being such a drip? Do you think I'll ever enjoy, I mean really enjoy things that other people do?"

"Why would you want to?" he asked.

"Because I want to be like everyone else," I said. "And I want to enjoy my life."

He reached over and took my hand. "Not a chance," he said. "You'll never be like everyone else. But that's not a bad thing. And you *do* enjoy your life. It's just a hard time now. You'll get through this."

"How do you know?" I asked.

"Because you're a tough girl," he said.

I didn't feel very tough. I felt like mush. I felt like dissolving into air. I felt like going away forever. I really felt like dying.

Back in New York, the family was trying to regain its equilibrium. Teri continued school as she had planned, with social work her major. At home, Bibs waited each day for both Jessie and Teri. It was easier for all of them without me there. There were boundaries I kept that my sister did not. So with me gone, no one worried about the kids making noise, they all ate together, and at night after dinner Gordon and Teri could be alone while Barbara took care of Jessie.

One of Barbara's greatest gifts was that her heart needed to mother in order to beat. My sister had inherited all my mother's great graces. Now those assets served us all.

Teri and Barbara lived together as sisters with the doors between apartments left open. My mother and father visited everyone each night. Gordon and my father sat apart and talked for hours.

Teri called me at least once each day to tell me how she was doing and I called Bibs each night to make sure everything was really okay. Teri was doing her automatic writing, but not as regularly, and so her Spirits asked her to make a firm commitment. They asked that she get up early and do her writing before her day began while she was still clear and fresh. Teri wasn't happy about it. She thought they expected too much from her. But she did it anyway. She began getting up at six to do her writings before she dressed to drive to school.

"Biology class is driving me crazy," Teri told me when she called. "The teacher keeps drawing a fetus on the board. I can't stand to look at it."

"What are you studying?" I asked.

"Genetics," she said. "And the probabilities of abnormalities being passed down in a family line."

"Anything interesting or applicable?"

"At least I found out that SIDS isn't genetic," she said. "But it does run in families. The problem is that SIDS wasn't a classification on a death certificate until 1978. But if they trace familial lines back, they usually find a baby who has died."

"But if you track back far enough, it only stands to reason that you'd find a baby who died of something," I said.

Teri had been attending SIDS meetings with Gordon while I was gone. Lois recognized her strength, motivation, and intelligence and asked if she would meet with the Board of Trustees of the Sudden Infant Death Syndrome Foundation to offer her help. Because SIDSF was a strictly volunteer organization, there was always a great need. Teri could help them in many ways. She could be a treasurer, a secretary, a fund-raiser; she could help with the newsletter. She hadn't been a SIDS parent for a year yet and so she couldn't apply to be a Parent Contact. She needed more time to heal herself before she could help to heal others.

Finally she decided she wanted to be an educator. Because if no one could stop these babies from dying, at least she could help stop some of the suffering of the parents. She'd let them know they weren't to blame.

Teri would have to work with the SIDS center and go out into the community to educate doctors, nurses, EMT workers, emergency room staff, and anyone else who was in a position to cause damage by not knowing how to discriminate between SIDS and child abuse. Especially the first response teams. So three months after Gregory died, Teri became educator for the Long Island chapter of the Sudden Infant Death Syndrome Foundation.

Teri also told me the problem with the house wasn't getting solved. Aunt Josie and my mother had gone over and done their ritual, but the next time she visited it, she got sucked right back into it again. She almost forgot to pick Jessie up from school, and that did it. The house had become even more of an enemy.

In the writings Janith told Teri to make sure that she continued earth things as she began her journey inward. Janith stressed that it was important to maintain balance. She said Teri was in a huge transformation period and that truth would help her through the tests that would follow.

"Did you hear that, Mom?" Teri asked horrified. "The tests aren't over."

During the next two weeks I spent a lot of time alone. I walked on the beach, but the sound of the waves just threw me back into myself. I had a hard time feeling anything. I couldn't feel the sand on my feet, I couldn't feel the wind in my hair, I couldn't feel the sun on my skin. We went out with friends to restaurants to eat each night, but all the food tasted like mashed bananas. Still, I tried to heal myself, I tried to nurture myself, I tried to find some beauty in my world. None of it seemed to be working. Even when I tried to meditate, nothing happened.

Then one afternoon, when I was standing on the balcony, staring at the ocean, as I had for hours every day, something happened. . . .

I saw a school of dolphins leaping up and playing in the waves. One of them came very close to shore, and suddenly he seemed to flip around to look at me. I heard a sound, a high-pitched call that seemed to beckon me. Then the dolphin plunged under the water. For the next ten minutes he dove and flew up into the air, dove and flew up again, and each time he did a funny flip and spin, made his sound, and looked at me. I watched, fascinated. *Play with me,* he seemed to say. Instinctively, I laughed.

Suddenly I was carried on the sound of my own laughter to a place high above, where everything looked completely different. Standing on that balcony in that one frozen moment, everything seemed to be exactly as it should be. Perfect. And for that one moment my heart completely understood.

When the dolphin finally disappeared, I stared down at the ocean beneath me for a very long time. I felt a deep inner peace as I watched the constant rhythm of the waves as each broke on the shore. I had no thoughts. But I focused my attention harder and tried to listen to what the ocean had to say. I tried to really hear.

Eventually I did. It could have been a whisper, but it sounded like a roar. *If one wave were not to break, it would stay the rhythm of the Great Waters.*

Those days in Malibu were very lonely days for me. I counted the hours until the kids could come out. I prayed for the time to pass quickly. Away from the scene of their nightmares, I hoped they'd be able to renew their dreams.

It was three weeks before they arrived. I was so excited, I had gotten up at dawn to wait.

Jessie was the first one I saw walking up the path of the beach house. I opened the door and she came in, still rubbing her eyes. Her fine blond hair was matted from sleeping and her skin was pale. "Hi, Jess," I said, bending down and kissing her. "How was the plane ride? Did you like it?"

"We drove inside the clouds," she said. But she was more pensive than excited, and seemed older than she had been when I left New York.

Teri and Gordon, carrying their suitcases, followed her inside. Teri had gotten thinner, and she looked older too. More grown-up. I hugged her tight and then hugged Gordon. "I'm so glad you came," I said, feeling alive again. "How long can you stay?"

I caught them exchange a glance, but it was Jessie who answered. "We can stay really long because Daddy *never* has to go to work again."

"What does that mean?" I asked as we all walked into the big room and sat on the couch. Through the large glass doors leading to the beach, the sun cast an orange light.

Teri explained. "Gordon's van was robbed last week after one of the jewelry shows. They took everything, so until the insurance pays, there's nothing to sell."

Gordon shook his head unbelievingly. "First Greggy, then the house, after that the car, and now my job."

"What happened to the car?" I asked. No one had mentioned a car before.

"When I took it into the repair shop last week, someone stole the stereo and the tires," Gordon explained. "The transmission was already shot, and so the mechanic said it wasn't worth keeping."

"Well, once this passes, your luck has to change," I said. "Nothing stays the same for too long."

"I hope you're right," Gordon said.

That morning while Teri and Gordon unpacked in one of the downstairs bedrooms, I took Jessie outside on the deck with me to show her the sea gulls and the sailboats.

When we came back in, Mario was sitting at the dining room table, reading the papers. He had set out all kinds of fresh-baked croissants, rolls, jellies, and jams. The weather was perfect and a warm breeze was blowing through the open doors.

When Teri walked into the dining room, she kissed Mario in greeting.

"How are you?" he asked her. He stood then to shake Gordon's hand. "How are you both?"

Jessie hung back, holding tight to my hand.

Teri sat at the table next to Mario and said, "We're as good as can be expected, with all that's happening."

Mario smiled at Gordon as he sat down next to Teri. Mario thought of Gordon as a new species of man, one who could adapt gracefully to marrying an independent woman. He himself could *live* with one, but marriage? Out of the question.

Jessie and I sat at the other end of the table, and as I buttered a roll for her, Gordon was telling Mario about his reluctance to sell the house, and how everything in his life seemed to be falling apart.

Teri added, "This whole year feels like such a waste. I was pregnant and the baby died, we bought a house and we have to sell it, we got a car and now it's gone, and Gordon has no job."

"Thank God we're young enough to start again," Gordon said, trying to make light of it.

"You know why all of this happened?" Mario asked.

"No," Teri said, "why?"

"Because you both decided to sell out, to give up being free spirits and become responsible members of society," he said. "A real trap."

I made a face. "I thought you would come up with something profound," I said.

"It is profound," he said, smiling. "And one of the great tragedies of youth. All of us live our lives trying to avoid danger. But nothing happened to Teri when she jumped a Greyhound to California, nothing happened to her when she was living on the Rainbow bus, nothing happened to her while she was living with Gordon and running on a sandy beach out in the world. It was when she bowed to convention, got married, when she was at home, safely asleep in her bed, that the most dreadful assault occurred."

"It wasn't an *assault,*" I said, "it's just part of the plan according to most of the ancient wisdoms, and an opportunity for evolution, according to Teri's Spirits."

Teri huffed. "Another friggin' opportunity for growth."

Mario said, "I don't know anything about Spirits. I'm not even willing to believe in them, so I'm no expert."

Teri laughed. "I don't believe in this any more than you do, Mario. In fact, if Mommy or Gordon were doing this, I wouldn't go anywhere near them. In fact, I'd probably try to commit them."

"Smart girl," Mario said, smiling.

Gordon was completely comfortable with his belief system. He didn't defend it, he just behaved as though it was just the way things were. "Janith is a pretty name, don't you think?" he asked aloud.

"I think its origins are Celtic," Mario volunteered. And then, mulling it over, he repeated, "Janith . . . Janith."

Jessie looked up from her plate. With her mouth full and one hand holding a roll, she extended the other, palm up. "Who's *Janith*?"

"Chew," I said, "so you don't choke. Janith's Mommy's angel."

Jessie frowned. "Why does she have that name?" she asked.

I looked at her, trying to figure out what she meant. "We have to call her something, or how would we find her if we wanted to talk to her?"

Jessie started to laugh. "You're gonna talk to an angel with your mouth?" she asked. "And she *went* someplace?" She didn't even wait for me to answer before she added, "That's so silly."

"Why, Jessie?" Teri asked. "Don't you have an angel?"

Jessie nodded. "But I can't say her name," she said, "not with my mouth."

"What does she look like, Jess?" I asked.

"You're *fooling* with me, right, Mama Carol?" she said, smiling.

"No," I said, "I'm not. I really want to know."

Jessie shook her head and breathed out hard. "She's all sparkly, that's all. If I say how she looks, it's lying," she explained.

I frowned now. "Why?"

"You can't say how an angel looks," Jessie insisted. "You just feel her in your heart and you see her in your eye."

Gordon interrupted now. "Carol, maybe tonight we could ask Janith some questions. There are still some things I'm not clear about."

"You're going to talk to Mommy's angel, Daddy?" she whispered, making a face.

Gordon nodded. "Yes, Jessie."

"But how can your heart *feel* what she says?" Jessie asked.

Gordon said, "My heart *can* feel when she's in the room, Jess, and sometimes grown-ups need to be reminded that they have angels of their own."

"This angel writes with Mommy's hand," I said, "so she can tell us the answers."

"That is so silly," Jessie said, her eyes twinkling. And then she wriggled down from her seat and walked over to her father. "Daddy, come play with me?"

Mario left after breakfast because he had a business meeting in Los Angeles. That day Gordon spent the afternoon building sand castles while Jessie sat next to him, watching. She didn't run and jump. She didn't go near the water. Every time I looked out the window at them, I expected to see her playing, hear her laughing, watch her running. But I felt as though I'd gone deaf.

Teri and I spent the day trying to catch up on everything that had happened since we'd last seen each other. Teri pointed to the shoreline. "It's so hard for me to believe that it's only been four years since Gordon and I met in California," she said sadly, "only four years since we planned our life together. Now it's so different from what we dreamed and planned, it could have been a different life."

"It *was* a different life," I said.

Teri looked over at me. "You know, Mom, I feel like I've been hijacked by Fate. I boarded a plane for a certain kind of life and I wound up on a different plane of consciousness."

"Sounds right," I agreed, laughing. "And it's true that tragedy plays tricks with time. It breaks it down into eras and periods. Like everything from now on will be before Greggy . . . or after Greggy."

We sat quietly for a while. I was watching Gordon as he tried to get Jessie to build with him when Teri said, "You know, Mom, it means more to Gord than it does to me that he lost a boy. I mean, I lost my baby, but he lost his son."

I reached over and patted her hand. "Honey, maybe in time he can have another. Maybe he can have a son again."

Teri frowned as she glanced over at me. "It's not that I don't want another baby, because I do," she explained. "I want another baby for all the same reasons I wanted Greggy. But it seems crazy to put myself through that again. I can't do it."

"I'm not talking about now," I said. "I'm talking about later."

"I'd rather adopt a baby," Teri said. "A two-year-old. I don't ever again want to take a chance on a new baby."

"Is Gordon okay with adoption?" I asked. "Or does he want his own?"

"It will be our own," Teri defended. "It just won't be our biological baby. It will be some little boy who needs us as much as we need him."

"Gordon wants that too?" I repeated.

Teri rubbed her eyes and looked sad. "Gordon would like to try again. But I can't do it, Mom. Not only for myself. What about Jessie? Nobody knows what caused Greggy to die, how can we know it wouldn't happen again?"

I wanted to say something that would comfort and help, but I could only say, "Sometimes in order to live your life fully, you have to walk through your fear. . . ."

Teri sat up straight, startled. "What are you saying, Mom?"

"You can't live life afraid," I said. "And you can't wait until your fear disappears. You have to be willing to take another shot. You have to be able to conquer your fear."

"Never," she said. "No chance."

Now I watched as Gordon picked Jessie up and ran toward the ocean. When he lowered her feet gently into the surf, I expected to hear her squeal. But there was nothing but silence.

Teri had been watching too. "Jessie's been so sad since Greggy died," she said. "I hope this trip helps her."

Later, as the Malibu sun was setting purple and pink across the evening sky, we ate dinner in the dining room. Then Gordon took Jessie out on the beach to take some pictures. Teri, who had loved nature so, hadn't yet set foot on the sand.

After Mario went upstairs to work and Jessie was in bed, Gordon, Teri, and I put some soft music on in the living room, lowered the lights, and began to meditate. We wanted to see if Janith was as accessible in California as she had been back home in New York. Gordon asked the questions that he wanted Janith to answer.

I had begun to think of these sessions with Janith in the same way I thought about sitting in a classroom with a philosophy teacher who could answer any question I could think of about life. She was a terrific teacher who was helping rebuild my belief system with a stronger foundation than ever before. This time the room turned pink again, and I saw light atoms of swirling energy but no distinct features. Still, I knew Janith had arrived because my body and mind felt different, even before Teri said, "You can ask the questions, Gord, my arm feels tingly."

Gordon spoke to Janith the way he would speak to anyone else he respected. He wasn't formal, he talked without reserve. He sat up straight but kept his eyes closed when he asked, "Janith, why did our first experience with death have to be our son?"

It did not have to be, you chose it to be, for the highest outcome of your life and purpose, according to plans once made. . . . It was important for the lessons to be learned well, that it was planned in this way.

"How can Teri and I begin to trust again?"

Slowly. One step at a time. Gently. Do not push yourself, for trust comes as the waves to the shore. It doesn't come as you push, it comes as you allow. . . .

I could hear the catch in his voice when Gordon asked next, "Is my baby safe and happy?"

Oh, yes. I may say that all the babies who die of this "SIDS," as you call it, are peaceful high Spirits of a wise nature. And when they transcend the lifetime on earth, they return to their place of greatness.

His next concern was, "Did the baby feel any pain, Janith?"

Pain was not in purpose for the lessons to be learned for any of these babies. That is why they choose to go in such a quick and easy fashion.

When he asked about Jessie, I could hear the pain it still caused him. "How can Jessica, who's so young, ever recover from this kind of wound?"

Children are much more open to accepting the gifts of the wound, not only the wound itself. She will become a flowering personality by this experience. And it has etched into her soul a lifetime of service and compassion for others.

Gordon turned to me then. "Do you have anything you want to ask Janith?"

Teri sat, her eyes still closed.

I nodded. "I'd like to know what happens on a spiritual level to a family once a child within it dies."

We must begin first to talk about what happens to a family when they begin to come down to earth together. And that is: the components of the group karma are all formulated, contacted, appropriately placed. When that one being or "child" decides it is time, as planned, to leave, depending on how connected these ones on earth are with their Spirits, they will either know or not know that this is part of the plan.

My head was swimming with questions, but all I could ask was "What kind of plans did we make? What kind of karma are we working through?"

Patience, Carol. It is not time. When it is time, you will know.

Be with the Light,
Janith

Chapter Ten

*T*he child within is our life-force, the part of ourselves that creates the dreams which shape our adult lives. It's that part of our soul that absolutely requires beauty and needs to hide from suffering in order to preserve itself.

Disneyland is a place which heals that child, which reminds us of the magic. All of us needed to go there to help Jessie reclaim her childhood, so we could reclaim our own.

During the ride down, Jessie didn't talk much. Gordon asked, "Aren't you excited, Jessie? You'll meet Mickey, and Goofy, and see Cinderella's castle."

She hugged her yellow blanket closer to her face and didn't answer him.

"She just doesn't know what to expect, Gord," Teri said.

I was sitting in the backseat next to Jessie. I turned to her and asked, "Do you know that the place we're going is a magic place?"

Releasing her hold on her blanket, Jessie looked up at me and asked, "Are we going to see God?"

Teri turned around. "God, Jessie?" she said. "God is in heaven, not in Disneyland."

"Oh," Jessie said. She sounded disappointed.

"Did you want to ask God something, Jessie?" I asked. "Did you have something you wanted to talk to Him about?"

"No," Jessie said. She held her head up high when she said, "I want Him to tell *me* something. I want Him to *answer* me."

"About what, Jess?" Teri asked.

"Mommy," she said impatiently, "I told you too many times."

Gordon had been following the signs, and hadn't been paying attention. He said, "Jessie, did I tell you that Uncle Doug is going to meet us today at Disneyland?"

"Who's Uncle Doug?" Jessie asked.

"Daddy's brother," Teri said.

Jessie put her head down for a minute and then crawled over next to me and leaned against my chest.

I stroked her hair and we rode in silence for the next few minutes.

"Mommy?" Jessie asked. "Do you have a brother?"

"Yes, Jess. Uncle Danny is my brother."

I could see where Jessie was going, so I said, "I don't have a brother, Jessie."

Jessie looked up at me. "Not even a dead one?"

"Nope," I said. "No brothers . . . but Aunt Barbara is my sister."

Jessie sat up again and looked at me. "I don't want any more brothers either," she said. "Only sisters."

Jessie was wide-eyed in Gordon's arms as he carried her from the car through the front gate at Disneyland. She smiled when she heard the music. "Great music, isn't it, Jess?" Gordon asked her.

She just nodded.

The old-time movie house and the old-fashioned shops lining both sides of Main Street took us right back in time.

Jessie, sitting silently in a stroller we'd rented, was looking toward the tall red watchtower. She pointed to a group of children playing.

"Great, huh, Jess?" I asked.

Jessie shrugged her shoulders and pulled her tattered yellow "blankie" closer to her chin.

Teri and I looked at each other, both of us having second thoughts about the wisdom of this trip, when we heard the loud music of a marching band. Drums, flutes, saxophones. Suddenly, magically, walking out of one of the side streets ahead of us, life-sized Disney characters appeared. There was Goofy, Donald Duck, and Mickey and Minnie Mouse.

Jessie sat up straight, looked at them, and then rubbed her eyes. She turned to Teri and me for a second, puzzled, and when she turned back again, Mickey Mouse and Donald Duck were coming right toward her. Jessie stood up. "Oh God!" she said with disbelief. "Oh, my God!"

We all burst out laughing. Gordon pulled out his video camera. Jessie said, "Mommy, quick, take me out of here."

Teri lifted her out of the stroller and put her on the sidewalk just as Goofy and Minnie came close. Goofy grabbed the end of Jessie's blanket and began to pull at it.

Jessie laughed at him, a big, full-hearted laugh. "Let go," she screeched, still laughing. When Goofy leaned down to talk to her, she threw her arms around his neck and hugged him. Her eyes were shining with excitement.

The rest of the day was a dream. Jessie started talking, really chattering, pointing, running, laughing. She seemed like her old self, and Teri looked both happy and sad about it.

"It worked," Teri said to me as we approached Cinderella's castle. "I was afraid she had lost her laugh."

"She just had to remember," I said. But I was concerned about Teri. There was something in her walk, the way she aimlessly swung her arms. She should have been holding a baby.

I lifted Jessie up to walk over the bridge at the entrance to Fantasyland. It was my favorite place. She put her cheek against mine and we both hummed, "Some day my prince will come."

Doug was waiting for us at the far side of the bridge in front of the enchanted castle. He was taller and lighter than Gordon, the older brother. I turned to say something to Teri, but she and Gordon were already running, holding hands, across the bridge toward Doug. They hadn't seen him since the baby died.

Doug hugged Teri first. She looked so small in his arms. Then he reached for Gordon and held him in a tight, long hug. When Doug let Gordon go, he turned to greet me. Finally he looked at Jessie and lifted her up. He threw her into the air and laughed. "Boy, am I happy to see you, kiddo!"

Jessie was telling Doug about Goofy as he carried her.

Then, in front of us, I saw the blue and gold circle of a whirling carousel. "Look, Jessie," I said. "Come with me."

There's a place in my heart that flies on the backs of the beautiful pastel and gold carousel horses. Spinning round and round, reaching for the brass ring, imagining the long, golden manes flowing as the carousel spins, seems to take me away to a time in my childhood when all things were possible.

I used to imagine that if I chose the right horse, the real magic steed hidden beneath the carefully carved wood, I could take off and ride high enough to reach the clouds. Through those clouds were the magical kingdoms I visited in the stories my father told. Now I climbed back into my childhood with Jessie. "Which horse?" I asked her. "It's important to pick the right one."

She looked at me and laughed. "I know that, Mama Carol. It has to be the special one."

I took Jessie's hand and we quickly ran around the outside of the carousel. "Which one, Jess?"

"I'm looking, Mama Carol," she said. "I'm trying to see.."

Suddenly she stopped, and pointed. "That one, Mama Carol, that one on the inside." It was a regal pink horse, its mane pure white. She wore a harness of carved pastel flowers and golden reins. Jessie and I jumped on the platform and ran toward her, afraid that one of the other children would get there first. We were breathless when I lifted Jess onto the golden saddle and mounted behind her.

The music began, loud and jubilant, and the horse began to rise. "Oh, Jess," I said, "we can't reach the brass ring from here."

Jessie hollered back above the music, "It's okay, Mama Carol. It's not a real brass ring. The real one is in the sky. Close your eyes."

And so I did.

With Jessie's hair blowing in my face like the ticklings of angel fingers, the magical steed who looked frozen in flight became the unicorn who carried us away from our unhappiness and helped fly us to magic lands.

When the spinning stopped, I jumped down and reached up for Jessie, but Doug was right behind me. He lifted her carefully, and she looked right into his eyes. "Did you ever see my brother?" Jess asked. "Gregory Thomas?"

"No," he said. "I never did."

"He was a very nice baby," Jessie said, smiling. "You could kiss him a lot. But he died now. . . ."

"I know, Jess," Doug said.

Jessie looked over at me and smiled. "God took him back to live with Him. But he's going to make up with me and send me a new baby."

Teri heard her and said, "Not for a long time, Jessie. Mommy has to finish being sad about Greggy. Then maybe we can adopt a little boy baby who has no mother or father or big sister."

Jessie shook her head. "I don't want a boy baby," she said. "I want a sister."

"Why, Jessie?" I said. "Boy babies are nice. Look how much you loved Greggy."

Jessie's voice was firm. "Boy babies die. I want a sister."

Teri walked up close to her and held her little hand. "All boy babies don't die, Jessie, a lot of them grow up," Teri explained. "You go to school with little boys, don't you?"

Jessie pursed her lips. "But there's more girls in my class, there's not so many boys."

Teri just looked at me.

Later that day Jessie and I flew high in the air on the gray Dumbo ride, and Teri and I took her through the dark caverns of Alice in Wonderland. She hid her eyes and screeched when she saw the Queen of Hearts and laughed out loud at the Mad Hatter's tea party. Teri and I watched through the windows when Jessie hung tight to Gordon and then to Doug as the yellow submarine submerged.

But afterward, when everyone else went into the Haunted House to see the holograms, Jessie and I waited on a blue bench outside, eating ice cream and talking. There were children throwing coins in a wishing well in front of us. "What's that?" Jessie asked.

"A place to make wishes," I said. "You throw a coin in, close your eyes, and make a wish for something you really want."

"Who listens?" she asked me, brown eyes wide.

"What do you mean?" I asked her.

"Who makes the wishes come true?"

I thought about it, and then I said, "I'm not sure."

She wrinkled her nose and made a funny face. "God again?"

I laughed. "I really don't know. But would you like to make a wish?"

She shook her head no. "I'm not talking to God. I'm still mad."

On our way to the car there was a pink and purple glow around the castle. Small yellow lanterns lined the streets and brilliant shining fireworks exploded in the dark night sky. Jessie had fallen asleep in Doug's arms, and Teri and Gordon were walking together in front of me, holding hands. I watched as Gordon turned to smile at Teri, but it was no longer the innocent smile of young lovers, it was the smile of war buddies.

By the time we reached Malibu, I was as tired as Jessie. Mario was sitting outside, reading by the light of the lanterns on the patio. Gordon wanted to walk on the beach with Doug, and Teri wanted only to be left alone so she could stare at the night sky and think about Greggy. I decided to bathe Jessie and put her to bed.

"I want to dress myself," she insisted after her bath.

I sat on the bed and watched her struggle into her pajamas. She had always been fiercely independent, from the day she was born. I wondered what she was thinking.

When she climbed into bed, and I sat next to her, to kiss her and tuck her in, she asked, "Is Disneyland really a magic place? Can wishes really come true?"

"It's earth magic," I told her, "and some wishes can come true."

"Mama Carol," she said, and her voice was soft and hopeful, "can we go back tomorrow and get my brother baby back? Can we make a wish for Gregory Thomas?"

I bent down and kissed her forehead. "Some wishes are too big for earth magic," I said. "And I'm afraid that's too big a wish."

Jessie looked sad. "God again?" she asked.

I nodded.

Jessie reached out to touch my hand. "Mama Carol, want to hear a secret?"

"Sure," I said, not sure I did.

"Gregory Thomas can't come to see us," she said, "But I can go to see him."

My heart almost stopped, but I tried to keep my voice even when I asked, "You can, Jessie? How?"

"In my dreams. I can go to my Father's land," she said, pointing up toward heaven. "It has rainbows and toys. And sparkly water like soda. And there's balls almost like real balls that you can throw. Gregory Thomas is there."

"Really, Jessie?" I said. "What do you guys do?"

"We play in the water," she said sincerely. "We suck the water into our mouths and blow stars at each other. . . ."

Late that night, after I'd fallen asleep, something startled me and woke me up. I opened my eyes to get my bearings and looked over at Mario fast asleep next to me. Alert now, I sat up in bed. I listened. *Chanting? Dancing on the beach?* I slid out of bed, careful not to disturb Mario, and tiptoed outside through the French doors onto the balcony. There, lit by moonlight, I saw a strange vision.

On the beach beneath me there appeared a small Indian village. At the center was a campfire crackling, orange fire burning bright, illuminating a circle of hard-dancing warriors wearing white-feathered headdresses. By the beat of their drums and the rhythm of their rattles, I knew their dance was a dance of mourning, not of celebration. Over to the side, standing apart, half hidden behind one of the tepees, stood a tall Indian warrior dressed in deerskin. His chest was bare, his face hidden in the shadows. Across the sand, closer to the water, I saw a young Indian girl dressed in white-beaded deerskin, sitting on the sand with legs folded beneath her. Her arms were extended, her face raised to the sky. As I watched, rising out of the waters in front of the young woman there appeared an old woman, her dark face deeply etched with lines. Her hair was long, white, and braided. She walked toward the young Indian girl.

The old woman stood over the young girl, and I watched her lips move, I watched her speak. But I couldn't hear what she was saying. The young girl nodded her head in understanding. She raised her face to the heavens again. She seemed to be listening. After a few moments she lowered her head, pounded the sand with her fists, and shouted aloud. Then she covered her face and began to cry.

I almost flew off the deck to comfort her. . . . Then I saw another Indian brave coming through the shadows. He, too, was bare chested, he also wore deerskin trousers and had one long dark braid, but he seemed much younger than the Indian behind the tepee. I looked over toward those shadows again. My vision cleared. Now I could see that Indian's face. I looked closer. . . . He was handsome, fine-featured . . . closer still . . . now I could see his eyes . . . Oh, Lord, those eyes again. He was the Indian in my dreams. I quickly spun around to look at the girl. Now, across from her on the sand, the young Indian brave sat. I tried to get a closer look at him . . . Gordon?

"Jesus," I said aloud as I rubbed my eyes.

"Carol?" I heard Mario call from inside the bedroom. "Carol? Where are you?"

The following morning at breakfast I asked Teri if she'd heard anyone out on the beach during the night. "We were out there, Mom," she said. "Me and Gordon."

"What were you doing?" I asked her. I didn't dare tell her what I had seen.

"It was amazing, Mom," she said. "We were meditating. And I saw this beautiful young Indian woman with a beaded headband and long, dark beaded braids. The details were so clear. She wore a white-fringed deerskin dress, and in her arms she held a swaddled baby. There was a bright yellow light around her. Behind her I could see burned tepees and fallen Indians in a campsite. And I knew the baby she held was dead. But she didn't clutch it to her chest, she didn't hug it to her. Instead, she held it high above her head like an offering. I watched her face, Mom. I could see it clearly. Her expression wasn't sad, it was triumphant." She stopped long enough to take a breath before she added, "I had the feeling it wasn't the end of her life, it was just the beginning."

"You seeing things?" I teased. "How come you're not frantic and frightened?"

Teri smiled at me. "I don't know, Mom," she said. "It was kind of familiar. Besides, it wasn't scary."

Gordon smiled. He was quieter than usual.

"And you, Gord?" I asked. "Did you see what Teri did?"

Gordon took a deep breath. "I saw the campfire, Carol. I saw the tepees. I even saw Teri sitting cross-legged on the beach. But then I lost my bearings or something. Because I can't really remember."

"I had to wake him up," Teri said. "He fell asleep . . . right on the beach."

Gordon looked troubled. "I don't think I fell asleep. I can still smell the village after it was burned. Something happened there."

Teri, Gordon, and Jessie stayed with us for the next two weeks. Each day they seemed to be able to play a little more, they seemed a little freer, I saw a little less pain. I played with Jessie on the beach while Teri and Gordon spent some private time together. And I took Teri and Jessie shopping in discount houses in Los Angeles and posh shops on Rodeo Drive while Gordon and Mario spent some time playing backgammon together and talking man talk. Teri and I talked about her place in SIDS, her writings, her courses, her future.

Then on their last afternoon, while Jessie was out with Gordon, I watched from the balcony as Teri walked along the beach. Her head was down as she slowly traced the shoreline with her bare feet, occasionally stopping to dig her toes into the wet sand. She looked up when the sea gulls cawed, and searched across the water as the sailboats, like angel wings, skimmed across the bright blue ocean. She collected driftwood and shells to put in her pocket and polished a shiny stone on her weathered jeans. Then it happened. She stopped. Turned toward the ocean, peeled off her shirt and her jeans, and ran fast and full into the ocean. I wondered what she was doing. She began to swim. Out, out, out. The terror I felt almost stopped my breath. I can't swim. I couldn't stop her or help her if she needed me now. She was in too deep. My head was screaming, my heart was pounding, I wanted to run. I was frantic. Then I saw the dolphin again. He leaped up, he made his sound, he looked at me. As though on cue, Teri turned back and started to swim toward shore. I began to breathe again.

"What were you doing?" I yelled, running down to the beach with a towel in my hand.

"I wanted to see if I could still do it," she said.

"Do what?"

She shook her head. "Get past my fear. Go deep. Trust life again," she said, smiling. "I wanted to see how far out I could go and still get back again."

I smacked her playfully. "You scared the shit out of me," I said.

But I finally understood why we had to come to California.

Nature is another face of God.

The god of the East Coast in winter is a harsh and Spartan god. Cold, brittle, colorless. He's a god of sleep and endings. But the goddess of the West, oh, the goddess of the West is a goddess of beginnings. A beautiful, bountiful, regenerative goddess. She nourishes the rich brown of the mountains, colors the vibrant green of the valleys, breathes out the bright blue of the ocean, provides the warmth of the red rising sun. Mother Nature on that day shone with the face of that compassionate and loving Goddess. She was the creator, the protector that any wounded child could run to. She was a healer.

The night before they left, Teri agreed to have one more session. So after everyone else was asleep, Gordon, Teri, and I went out on the beach to talk to Janith. Under the cloak of darkness, lit only by the bright stars in the sky, we sat in a circle. Teri held her pad on her lap.

Gordon asked, "I'd like to know why our whole life is falling apart right now."

According to plans once made, you are being born again. You must die before you can be born again. Do you not see that this must happen on the outside as well as on the inside?

Gordon smiled. "That makes sense." he said.

"Only if you believe that business that Janith calls 'plans once made,'" I said.

Teri said, "I can't imagine ever making any plans like these. When did I make them? Once made *when?*"

In the time, in the space, provided for rest, for evaluation, for planning. It is after death. Sometimes it is in dream state as a person is alive on earth, plans are being formulated, plans are being thought of, plans are being lived out. In the space between life and death is where most decide what the next step will be in their growth process.

Hopkins wishes to say his karmic debt has been repaid, and he had been called to another time and space. He wishes you well and is grateful for your allowance of his protection when you most needed it.

"Wow," I said, "I guess you must be stronger than you know if Hopkins could move on."

Teri shrugged. "I just want to know if that means we should sell the house," she said. "I want some clear and practical advice. I know Janith can't interfere with destiny, but philosophy doesn't really help me. In order to trust this, and see how it can help on earth, I need some concrete information."

There is an earth companion of the angels, who is called Suhamaraan. Suhamaraan has had many incarnations on earth and has offered to help with the more concrete aspects of human experience. His last lifetime was in Ethiopia, where food was scarce but Spirit was plentiful. He was a skinny black man with a very good and evolved soul, and he may help greatly with the information that you wish, if you allow. You may ask him of your concerns.

Teri asked about the house. And this time Suhamaraan answered.

Welcome, Teri and family. Things are seemingly dark now, but as you walk forward, the fog will clear. The house you occupied has seen many unresolved pains. You could never change this, no need to try. You are called to be with us in order to help us help others. This is your divine right. Your life will slowly begin to fall into place. Your home and your self are quite important now. This is where the work must be done before other work is begun. The house will sell for eighty-four thousand dollars. This is good. You will sell it and move into your greenhouse (growth house).

Teri laughed. "He thinks I'm a plant," she said.

What makes you think plants are different? You will know immediately this house belongs to you. Love has been there for many years.

Be with the Light,
Janith

* * *

The day after Teri and Gordon returned to New York, Gordon hammered a big for sale sign in the front yard of their house. He also called real estate agents and told them to put it on the market. While they had been in Malibu, someone had broken into their house and stolen Gordon's computer and all his photography equipment. That was the last straw. He wanted to sell the house as soon as possible. Both of them felt it was time to start a new life. Moving out of their old life was the first step.

Teri began to have difficulty applying herself at college. It wasn't only that her mind didn't seem as sharp as it had, but the courses she was taking seemed to have too little practical value. The psychology courses seemed too limited, and none of them addressed the states of consciousness that mirrored her experience. So Teri began to read and research many of the spiritual teachings. Soon she felt pulled in too many directions. When she spoke to me, she told me she would have to make a choice soon in order to do anything well.

She was also getting excited about finding a new place to live. Living at my house had offered her time to recuperate, but now she was getting restless. She wanted her own territory. Jessie did too. She wanted her own room again with her own toy chest.

Gordon pored through the want ads, went on interviews, and tried to find another job. His real love was photography, but all the money he had was invested in their house. Suhamaraan had said that a job would be offered to him, so he looked as he waited for his opportunity.

The insurance money for their old car helped them buy another. They chose a little Sunbird, a used one, with only fourteen thousand miles on it.

The week before I came home, Teri got a bid on the house and my father's boss offered Gordon a job working as a kitchen cabinet salesman, with the promise of promotion and an opportunity for design and management. Gordon accepted, more because he would get a chance to be with Poppy than anything else. By the time I got there, they had a car and Gordon had a new job. Life seemed to be moving forward again.

Malibu had been the perfect place for me to begin to heal. I had enough rest to last a lifetime and I was looking forward to being in the middle of my family again.

Everyone was waiting at my house the night Mario dropped me off at home. He shook hands with my father, kissed my mother in greeting, and announced to Danny and Teri, "I've returned the Queen of France safely back to her kingdom. I've done my duty. Now I must return to my own kingdom."

I unpacked my suitcases and handed out the presents I had brought. We all had a lot of catching up to do, and we talked late into the night.

At one point I noticed my father had disappeared, and I went in search of him. I found him sitting in my study, listening to music and smoking a cigar.

"How did it go, Carol," he asked.

"Good," I said. "Good, Daddy."

He shook his head. "It was the best I could do, baby," he said. "I was out of my league. I was afraid you were running wild with some of your concepts. I was afraid you were losing control. I did what I thought was best, but I'm not sure it was the right thing."

At that moment my father had the same pained expression on his face he'd worn when I was a child and he had to decide my punishment. One particular time stood out in my mind.

I was about nine years old and I don't remember what I'd done. What is still crystal clear is the picture of my father and me sitting on the edge of my bed while he explained his predicament. Again he was shaking his head, asking me to try to understand his struggle and why he felt he had to hit me. As he often had, he used a story.

"Baby," he said, "consider this: If somebody gives you a Thoroughbred horse, a spirited animal, one you know can be a winner, are you not remiss in your duty if you don't train that animal to be all it can be? Then, whose fault is it if that horse doesn't win? If you haven't put the time and effort into her to run her through her paces? You have to know when to hold the harness slack enough to give that horse its head, to let her feel her power, but it's just as important to hold that harness tight, to pull it back sometimes, to keep her from running wild. . . . Raw power is nothing without discipline. Now, you never want to pull that bit in her mouth so hard or so often that you break her spirit, that would be a real tragedy, but if you give her less than your best, you've dishonored the precious gift you were given. You've proven that you weren't worthy, and you've cheated her because she never had the chance to be true to her nature, to be all she could be. Now, that's a sin, baby, that's a sin. . . ."

With my father, all lessons had something to do with the "animal kingdom." My mother tried to tell him I was just a little girl, but he couldn't hear it at the time. He just thought she was being soft, that she didn't understand. He'd had no father himself, no one to model himself after. So everything he'd learned was learned from Indian lore, the animals, or from the Greek myths.

I understood his predicament on that day when I was only nine, and I understood it now. I walked over and hugged him. "It really is okay, Daddy."

"It was much too heavy-handed," he admitted, looking pained.

"Don't do this to yourself," I said to him. "We're all just winging it. How did you make out while I was gone?"

He flicked his cigar ash into the large ashtray on my wicker coffee table. "I read. I hope you don't mind, but I asked your sister to lend me some of your books. And I listened to some tapes."

"What kind of books? What kind of tapes?" I asked.

"Those," he said, pointing to my New Age shelf.

I smiled. "Did any of it make sense?" I asked.

He nodded. "Some fine thoughts," he said. "I especially liked that nice Jewish boy, Ram Dass."

I laughed now. "There's hope for you yet, Daddy," I said.

He laughed too. "It's never to late to learn," he said. "In fact, I'm toying with the idea of taking a course up at the college here."

"What kind of course?" I asked.

"Anthropology, I think," he said. "Cultural anthropology. I'd like to learn a little more about the Aborigines and other tribal peoples."

"College, Daddy?" I said. "That should be a kick for the class."

He looked thoughtful. "I always wanted to go to college. I always loved learning."

"Hey," I said. "Then do it. Seventy years old is a great age for a wise man."

Two days later a real estate broker called Teri with a list of affordable apartments in the area. When Gordon got home from work that night, the agent came to pick them up. The first one they went to see was in a large apartment complex a few towns away. It was a new, spanking clean, modern apartment with three bedrooms and a new kitchen. But both Teri and Gordon were uncomfortable in it. "No," Teri told the agent. "I don't know why, but I can't take this one. It doesn't feel right."

Next they looked at a small natural cedar cottage right on the canal. But both Teri and Gordon looked at the water, thought of Jessie, worried, and said almost at the same time, "No way."

The agent was getting discouraged. On the way to the last apartment she told them, "This one is in a private house, upstairs. It has only two bedrooms and it's not new. Honestly, it's not as nice as the others. It needs paint. They have kids who've been living in it and, truth is, they've made a mess of it."

Still Gordon and Teri wanted to see it.

This apartment was in a house right around the corner from mine. It was dark by the time they drove up, so they didn't get a good look at the outside. All they could see was that it was a large two-story house.

As they walked upstairs, the agent in the lead, Teri looked back at Gordon. There was a nice smell in the house, the smell of home cooking. Upstairs, the rooms were large. The walls in the smaller bedroom were covered with warm yellow Sesame Street wallpaper. It was furnished in Kid's Stuff, a crib, a toddler bed, and a toy chest. Gordon reached for Teri's hand. The living room was large enough to hold all their furniture and Gordon's aquarium. As Teri looked around, she knew that all the windows facing east would make the living room bright and sunny in the morning. But what finally did it was that Gordon spotted a Native American dream catcher hanging on the walls of the master bedroom. He smiled at Teri. "We'll take it," Gordon said.

The following day Teri took Jessie and me over to show us the house. It was then, in the daylight, that we saw what she hadn't the night before. The house was painted a bright forest green.

Teri burst out laughing. "I didn't think they meant it literally," she said. "I didn't think when they said we'd move into a greenhouse, it was as simple as a green house. I thought it was a metaphor."

Once we went upstairs, we found the young woman who lived there cleaning out her cabinets, already packing. "We're moving because we just bought a new house," the woman explained to us as we stood in the kitchen. Then she glanced around and told Teri with some regret, "It doesn't look like much, but we had a lot of good times here. This is a good house, there's a lot of love."

Jessie wandered into the yellow bedroom. There, sitting on the floor, playing with blocks and other small toys, was a little boy about two years old. In the crib there was a smaller baby playing with a mobile. Jessie stayed and stared.

When we were ready to go, Teri had to walk inside and lift Jessie up to take her with us. She waved to the kids as she went.

Once we were outside again, Teri asked Jessie, "Do you like our new apartment?"

Jessie was jumping up and down, laughing. "I really like Sesame Street and I like those babies," she said. She looked a little worried when she asked, "But where am I going to fit my bed?"

Teri smiled at her. "Right against the wall where the baby's crib is now," she said.

"Where will the baby sleep, then?" Jessie asked.

Teri and I looked at Jessie, then at each other. It was a moment or two before we got what she meant.

Then Teri kneeled down in front of her and explained, "Oh, Jessie, that little boy and the baby can't stay in that apartment. They belong to their mother. They have to go with her."

Jessie frowned. Then she stomped her foot hard against the ground. "Then where's *our* baby?" she asked.

"Honey," Teri explained, "you know about Greggy. Remember?"

Jessie breathed out hard. "I'm not saying about Gregory Thomas. I know *he* can't live with us. I'm saying about the other baby we're going to get. The *sister*. I told you, Mommy. . . ."

"Honey," Teri said patiently, "I didn't tell you we were going to get another baby—"

Jessie cut her off. "I know that," she said. *"God* told me."

Teri stood up. She smiled at Jessie. "Okay, honey. Let's see what happens."

Jessie took Teri's hand and looked up at her, smiling. "You're going to really like my new baby," she said, skipping.

In the weeks since Teri and Gordon had put their house up for sale, they had gotten several bids. All were lower than Suhamaraan had told her. Still, she and Gordon were eager to sell the house, so they accepted all offers. But one by one each deal fell through. Gordon was getting nervous because until their house was sold, they were forced to pay both the mortgage and the rent on the new apartment. They wouldn't be able to do that for more than a few months without having to let the bank foreclose and lose all the money they had invested.

* * *

Each night Barbara or I took turns watching Jessica, while Teri, Gordon, and Danny went over to the apartment to clean and paint everything, except for the yellow room. Jessie wanted that to stay just the way it was.

On the night before they were to move in, as I was tucking Jessie into bed, she said, "Mama Carol, there's a brown cloud in my eye. It has eyes and a mouth." Then she giggled. "And ears."

"Sounds like a fun cloud," I said.

"He's not," Jessie said. "He's mad."

"Why?"

Jessie opened her eyes and looked straight at me. "His mommy and daddy are selling his toy box."

"No mommy and daddy in their right mind would do that," I said.

She sat up. "They would too. They left it in the house. And they're selling the house," she said, her voice filled with intensity.

"Is that little cloud like *you?*" I asked.

"A little," she said, shrugging her shoulders.

"Well, you don't have to worry," I said. "Mommy and Daddy didn't sell the house yet. Nobody wants to buy it."

Jessie shook her head. "Oh, yes," she said. "That lady does."

I knew better than to argue with her. "I'll tell Mommy and Daddy," I said. "I'll make sure they know."

"They better hurry," she said. "That lady's coming. . . ."

The whole family came to help with the move. Danny and Gordon moved all of their furniture in a single day, and that night Teri and I hung curtains and fixed beds and put towels in the bathroom. When we finally sat down to eat the dinner that my mother had cooked, the phone rang. Teri answered. It was the real estate agent.

"Oh, God, you're kidding" was all we heard her say.

"What happened?" I asked when she hung up.

"Somebody just offered eighty-four thousand dollars for the house," Teri said. "And the agent said if we'd accept the offer, they wanted to move in right away."

Gordon walked into the kitchen. "Did you say the house sold?" he asked. "What about the mortgage?"

Teri's eyes were shining when she said, "They have cash. . . . The agent says they have a very large down payment."

My father asked, "Who is it, baby? Is it a local family?"

"No," Teri said. "It's just some lady with two sons."

I heard Jessie before I saw her standing in the doorway. "I *told* you, Mama Carol."

Gordon and Danny dropped everything and went to get Jessie's toy box.

Just before the closing, Teri went back to clean their old house. As she pulled into the driveway, she felt happy; things were finally turning around. She pulled her jacket tight around her as she got out of the car. The weather was still cold.

Walking up to the front door, she stood back for a moment just to look. White matchbox house with black shutters. It's still a cute house, she thought.

Teri took a deep breath as she opened the front door. She could still smell the newness of it, fresh paint and rugs; they had hardly lived in it at all, she thought with some sadness. As she walked toward the kitchen to get the mop and broom she had placed there, she felt even sadder that they were getting rid of the only place they had shared with Greggy.

Opening the broom closet, she ran her hands over the new oak cabinets, remembering how excited she had been when they had first been put in. How grateful she had been that Grandma and Poppy had chosen to buy them. The shine was still on the blue Formica countertop she had picked out. She began to wonder if they were doing the right thing selling the house.

Teri put the broom down and walked through the living room straight into Gregory's room. Visions and memories set themselves free in her mind. His little face as he awakened in his crib, the lullabies she sang him while sitting in the rocking chair in the middle of the night, the look of the sun as it made rainbows on his light blue walls. She cried then, but they were hot, dry tears. Tears of acceptance. Tears of good-bye. Once they sold this house they were getting rid of everything concrete that represented Greggy. Now there would be no place, no stone, no house, no mark that he had ever been on earth. It was harder than she expected.

Her misery helped to propel her. She scrubbed floors, washed windows, cleaned corners of the rooms until the house shined. She wanted the people who moved into it to be happy. Several hours later she had finally finished. It was time to go.

She stood on the stoop for one last look around the grounds. The trees that were so green and full in summer were completely bare now and brittle brown. The silvery frost covered and matted the old grass on the lawn. Her white fence had rusted. Fondly she turned to look at her favorite tree. A huge oak, the tree that had offered her sanctuary in the first wintery rain. She ran her eyes over it, along the branches and up toward the sky.

And screamed!

A cat, a dead cat, a skeleton, with bony front paws was propped in the fork of the tree's huge trunk, its empty eye sockets staring straight at her.

Teri remembered the old superstition that a cat could suck the breath from a newborn baby. Her heart was racing. She was terrified again. "You can have this fuckin' house," she screamed into the wind. "And all that comes with it!"

Chapter Eleven

Easter morning promised a beautiful spring day. The trees and grass were vibrant green and all around us the flowers had begun to bloom. Barbara had gotten up early to hide the Easter eggs outside under the bushes so the kids could hunt for treasures. We were cooking a big Easter dinner. The spaghetti sauce was simmering on the stove and the fragrant pork roast and prime rib were already sizzling in my oven. Everyone was coming over. I was hoping it would be a good day for Teri, the beginning of new hope.

Teri hadn't gotten dressed up and Gordon wore a jogging suit, but Jessie was wearing the long white dress I had bought her in France the year before. With a crown of silk flowers around her fine blond hair, she looked like a fairy. "Like my shoes, Mama Carol?" she asked, eyes alight, wiggling her toes in her new white sandals.

"Love 'em," I said as I bent to kiss her. I hugged Gordon in greeting as he walked in, but Teri looked so fragile, I just smiled at her.

"Did Dan get here yet?" Gordon asked.

"Any minute," I said. "He's picking up the pastry."

Jessie was pulling at Gordon's hand. "Let's get Chris, Daddy," she said. "Let's do the treasure hunt."

The dining room table was set with a pink linen cloth and in the center, an arrangement of cut spring flowers. Teri sat down and pushed one of the plates away. "Do you want some tea?" I asked her. "And would it help to talk about it?"

"I feel so sad today," she said. "The birds are singing, the sun is shining, and if Greggy were here, he would have been seven months old."

"Holidays are always rough" I said, trying to comfort her.

"It's so much harder when the whole family is around, without Greggy. I wanted to stay in bed and hide. But I couldn't because of Jessie."

"I know," I said. "She seems excited."

Teri nodded. "She still talks about Gregory every day, but in the last week, all she's been talking about is the new baby God is going to give her."

"That must be hard for you," I said.

"I can't do it, Mom," she said. "Not for Jessie, not for Gordon, not for anybody. I just can't put us through that again."

From outside, through the open window in my living room, I could hear Jessie and Chris laughing each time they discovered another colored egg or small treasure. Teri heard them, too, and said, "I hate that Greggy's not here. I want to be happy for Jessie, to be thankful for all that I have, but I'm not. I keep thinking that in millions of homes all over the world there are babies sitting in high chairs, sleeping in cribs, rolling around in playpens, and lying in their mother's arms. They're happy and healthy, all of them. And their mothers are having the kind of Easter that I should be having. It's not fair."

Then Jessie came flying into the living room with Chris behind her, to show Teri a silver bracelet wrapped around a pink egg she had found. But she took one look at Teri's expression, and kissed her instead. "Poor Mommy," she said, and she turned to Chris, "Mommy misses my brother, Gregory Thomas. Today she doesn't care about eggs. Let's find my daddy."

When Jessie ran back out of the room, Teri smiled a little. She looked at me, a small child again, and said, "I'll give up chocolate bunnies and colored eggs forever. I just want the Easter bunny to bring Greggy back to me."

Then the front door opened and my mother and father, carrying loads of food, came struggling in. Mother always made hot antipasto with fried artichokes, zucchini, and stuffed mushrooms. My father had baked several pies for dessert. I got up to help them just as Danny pulled up in the car.

Suddenly the house was in complete chaos. Everyone was talking at once and all the kids were running in and out as Barbara and I began to serve the food.

Once the ravioli and the roasts had been placed on the table, my father stood and raised his glass to say grace. "Thank you for every-thing we have, and for allowing all of us to be together," he said.

During dinner, everyone was quieter than usual, though Gordon and Danny sat next to each other and talked. I noticed Teri wasn't eating. When I was clearing off the table, I heard Gordon whisper to Teri, "Why don't we go into Carol's study and see if Spirit can make you feel better?"

Teri nodded and they both looked at me. I went with them. In the study I put on some music and pulled the shades down so the light was dim.

We always began with a prayer for protection and asked only for information that would serve the greater good of everyone. I had begun to feel different when Janith was around. The air seemed thinner, my body less heavy, my heart happier. Always, within sec-onds, Teri's hand flew across the page.

Gordon asked for any suggestions Spirit had to help, and the writings began. . . .

Teri, there is no greater pain on earth. It remains good to speak with yourself of the missing. A normal and right way past human death. Sometimes life plays tremendous games with the human soul and it may find it hard to comprehend the goal of the game to be one of self-fulfilling self-love providing pain, pain providing growth, and growth providing love of Light, and back around the circle. Very popular are merry-go-rounds. This speaks to a part of the higher consciousness in all. This will be the first of only a few holidays without another baby. Your time is meant for healing purposes, not for a wait of no reason.

There is no way to see your own future, but I may tell you that your daughters will fill the hole that your son left. A child will come in time. Love is important and laughter is healing. Laugh at yourself, laugh at us, laugh at the world as well as cry for it.

Suhamaraan

Dear child, life is a series of pains. The joys are only a counterbal-ance to make room for the times of growth pain. This you are coming to know. Joy feels good. Yet, suffering enhances love for other. In this way it remains fine. Go be with people and live your life. That is all you are doing, no different than any other.

Be with the Light,
Janith

* * *

Teri opened her eyes. She was angry. "I can't believe just like that, they're telling me I'm going to have another baby. What happened to cocreation? Where's my choice, my free will, in all of this?"

Gordon said, "You probably do have some choices, but not the ones we think we do."

Teri felt her hand begin to tingle again. She picked up her pencil and Suhamaraan explained.

Plans once made have openings, as does a screenplay. Walk in, write in. You have certain freedoms, that is the freedom of choice which is not filled in before birth.

"Why did I have to trade them for Greggy anyway?" Teri asked, annoyed.

If we could feel physical pain, we would feel it now. Right in our third eye. You are slinging guilt. We were not your trade, you were your trade. But all will remain of Divine Right Action, as it has been worded. Not very nice to do to us as others do to you as parents!

Suhamaraan

I thought he was funny, but Teri didn't, so she asked Janith, "How can I stop the missing from hurting so bad?"

It is important to remember that the missing is only on the physical plane. If you can reach into other planes of consciousness, you will not have that missing as greatly. It is quite important to remember that once "out of body" does not mean "does not exist." Your son is just out of body. That means you need to get out of body in order to connect, to reach, to touch, to feel, to stop the missing. You must be able to meditate to do this. Or it can be done in dream state.

Gordon was pleased by the answers. They seemed hopeful. He suggested to Teri, "Why don't we try to reach Greggy? Maybe it will make you feel better."

All of us closed our eyes. Behind my eyes I immediately saw a unicorn. And when I jumped on his back he flew me up through the clouds again to the magical kingdoms. Greggy was there, his essence. Again I had that feeling of boundless freedom.

After about twenty minutes, when Gordon was finished and had opened his eyes, I asked, "What happened for you?"

He looked sad. "It's always the same, Carol. It's always the snow.

I love snow. But before I get a chance to really feel it, I'm walking in a valley again. A bright green valley. And I miss the snow."

Finally Teri's eyes were open.

"Do you feel any better?" I asked her,

Teri smiled. "I felt as close to Greggy as when I was pregnant. It wasn't as good as holding him in my arms, but it sure was better than that terrible emptiness."

"And the things they said, did that help?" I asked her.

"Some," she said. "Part of my pain seems to come from believing that something went wrong. If everything's just the way it should be, then some of my need to make it right seems to disappear."

It was a particularly sunny day in April and my front yard was blooming with flowers. I thought about washing my windows, but then decided to just wait until the feeling passed. It was too beautiful a day to work.

When Teri stopped by on her way home after dropping Jessie off, I was sitting on my front stoop, drinking tea. She sat next to me. "I talked to Lois last night," she said. She reached over, took my cup, and sipped some tea. "She told me how she made her decision to have another baby."

"How?" I asked, taking my cup back.

"Lois said when she realized she would have given her right arm for one more hour with her baby, she knew she had to try again."

Teri's eyes were shining and her cheeks were aglow from the sun. "Is that how you feel?"

"Mom, I would give anything for another hour with Greggy."

"What does that mean, honey?" I asked gently.

"It means it was all worth it," she said. "It means I have to try again."

"Are you sure?"

Teri bit her bottom lip. "I'm more scared about this than anything I've ever done. But Gordon wants another baby and Jessie needs a brother or a sister."

"And you, honey?" I asked. "What about you?"

Teri said softly, "My arms feel so empty, Mom. . . ."

All I could do was hug her.

*　　*　　*

Three months later Teri stood in my doorway and told me, "I'm pregnant." I was sitting on the couch in my living room.

I didn't know whether to laugh or cry. Instead, I found myself staring out the window. There were half a dozen squirrels running in circles and playing with each other. They were chasing each other up and down my big oak tree. Without a word to Teri, I got up and walked into my kitchen to grab some bread and honey-roasted peanuts. Then I tossed them out the window to the squirrels.

"Mom?" Teri said. "Did you hear me?"

I turned to look at her and tried to smile, but at that moment I felt a silent scream of terror fly up from somewhere deep inside.

One of the squirrels hanging upside down from the tree started to holler, bark, call. It startled me and brought me back to earth.

Teri was kind. She walked over to the window and put her arm around my waist. I put mine around hers.

"They don't seem to have to plan," I said, looking outside, while trying to sort out my emotions. "And it seems to work out for them."

Teri laughed then, a funny, childlike laugh. "I wonder if they think God threw the bread," she said. "I wonder if they think heaven rains peanuts."

I turned to look at her. "Are you okay?"

She nodded. "Are you?"

"Of course, honey," I said.

"You're lying, Mom," she said.

"I'm a wreck," I admitted.

We hugged each other.

Then we walked inside and sat down at opposite ends of the couch in front of the big picture window in my living room. Legs up, we faced each other. "How do you feel about having another baby now that you're really pregnant?"

Teri laughed. "You're jumping to conclusions again," she said. "Before, I thought being pregnant meant having another baby. Now all I know is I'm pregnant. Another baby doesn't necessarily follow."

"You really feel that way?"

"I'm no longer innocent, Mom," she said, but she was smiling good-naturedly. "In fact, even if I have a baby, there's no guarantee it will stay."

"How can you think like that and still make plans?"

"Are you kidding, Mom? Haven't you learned anything from Greggy?"

"Of course. But without a dream of a baby, or plans for the future of that baby, how can you and Gordon be happy about it?"

Teri frowned. "That's the problem," she said. "I'm starting to get really pissed at Greggy now for wrecking my feelings about this pregnancy."

"Did you ask Spirit about it?" I asked.

"Yep," she said. "Gord asked. And Suhamaraan said this baby was coming only to give and take love. He said she would stay and bring us peace and forgiveness for the other plans once made."

"Do you believe it?" I asked.

"Well, he was right about the job, right about the car, and right about the apartment, so I'm hoping they're right about this."

"Do you have a name picked out yet?" I asked her.

"Wampum Indian baby," Teri teased.

"Be serious," I said.

"Okay," Teri said.

"It's kind of soon, but Gord and I figured that if it's a girl, like Spirit suggested, we'd call her Ashley Nicole."

"And if it's a boy?" I asked.

"I'm not even thinking about that," she said. "But if it's a boy, Gordon wants to name him after Poppy. He wants to call him Tommy."

"Did you tell Jessie about the baby yet?" I asked.

"Yes," she laughed. "Gordon and I spent hours choosing just the right words, trying to be careful to present it perfectly. But Jessie listened to us and then with her hands on her hips and a smart aleck grin, she said, 'See, Mom, I *told* you God wanted to make up with me.'"

Chapter Twelve

T he beginning of Teri's pregnancy was wonderful. She never got tired, had no morning sickness, and gained very little weight. But after a few months of attending school and doing homework, educating for SIDS, and doing her Spirit writings, she found she had too little energy for all she had to do. She wanted to stay healthy and feel well. And so she knew she had to make a choice. She struggled with her options, and finally decided she would sacrifice least if she quit college. She could always continue later. More important right now was the time to spend with Jessica. Teri wanted it to be special.

When she picked Jessie up from school now, she took her to the park, spent hours with her there, fed the ducks, and had small picnics. Teri felt it would be soon enough that Jessie would have to share everyone's attention and worry again.

The new apartment really seemed to be healing for Teri and Gordon. Teri had the freedom to walk around the block with Jessie to visit me and the apartment was small enough for her to keep clean without too much effort. Old school friends visited some afternoons, and she and Jessie began to spend long summer days at the village beach. My mother and father stopped at their apartment on the way to my house each evening, and Gordon and Poppy had gotten even closer now that they were working together.

One afternoon I was sitting on my couch, daydreaming, staring out the large picture window, when I saw Teri and Jessie walking down the street toward my house. I marveled at how grown-up Jessie was beginning to look. Denim jeans, ruffled pink blouse, and a matching pink headband on her cornsilk-blond hair. She was getting so much taller and she walked with such purpose. Teri was walking next to her, wearing jeans and a pink T-shirt. She looked more like an older sister than her mother. I noticed that Teri had finally gotten some of her color back; her skin was a golden tan, and her auburn hair was shining.

I watched as Jessie stopped on my front lawn and plunked herself down on the grass. She began to play with a small dandelion. Teri sat down next to her, leaned over, and said something to her. The next minute Jessie stood up and put her finger to her lips. A secret. Teri covered her eyes while Jessie ran around the side of my house until she disappeared from sight. Teri peeked but covered her eyes again as soon as she saw Jessie rushing back toward her.

Jessie's hands were hidden behind her back. She stopped a few feet away from Teri. Then she slowly tiptoed closer.

From behind her back she pulled a long yellow daffodil, stem and all, and placed it carefully in Teri's hair.

Teri uncovered her eyes, felt the flower, and laughed out loud.

Jessie put her arms around Teri's neck and kissed her on the lips. By the time I blinked again, Teri had tackled Jessie, threw her on the grass, and was tickling her.

I opened my front door to call to them, but all I could see was Jessie's flailing legs and all I could hear was their squealing laughter. In that moment my heart flew back to me on wings.

Jessica's third birthday was in the middle of July. God must have been particularly fond of Jessica on that day because the weather was exquisite for her party. The azure summer sky formed a perfect background for the fluffy cotton-candy clouds that looked like smiling faces as they floated overhead.

Teri, Gordon, and I hung green and yellow streamers across the big tall trees in my backyard, and the balloons we placed all around seemed to dance in time with the music that was playing on the big stereo that Danny set up.

Several of Jessie's friends from nursery school came carrying brightly wrapped presents. They all ran around on the grass, some playing ball and others croquet. They all laughed as they sat around the picnic tables and watched the magician Teri had hired pull rabbits out of her hat, and coins from behind their ears.

Jennifer, Christopher, my mother and father, Barbara, Danny, and several of our friends also gathered to wish Jessie a happy birthday.

When it was time, Teri carried out a big sheet cake covered with whipped-cream and butter-cream flowers. Everyone sang as Teri lit the candles.

Jessie was kneeling on the picnic bench, ready to blow them out.

"You have to make a wish, Jessie," I reminded her.

"I know that, Mama Carol," she said.

Jessie squinted her eyes tight and clenched her fists before she blew all the candles out with one hard breath.

"What did you wish?" I asked her.

She looked at me with a sharp intelligence in her light brown eyes and smiled. "It's a secret," she said. "I can only tell Mommy."

Teri moved closer to her, bent toward her. Jessie whispered in her ear. I watched Teri's expression for clues, but all I could see was uncertainty.

"I don't know, Jess," Teri said softly.

"I know it's a big wish," she said, smiling at Teri.

Jessie and her friends ate some cake and then went inside to play with her new games. Barbara and Jennifer went with them.

"What did she wish for?" I asked Teri.

Teri looked down at her hands. "She wants Greggy's music box," Teri said softly. "The one with the little caged bird."

"You don't want her to have it?" I asked.

"Well," Teri said, struggling with her emotions, "I don't have anything of Greggy's left, except the tin can. . . . Both Gordon and I wanted to keep that music box."

"Then don't let her have it," I said, touching her hair.

Teri looked troubled. "But she deserves it," she said. She looked at me with tears in her eyes. "Mom, from the time Jessie was a baby, she fought so hard for everything. She fought so hard to live."

Teri talked to Gordon.

Jessie got the music box.

That night, just before Jessie was ready to go home, she came over to kiss me good-bye, and she whispered, "I'm going to have such a happy life, Mama Carol, because almost *all* my wishes come true."

The first real scare of Teri's pregnancy came during her fourth month. She had gone to Dr. Bures for her prenatal checkup.

She was lying on the examining table, a paper sheet over her belly, thinking how great things were going. She hadn't gained much weight, her circulation was fine, and her blood pressure was good. When Dr.

Bures came into the room to check her, she confessed that she'd been feeling so well that it was even hard for her to believe she was really pregnant.

"Maybe hearing the baby's heartbeat will convince you," he said, smiling.

He pulled down the sheet and placed the cold round fetascope on her slightly swelling belly. He looked intent as he listened. Then he moved it over a little and listened again.

Teri began to feel anxious. "Nothing?" she asked.

Dr. Bures ignored her. Moved the fetascope again. Pushed harder, listened more intently. He looked worried.

Teri touched his hand. "Is something wrong?" she asked.

Dr. Bures pulled the earphones out of his ears and stood up. But still he didn't answer her. Instead, he walked over to the door and shouted to his nurse. "Bring me the Doppler machine." He sounded impatient, which he almost never did. "I don't know what takes them so long," he muttered as Teri lay paralyzed with fear.

The nurse rolled in the new machine. Dr. Bures grabbed a tube of jelly from the cart and spread it on Teri's belly. Then he turned on the machine and placed the small microphone over the same spot he had put the fetascope. Almost as soon as it hit, Teri heard the sound. A small thump, thump, thump. Dr. Bures pushed a little harder. A strong, loud thump, thump, thump.

They both laughed out loud. Then Teri patted her belly and said softly, "Thanks, baby."

Dr. Bures ran his hands through his salt-and-pepper hair and said, "I don't know how we're expected to hear anyway. At this stage the baby's heart is only the size of a quarter." But he was obviously relieved.

Once Teri was dressed, she went into his office and sat down.

Dr. Bures, already seated, was rummaging through some papers on his desk. "I figure your baby's due date to be around March tenth," he said. He looked up at Teri and added, "I'd like to schedule you for a C-section on March third."

Teri was disappointed. "Can't I try a vaginal delivery again?" she asked. "I had Jessie naturally. And I might have been able to deliver Greggy without a C-section if he were a different baby. I've read where women can have vaginal deliveries after a C-section."

Dr. Bures hesitated and then he shook his head.

Teri tried again. "Dr. Bures, it was so much easier with Jess. I had such a hard time with Greggy. I felt so sick."

But Dr. Bures said, "I'd rather not take any risks with you. You have a small pelvis. My guess is that if your first one had been any bigger than five pounds three ounces, you'd never have delivered her vaginally either. And after the last trouble, I think it's too big a risk."

So Teri agreed. And it was scheduled. On March third she would have her second C-section and hopefully a new and healthy baby.

A plush carpeting of fallen brown and yellow leaves covered the streets and lawns. With Teri's growing belly came her expanding awareness that she would soon have to leave their apartment to find a bigger place to live. Besides, that long flight of stairs was too dangerous for a little baby. If ever it should fall down . . . They began looking at a few apartments and small houses, but nothing charmed them. The ones they liked were too expensive, the ones they could afford were too far away.

Teri continued her automatic writings. We kept track of them by date and time. So far there was no repetition and much of the information was new. Teri had given up the idea that it was her own mind and had learned to trust them.

Then one morning, as Teri and I were sitting again in my study, her pads resting on her swollen belly, we asked if her Spirits had anything they wanted to tell us.

Teri, we would like to talk through you in words soon. Please allow this to be possible. It will be much faster and more efficient. This will not harm you or your child.

Once you become what some call a "trance channel," validity appears to be obvious for human livings. Writing does not have the same validity as talking.

You may allow us small amounts of time at first. A tape can be played to record our works. Carol, you or any other such person may sit and ask questions of mutual interest. Teri, please allow this for yourself. This does not have to be an instant decision, take some time to do what you must in order to feel comfort with it.

The vibration in your arm at the time of writing is different, that is why the feeling changes and sensations change and writing changes. Similar to what happens in the voice box, very same, just different part of the body.

Be with the Light,
Janith

*   *   *

Janith will not talk until you give permission. Until you are comfortable. We can take a slow advance. Continue to write with us and one day when you feel you may allow, ask to begin the talks. We will inhabit only your thoughts as we do now, at first, so you may understand. But later, when Janith comes, she cannot speak without total inhabitance of the body, therefore you will not remember. This will not happen until permission is given by you. No walk in will occur for any extended length of time. Do not worry about your accuracy. This is good and right.

Suhamaraan

"Forget it," Teri said when she saw the writings. "I'm the girl who didn't even want to share her room as a teenager. I'm the one who needs a bigger house 'cause I don't want to share my space now. And they're asking me to share my body? No way! Not possible! Can't do it."

"What are you afraid of?" I asked her.

She frowned at me. "There you go again, making things seem normal that aren't," she said. "Be serious. I saw *The Exorcist.* I'm not going to take any chances. Besides, I don't want to look and sound all weird and twitchy like those channels I've seen and read about. No way."

"Teri," I said, "spirit communication is completely different from demonic possession. And the purpose is different. I'm sure Janith would never let something like that happen. But if you're really uncomfortable with it, then don't do it. Tell them no."

Teri looked at me. "Really, Mom," she said. "I'm serious. I know I can't do it."

"Then tell them to forget it," I repeated.

Teri shook her head. "I'll think about it."

Two months later Teri and Gordon found a big colonial house that they could rent reasonably. It had four bedrooms, a large eat-in kitchen, a playroom, a den, and a huge sunroom. It also had a big backyard. It was close enough to Gordon's work, and not too far from my house or my mother's.

Within two weeks they moved in.

A few days later Teri was sitting at her kitchen table, writing letters. She and Lois were organizing a SIDS seminar at Stony Brook

University to educate doctors, nurses, and other health care professionals. Teri was sending out invitations to them as well as requests for speakers from members of the scientific community. Jessie was singing as she wheeled her dolls in a stroller around the playroom. Suddenly Teri heard Jessie scream.

Her heart stopped as she raced toward the playroom.

Jessie was kneeling on the floor, holding one of her dolls and rocking it. Her little stroller had fallen on its side next to her. "Oh, God," she cried, looking up at Teri, "my baby's *dead!*"

Teri's heart was still pounding as she stood in the doorway. When she caught her breath and saw that Jessie wasn't hurt, she kneeled down next to her. "Jessie," she said, tears in her eyes, "your baby's not dead. Babies don't die just because they fall."

Jessie wiped her eyes and looked at Teri. "But babies just die in their crib?"

Teri reached over and hugged her. "Sometimes babies die. But when they're meant to live, they live," she reassured Jessie.

"Is our new baby going to live, Mommy?" Jessie asked.

Teri hesitated. "I hope so, Jessie," she said. "I really hope so."

My mother was happy about the promise of a new baby, but my father wasn't sure how to feel. One night we were all sitting around the table again, talking. My father was sipping the espresso coffee that I had made, when he asked me, "Do you think it's wise for Teri to have another baby so soon?"

"Dad," I said, "after Greggy, I don't think it's wise for anyone on earth to ever have another baby. But it's not my life."

"Of course not, Carol," he said. "And you know I would never interfere, but I was just wondering if those kids had given themselves enough time. How could they survive if it happened again? Maybe it's not wise to try to replace that baby."

I smiled. "I don't know whether you ever recover from something like that," I said, "and one baby can never replace the other. Each is different and the interactions could never be the same. Look at the difference between Jessie and Greg. Besides, remember when I fell off that horse? You were the one who made me get right back on."

He shook his head. "This situation is different. That was to help you overcome your fear so you could achieve mastery. That was so that you could overcome your fear so you could live a full life."

Then my mother said, "She's still going to have this baby baptized in church, isn't she? Even though the angel's here?"

"I don't see any reason why she wouldn't," I said.

My mother hesitated, looked at me, and then asked, "Who's going to be this new baby's godparents?"

"I don't know whether she's even thought about that yet," I said. "Why?"

"Well," she said, "your father and I were Gregory's godparents, but we never got a chance to do much. We should be this baby's godparents." She sounded as though she'd been ripped off.

That year, winter was especially cold. The first snow fell thick and white. I had just awakened and caught a glimpse of the fast-falling flakes through my half-open bedroom window. Snow had always made me feel lonely, from the time I was a child. While other children built snowmen and threw snowballs, I had always stood aside. Now, as I sat up in bed with my blankets still wrapped around me, I realized that for the first time in my life, when I saw the snow, I wasn't lonely anymore. I was sad, that was true. But still I smiled. It was Greggy, of course. Snow reminded me of Greggy. It made me think of him, it made me miss him, but now at least the snow had meaning.

With Christmas right around the corner, I talked to the family about what we should do. No one really felt like celebrating. Still, there was Jessie to think of, and Chris and Jennifer. Usually I bought a tall live tree and decorated it with lights and balls and tinsel. And I bought so many gifts, my father always used to shake his head and give a speech about moderation. That speech had become as much a tradition as the manicotti and fresh ham we always had, but that year it wasn't necessary to talk about how sinful it was to have so much when many others had so little. Because though I bought the tree and decorated it, I didn't have the heart to buy a lot of gifts.

So Christmas was quiet and thoughtful, and somehow more reverent than it had been before. I myself understood it better. Its sacredness and its message. Somehow we all got through the holiday. But the truth was that our Christmas wasn't in December that year, it would come in March. Our family wouldn't have a real holiday again until Teri and Gordon had their new baby. Then we could all celebrate.

* * *

In January, Teri and Gordon registered for a course in cardio pulmonary resuscitation in order to qualify for an apnea monitor for the new baby. Though even at the time the statistics claimed that there was a less than five percent layover between SIDS and apnea, some parents chose to use the monitors anyway. Research later clarified that normal babies had periods of apnea, and that there was concern only if the babies had "pathological" apnea, where they turned blue and lost consciousness.

A monitor couldn't prevent a real SIDS death, but it could alert the parents of a baby who stopped breathing for too long from apnea, though those babies would breathe again on their own anyway.

Teri wasn't sure what she wanted to do about the monitor; Gordon agreed that they should explore all the options.

That night, one month before Teri's scheduled delivery date, she came over to ask Barbara to go to the monitoring course with her. I already knew CPR from all my years of working pediatrics.

Barbara frowned. "Why would you want me to go?"

Teri smiled at her. "Aren't you ever going to offer to watch the baby for me?"

Barbara hesitated only a minute before she said, "Of course, but what has that got to do with it?"

"What are you going to do if the baby stops breathing?" Teri asked. "Or if the monitor goes off?"

"Die myself," Barbara said.

"Are you saying you don't want to come with us?" Teri asked.

"Oh, no," Barbara answered. "I just thought you could learn and then show me what to do. But if you want me to come, of course I'll come."

"Thanks, Aunt Barbara," Teri said. "I was afraid once I had this baby, I'd never get out of the house again because nobody would baby-sit for me."

"Don't be silly," Barbara said. "You know we'll help you with whatever you have to do."

"You and Gordon have decided to monitor the baby?" I asked.

"Not really," she said. "We just want to keep our options open. And if we don't take the course, they won't give us a monitor even if we want it—unless something happens."

"Makes sense," I said.

After Teri left that night, I was clearing away the cups and saucers and Barbara was still sitting at my dining room table.

"It was nice of you to offer to go with them," I said to her.

"I didn't offer," she corrected me. "I'd rather go to China on foot."

"It might not be too bad," I reassured her. "And it will make you feel safer afterward."

Barbara looked at me, her eyes searching. "Are you serious? Do you really think I'd watch that baby alone for the first year?" She shook her head. "And do you really think if I did, and the baby stopped breathing, *I* would continue breathing long enough to resuscitate it?"

I laughed. "Then why did you agree?" I asked.

"Love," she said. "Only because I love Teri as much as I do."

The following night Jessie was already dressed in her pajamas when Teri and Gordon came to drop her off and pick up Barbara. After they left, we sat on my living room couch and wrapped ourselves in a blanket, cuddling. I had put the video of *Sleeping Beauty* on my VCR and we were quiet as we watched it. But when the song, "Some Day My Prince Will Come" began to play, I grabbed my heart and said to Jessie, "God, I love this song."

Jessie looked up at me and frowned. "Mama Carol, you have to stop thinking about princes," she said.

"Why?" I asked. "I love the idea of a prince."

Jessie sat up straight and faced me. She was very serious when she told me, "Mama Carol, there are no more princes. Their time is passed."

I shook my head wildly. Then I wailed dramatically, "Don't tell me there are no more princes . . . I won't be able to bear it."

Jessie took a deep breath. Then she took my hand and very patiently explained. "Nowadays, princes are just good men who help people, like Daddy and Mario."

"I can't accept that," I said stubbornly. "I refuse to believe it. I need to believe there are princes in my world in order to go on."

Jessie was getting exasperated with me. "Mama Carol, even if there were princes, you still couldn't have one. You're too old."

I made a face at her. "Oh, give me a break, Jessie," I said. "I'm a very young grandmother. I'm practically a kid myself."

Jessie stood firm. "If I wanted a prince, I could have one. But you already did your life and you didn't do one of those princes in it."

"Okay," I conceded, "Okay, you win. I'll just have to forget about them being real and just dream about them."

Now Jessie was really upset. She waved her finger at me and spoke with renewed intensity. "No, no, no," she said, "I already told you there are no princes. If you dream about them, you'll be in big trouble."

"Why?"

"Because the shadow team will send somebody to fool you who looks like a prince," she said.

"What the heck is the shadow team?" I asked her. She looked wary, as though I were teasing her. "I'm not kidding you now," I said. "I really don't know."

Jessie's shoulders sagged with the weight of my ignorance. But still she explained. "There's an angel team and a shadow team. The angel team always wins 'cause they're the truth. But the shadow team can cause a lot of trouble in your life."

"Where did you hear that?"

"Everybody knows that," she said. "Ask your heart."

She said it with such confidence, I actually felt dumb. "Okay," I said, "okay, you made your point. You win."

Jessie smiled and settled back on the couch again, snuggled against me. I stroked her hair. After a few more minutes of *Sleeping Beauty*, she turned her face up to me and asked, "Mama Carol, when we finish this video, can we watch TV? Can we watch *Married with Children?*"

My second book was being published, and by the end of January I had to begin a publicity tour. Fourteen cities in three weeks. I would have to start with the *Regis and Kathy Lee* show in New York and wind up with *AM Los Angeles*. Mario had rented the house in Malibu again that year and I knew I could spend a month there and be home in plenty of time for Teri's new baby. Barbara would come with me. I hated going to strange cities and staying in hotel rooms by myself. Besides, Barbara knew how to dress me. Without her I would have appeared on TV dressed in sweat suits. But everything I had to do for the book's publicity was due to be finished by the third week in February. It would work out just perfectly.

Barbara had talked to me about giving Teri a shower before we went on tour, but Teri didn't want one. "Let's just wait and see," she said. So Barbara and my mother bought some things anyway and secretly put them away. Mario and I wanted to buy her a new crib, new furniture for the baby's room. Greggy's stuff was still in my spare room, but Teri wasn't comfortable using it or giving it to someone else. So it just stayed there.

Teri hadn't mentioned any more about letting Janith speak through her, and her Spirits didn't push. Janith had said that she would speak in a different cadence and with different vocal parameters than Teri. She told us that one day we might want to have Janith's voice studied in order to make a bridge between realms. It sounded exciting to me, but Teri just said, "They still don't get it, Mom, do they?"

I tried to sound as neutral as possible. "I guess not," I said. "There's nothing that would make you want to try it?"

She shook her head. "Not a thing I can even imagine right now," she said firmly.

In early February, Teri became president of the Long Island chapter of the Sudden Infant Death Syndrome Foundation.

A couple of weeks before Teri was due to have the baby, the producer of the *Donahue* show called to say they were doing an episode on the loss of a child. They wanted representation from SIDSF. Teri and Lois accepted because they felt it was an important step in educating the public. Gordon, along with several of the other parents, also wanted to go.

They sat in the back of the audience together. An audience filled with parents whose children had died. Parents of murdered children, victims of suicide, Mothers Against Drunk Driving, and a bereavement group called Compassionate Friends.

In front of them there was a couple representing SAD. "What does that mean?" Teri asked the woman.

"Sudden adolescent death," the mother explained. "It's when an adolescent dies for no reason. No accident, no drugs, no medical condition. The kids just die when they're in bed, or in school, or on a football field. When the autopsy is done, the pathologist can't find a cause." The mother looked at Teri, read her badge, noted her belly, and offered, "Our son died at sixteen. He was a bright, lovely boy."

Teri didn't know whether to laugh or cry. A year is one thing, she thought, but I can't worry forever. I'll never survive.

Teri was in a fog most of the show, unconsciously rubbing her belly, trying to comfort herself and her soon-to-be-born baby. But then Donahue asked a question about dealing with grief and Gordon raised his hand.

Suddenly, surrealistically, Donahue was standing, microphone in hand, right in front of Gordon.

Gordon looked around the audience. "Our son Gregory died three days after Christmas last year. He died of SIDS. And I guess what I want all of you to know is that you will have bad days, God knows. But also you will have good days. I want to say, please don't feel guilty about those good days." Donahue was about to walk away, when Gordon reached out to stop him. He looked into the camera and pointed to Teri. "As you can see," he said, smiling at her, "we're going to have another baby. . . ."

The following morning, Teri went into labor early. I didn't know it. I had flown to Texas late the night before for another day of publicity.

I was just waking up, stretching and getting ready to get out of bed, when the phone rang. I sat bolt upright. My heart skipped a beat. "Who is it?" I asked. "Is everything okay?"

"Mama Carol, God *really* made up with me," Jessie said in her soft sweet voice. "He sent me a new baby. And it's a *sister!*"

Chapter Thirteen

We drove straight to the hospital from the airport. But it was dark when we finally arrived. Even though I had canceled all my interviews that day, it had taken too many hours to get a flight back to New York. My heart hadn't stopped racing since I'd talked to Jessie that morning. Afterward, when I talked to my mother and Gordon, they had assured me that both Teri and the baby were fine. But still, I had to see for myself.

The night was clear and cold. Barbara ran in first; she couldn't wait to see Teri. But outside the hospital I stopped and took a deep breath. I tried to compose myself. I scanned the dark night sky for Greggy's star and made a wish. Then I took another deep breath and walked inside.

Once inside, the elevator seemed to be moving in slow motion. As I reached the third floor, even the doors opened slowly.

A hospital at night is so quiet, it feels like a church. I ran toward the nursery, trying to silence the clicking of my shoes on the shiny tile floor, when suddenly I came to a screeching halt. I *felt* that baby before I ever saw her.

Through the large window of a small private nursery I was looking at the cutest baby I had ever seen. Dark curly hair, chubby cheeks, tiny nose. Perfect. My eyes filled. Then I started to laugh. Laughed like when I was a little kid in church. I even put my hand over my mouth to try to stifle the sound, but then the baby opened her eyes and looked straight at me. My heart soared . . . and I knew if joy could burst the seams of a heart, mine was in real danger. Oh, God!

I thought, thank You . . . I'll never forget this moment for as long as I live.

The plastic crib was slightly tilted, so it had no name I could see; still, I knew who that baby was. Ashley Nicole . . . it was true, she did look just like Greggy, but she *felt* completely different. Though her left arm was taped to a tongue blade, and an IV was running in, I knew without a doubt that nothing was wrong with her. Because while Greggy had looked like angel fuzz, this baby looked solid, her pink skin bounded by sharp baby edges.

As I watched her chest go up and down, I could see she was having a little difficulty breathing, but that was fairly common for new babies delivered by C-section. I left the window, grinning broadly. Now I couldn't wait to see Teri.

Barbara was sitting on the bed and Teri looked wonderful. Her eyes, though tired from her labor and delivery, shone when she saw me. There were no harsh lines of pain on her face and she looked relaxed. The first thing she asked me was "How does she *feel* to you?"

I bent down and kissed her forehead. "She *feels* great to me," I said. "The most heavenly human baby I ever saw, but nothing like an angel."

Teri smiled a big, broad smile. "She does look just like Greggy, Mom."

"Yep," I agreed. "She does. But with Greggy all I could do when I first saw him was cry. This time the only thing I could do was laugh. And laugh . . ."

Teri put both hands up over her mouth; her eyes really sparkled now. "She made me laugh too, Mom," she said. "And she really looks pissed about that IV." But Teri's expression changed when she told me, "I want to hold her, but I'm a little afraid. I don't want to get too attached to her . . . just in case."

"Oh, shut up," Barbara said, cuffing her arm. "Don't talk like that."

"She'll be fine," I said, "lots of babies have some respiratory distress after a section. In a regular delivery the contractions of the uterus press a lot of the fluid out of the baby's lungs, but in the quick exit of a C-section, the lungs take a little longer to clear." I put my hand on hers. "Do you want to go down to the nursery and see her? We can walk you down. . . ."

"You think I can?" she asked.

"Sure," I told her. "It's been long enough since the anesthesia."

Barbara grabbed her bathrobe and helped her sit on the side of the bed. She didn't feel dizzy and didn't have a lot of pain. Once I helped her get into her robe and slip some moccasins onto her feet, we began the slow walk down the hall toward the nursery.

As we passed the nurses' station, one of the nurses smiled and said, "That sure is a pretty baby. She's the prettiest baby in the nursery."

Teri was walking slowly but steadily down the hall. At the window of the nursery she turned to look at her new baby. "Oh, my God," she said. "She *is* beautiful." I started to laugh again, but Teri walked right up to the door and knocked. "I want to hold my baby," she told the nurse.

Four days later, Gordon, Jessie, and I went to the hospital to pick up Teri and the baby. Teri was feeling well, so Dr. Bures released her early.

Jessie was so excited, she could hardly breathe. From the backseat of the car she clapped her hands and said, "I can't wait, Mama Carol," she said. "Does she look just like me?"

"Not so much," I told her. "She looks much more like Greggy."

"But she's a girl, right?" Jessie asked.

"Right," I said.

When we arrived at the hospital, I pulled the car up in front and Gordon went in to get Teri and the baby. I sat Jessie on the hood of the car and pointed to a window on the third floor. "Look!" I said to Jess. "There's Mommy."

Jessie looked up and waved. Teri waved back.

"Is somebody going to bring them down?" Jessie asked impatiently.

"Daddy will . . . any minute," I said, putting an arm around her.

A few minutes later we saw Gordon coming toward us. He was pushing Teri in a wheelchair toward the front door. She was holding the baby in the soft pink blanket and sleeper that Barbara had bought. But as soon as Teri saw Jessie, she motioned to me to take the baby.

Jessie walked up to Teri first, looked timid and shy. "Are you okay, Mommy?" she asked.

"Come here and give Mommy a hug," Teri said to her.

Jessie walked close and hugged Teri very gently. "Are you okay?" she asked again.

Teri smiled at her. "I'm a little sore, Jess," she said. "But I feel pretty good."

Jessie smiled. When I leaned down to show her the baby, she

walked over and looked. She stared. Then she very gently touched the baby's cheek.

I handed the baby over to Gordon, who strapped her into the car seat. Then he slid into the backseat. Teri sat next to him. "Come here, Jessie," Teri said, "come sit with Mommy, Daddy, and Ashley."

But Jessie hesitated. "I think I'll sit in the front seat with Mama Carol," she said, "so she won't be lonely."

We had all decided that for the first week after Teri got home, she, Gordon, and Jessie would stay at my house so Barbara and I could help her with the baby. Also, because Teri and Gordon's new house was bigger, with many more rooms, Teri would find it hard until she recovered to chase Jessie around and keep an eye on her.

That first afternoon we had hardly gotten Teri and the baby settled in my living room before Allan Keller, from the apnea monitor center at Long Island Jewish Hospital arrived. He had brought over a monitor and was ready to show Teri how to use it.

The baby was already sleeping peacefully in the lace-covered bassinet that my mother had decorated and placed next to the couch. Teri was sitting next to her, having a cup of tea. Gordon sat down next to her.

Allan walked over and looked at the baby. "Boy, is she pretty," he said. And then, looking at Teri, he added, "I'd like to show you exactly how the monitor works. I'd like to put it on her."

Jessie had been playing with her coloring books on the coffee table, but now she got up and walked over to me, took my hand, stood close by.

"Do you want me to wake her?" I asked Teri, pointing toward the bassinet.

Teri nodded. "You'd better," she said. "I want to make sure I get it right."

Jessica followed me as I walked over to the bassinet. I reached in and gently turned the baby on her back. She stretched and yawned and Jessie laughed out loud. "She looks like my baby dolls," Jessie said.

"She really does," I agreed. Jessie was standing at the head of the bassinet and she watched intently as I began to undress Ashley. Teri leaned over so she could see too. Chubby, creased little arms and legs. Big blue eyes squinting open and then slamming closed, baby stretches and yawns. Finally Ashley was naked.

Allan Keller leaned over and placed a wide gray Velcro belt around her tiny chest. That belt held the monitor leads. Then he began to arrange the long black wires that led to the machine.

Both Teri and Jessie had the same expression as they watched. They were frowning. But when Allan triggered the alarm to test it, Jessie was startled and began to cry. She ran over to Teri. "Don't worry, honey," Teri said, reaching over to hug her. "It's only a machine—like an alarm clock. And it will ring only if the baby stops breathing."

Jessie kept crying. "Is our baby sick, Mommy?" she asked in a worried voice.

"No, Jessica," Gordon answered. "Ashley is fine." I noticed, though, that he was hanging back, not really watching what was going on.

Allan handed Teri the baby now, and she was trying to navigate past the wires to wrap her in a blanket, but the wires kept getting caught. "Come here," she invited Jessie, who had moved out of the way. "Come here and hold the baby's hand."

Jessica shook her head. Then she stepped back away from Teri.

Suddenly Teri put the baby on her lap, unwrapped her, and quickly removed the straps and wires from her chest. "I can't do this," she said to Allan. "I can't. It's crazy. It will make us all crazy. This baby isn't sick. But with all these wires, everyone will think she is. And worse than that, on some level she might even get an idea she's sick. People will treat her different than a normal baby. And she is normal. There's nothing wrong with her except she had a brother who died. I just won't do this to her."

Jessie smiled our collective relief. Even Allan looked like he felt better. "If it is SIDS, a monitor won't help," he said.

"I know," Teri said.

Now Gordon spoke. "Maybe you should leave the monitor anyway," he said. "Just in case we change our minds."

Teri was quick to agree. "That's a better idea," she said. Then she pointed to the farthest corner of the living room and said, "Just put it over there if you don't mind."

Before Allan left, he walked over to the couch where Teri was still holding Ashley. "She sure is cute," he said, smiling.

Jessie walked over, slid onto the couch next to Teri and announced, "She's my sister . . ."

Gordon had to go back to work, so he walked out with Allan. When they shook hands I noticed that Allan held on a long time, before he let Gordon's hand go.

Teri was tired, so she put the baby back in the bassinet and went into my bedroom to take a nap.

For the next few hours Jessie circled the bassinet, whispered to the baby, and finally reached in and held her hand. By the time Teri came back out, Jessie was holding the baby, sitting next to me on the couch. Jessie was wide-eyed with amazement and chattering up a storm, telling Ashley all her favorite stories.

Teri walked over toward the couch slowly. She sat down next to Jessie and stroked Jessie's hair as she asked, "Well, what do you think of your new baby sister?"

Jessie looked up at her and smiled. "She really is a nice baby, Mommy. And she's really cute . . ."

"But?" Teri asked.

"She's not Gregory Thomas," Jessie said, shrugging her shoulders. " 'Cause I would *know*."

My mother was happy again, puttering around, helping Teri by sterilizing bottles, ironing baby clothes, and taking care of everything around the house. My father smiled and held the baby often. Barbara was thrilled again, and so were Jennifer and Chris.

Everyone in the family, as well as all our friends, were completely amazed at the resemblance between Ashley and Greggy. They could have been twins. But like Jessie, for me Ashley was completely different.

I trusted her from the day I first saw her, and each day my heart fell more in love. I was enchanted by Ashley. She was absolute magic for me.

My father looked at her with tears in his eyes, tears of gratitude, tears of healing. My mother couldn't wait each day to hold her and bathe her.

But in a very special way she was more than anything else Gordon's girl. Her eyes shone whenever he held her and she shared special smiles with him. She accepted him unconditionally, as Jessie never had, and every time she saw his face, it seemed to please her. Teri was thrilled with her, but still a little wary and so Jessie and Teri had grown even closer.

The night before they went home to their own house, while Barbara watched Ashley, Teri asked me to sit with her while she again did her automatic writings. She was grateful that she'd felt Janith so close to her during her labor and delivery. And she knew her healing had gone easier because of that. She asked Janith about it.

This pregnancy, this birth, this child's life, is not meant to be hard, she is content with plans once made.

Teri was worried because this baby was also too beautiful, seemed too perfect, like Greggy. Teri asked Janith if Ashley would live, if she would stay.

This child is quite beautiful and this is to show you that even the perfection of the physical will stay on earth if it is meant to. She has much purpose in her creativity. And you will become lighter, happier, and more insightful with her growth.

> *Be with the Light,*
> *Janith*

The following months passed quickly and Ashley began to grow as Janith had said, easily. She was a happy baby, no colic, enjoyed her formula, gained weighed quickly. She was alert, loved company, but didn't seem as needy or demanding as Jessica had been. She didn't exhaust Teri, she gave her space. She spent hours looking around and laughing at all the small toys that we bought her. She seemed completely entranced by life.

The realization that Teri's spirits had been so right again made her think about what had been asked of her. When they had first suggested she consider channeling, she had been very reluctant, but now she was at least willing to ask questions about it. Janith explained that when she was inhabiting Teri's body as a walk-in to communicate, another entity could not enter any more than when Teri's own consciousness occupied her body. They assured her again that it was her soul's purpose and that her future was to be a spiritual counselor. But still Teri was hesitant.

Each time we sat in session, through the difficult months of waiting for Ashley Nicole to grow past the age when Gregory had died, Teri's spirits helped with constant reassurances. But it was Jessica's observations that reassured me even more.

On Mother's Day, when Ashley was almost three months old, Jessie took me aside and asked, "Is Ashley as big as Greggy was?"

"Yes," I told her, "she is."

"But is she as *old* as Greggy was?"

"No, not yet," I said. "But pretty soon she will be."

Jessie looked thoughtful. "Mama Carol," she said, "will you tell me when? 'Cause I have a secret to tell you."

"Can't you tell me now?" I asked. "I won't say anything to anyone else."

She shook her head firmly. "It's not about *that,*" she said. "I have to wait."

On Father's Day, Jessie asked again.

Ashley was four months old.

Everyone was coming over to my house to celebrate with my father. But before they arrived, I was standing at the kitchen sink, peeling shrimp, and Jessie was sitting on my yellow Formica countertop, watching me. Ashley was behind us in a battery-operated swing that was rocking gently back and forth.

Jessica, dressed in a yellow flower print outfit, her straight blond hair in a ponytail, was swinging her legs back and forth. I started to sing "Old MacDonald," and she joined in, but suddenly she stopped and asked, "Is Ashley as old as Greggy was now?"

I turned to look at the baby. Her dark, curly hair was in ringlets all over her head and she was smiling at us and making baby sounds. "Hey, Ashe," I called to her, and she laughed again.

"Mama Carol?" Jessie said. "Is she?"

I looked at Jessie. I smiled at her. "She's older, Jessie," I said. "She's already older."

Jessie looked relieved. "Then I can tell you the secret," she said.

I wiped my hands on a cotton dish towel and leaned against the counter next to her. "Tell, I'm listening hard," I said.

Jessie held her hands up with palms facing each other. Then she turned them opposite and hooked her fingers together in a tight grasp. "Try to pull my fingers, try to pull my arms apart," she instructed me.

I reached over and put my thumbs in the crook of her elbows, one thumb in each. And I tried to pull her hands apart. But she held her fingers tight. "I can't, Jessie," I said. "You're holding on tight."

She nodded. "See?" she said. "That's how it was with Gregory Thomas."

"I don't get it," I said.

Dramatically and with great difficulty Jessica stretched her fingers. "My brother Gregory Thomas and I had to pull apart like this," she said, and her hands flew away from each other, one going up and one down, "so he could go up to heaven without his body, and I could stay on earth with Mommy and Daddy."

"That must have been hard, Jessie," I said, stroking her hair.

Her eyes widened. "It was *very* hard," she admitted, " 'cause I was a *sister.*"

I turned and looked over at the baby. Then I asked, "What about Ashley, Jess? What about you and Ashley?"

Jessie laughed . . . the sound of tinkling crystal. "Mama Carol, look in her eyes. Just look in her eyes. Can't you see? Ashley has no pulling."

During the summer Teri would take the kids to the beach and to the park almost every day, and when she'd stop by to see me, while Jessie ran around the yard, I'd sit on the front lawn with Ashley and get completely caught up in her fascination with a blade of grass. I learned to see nature through that child's eyes, and it was truly magical.

My father responded to her in the same way. Though he loved Jessie's sharp mind, her strong will, her ability with words, he loved Ashley's softness, her joy, her interest in the animal kingdom. He began to stop over at Teri's during the day to play with Ashley, to take her for walks, to explain to her, as he had to Teri, about nature.

Then one day when Ashley Nicole was almost six months old, Teri took the kids to the beach. They were sitting at the water's edge, playing, when a friend of Gordon's, a professional photographer, approached them. He asked for permission to take some pictures of the baby. Several days later, when the pictures had been developed, he sent them to Teri with an invitation from an agency that wanted her to model. Gordon and Teri laughed about it that night, and though they knew that was not what they wanted, they remembered some of the things that Janith had said. It was true. Ashley's life was turning out to be easy and beautiful.

Teri had said that she couldn't channel until she really trusted Spirit. Until at least some part of her healed. Now Gordon was happy with his job, they were comfortable in the new house, Jessie was well, and Ashley had turned out to be all they had promised. In gratitude and relief, on the day that Ashley was six months old, Teri chose to allow Spirit to speak through her.

During the first few sessions when Teri began to speak for Spirit, she was still "there," still conscious, still aware of what Spirit was saying. It was as though someone were talking to her on a telephone and she was repeating what they said. Teri's voice was her own and there were several pauses while she listened and then repeated what was being said. The only difference I noticed was that she used different words than usual, and spoke about different concepts. There was no change in her facial expression or in her body's movements.

But during the session that Teri first allowed Janith to come in, on the day that she first fully surrendered her consciousness to the greater consciousness, her voice changed and so did everything about her. . . .

We were sitting in my study, Teri in my leather chair with her legs crossed under her, and I, across from her, on the couch. Soft music was playing in the background, and I had set up a tape player next to me in order to record the session. On this day I was watching Teri carefully, to see if I could notice any changes, but she looked the same as usual. Sitting, meditating, with her eyes closed.

Slowly the room filled with a pink glow again, but this time instead of seeing the subtle energy of the angel, I saw Teri shiver, as though she had a chill. Then she smiled gently, the soft, sweet smile of a child in a beautiful dream. She tilted her head slightly and moved her hands in a graceful pose. Her face looked more translucent, and her body more relaxed, surrounded by a halo of pink light. Underneath her lids her eyes flickered fast, as though she were in REM sleep. I was certain, even before she spoke, that Janith was there.

Janith wishes to thank Teri for the allowance of this communication. It is important that we ask questions that are relevant to human earth point problems at this time. Welcome, Carol. Do you have any such questions?

"Hi, Janith," I said. It was funny to me that she felt so different from Teri. The quality of her voice was sweet but older than Teri's own. And she spoke with complete assurance. Some of the words were archaic and yet her sentences were exact and her inflections very different from Teri's. My head was swimming with questions. But first I wanted to know more about the realms of angels, more about their "culture."

I asked, as I would ask anyone from another place, "What language do Spirits speak?"

Janith answered, *"The language of Spirit is transformation, Carol."*

Then I asked, "How can we understand more about God?"

Janith looked amused when she said, *"To know ourselves is to know the attributes of God."*

"Can you give us some guidelines for good Spirit channel communications?" I wanted to know if she recognized what others called negative spirits. And I wanted her to allay some of Teri's fears.

Janith explained. *"Human minds, human souls, are capable of good judgment, Carol. They are capable of interpreting the spiritual not only on an intuitive level but also on a rational level. And Janith feels it is quite important to look at these communications not only with your mind's eye, but also with your mind. Are they causing harm? Do they interrupt with destiny? Are they taking from more than they are giving to? Basically it is much the same as a very good, very comfortable human relationship. Also, you must ask yourselves, is it a growing relationship? This must remain the most important test, if you will, of a good spirit communications relationship. For if it does not allow or precipitate growth, then it is and does become the worst form of stagnation, which is not good."*

That made perfect sense to me. I didn't want to ask too many more questions because I didn't know how being in trance would affect Teri. Also, I was eager to ask about her experience. I knew she would have questions to ask, so I said to Janith, "I'd like to take some time to think about more questions, and I'd like to ask Teri for her questions too. Do you have anything you'd like to say to Teri?"

Janith nodded.

"Teri, I am offering help. I am here to learn, yet I am not here to take. If ever our relationship becomes taking, I wish to dissolve it, and I wish for you to help dissolve it."

"Thank you, Janith," I said. I was touched by her nobility. As Teri's mother, it was reassuring for me to know that she would respect Teri and her needs. Now I could stop worrying.

After a few minutes Teri stretched as though she were coming out of a deep sleep. She opened her eyes and smiled. "I feel pretty good," she told me. "What happened this time that was different?"

"Janith," I said.

Teri frowned and looked at me. "What did she say? I can't remember anything."

I rewound the tape and let Teri listen. Watching her expression was at least as much fun as listening to Janith. She looked surprised, then approving.

"How was it for you?" I asked. "How did it feel from inside?"

She smiled. "I don't know, it was kind of like sleeping. Only now I feel better."

Teri was relieved, because when Janith entered, she entered gently and when she spoke, she spoke with a soft and lilting voice. She was glad to know that her movements became more graceful, her expressions more peaceful, her voice surer and more compassionate.

* * *

In the following months Teri and I got together so she could channel for about twenty minutes each day. Janith explained that Teri shouldn't spend more time than that in trance because the primary purpose of a life on earth was to live it on earth. She offered a formula: one-quarter spirit, three-quarters Earth. Often in the afternoons between my own writing, I copied many of the tapes over onto paper. I noticed there was still no repetition. Janith and I spoke about books and concepts that Teri had no knowledge of, and we could hold an entire conversation about things I wanted to know that Teri had no interest in. Janith always made me laugh as she taught me.

Teri was still struggling with what was fair and what wasn't in this world, and so during one of the sessions, she asked me to ask Janith about handicaps.

"Janith," I asked, "what is the purpose of being deaf?"

She answered, *"To hear with your heart."*

"And what is the purpose of being blind?" I asked.

"To see with your inside eyes."

"Is there a purpose for amputees?" Thinking of all those I'd seen in the hospitals over the years.

Janith answered, *"To learn to be whole from within, not without."*

As soon as Teri was really comfortable with Janith, we began to invite some friends over to ask their questions. The Spirit sessions were becoming much more fun because they had become much more interactive. We all knew that Janith was playing with us as well as teaching us.

My father hadn't mentioned anything about Teri's channeling, though I knew that Barbara had spoken to him about it. He had, since the year before, continued to read and explore my books on Eastern religion and mysticism.

My mother's approach was different.

One night while my father was watching the last quarter of a football game in my living room, my mother asked, "What's this I hear now? The angel's talking?"

"Yep, Mom," I said, smiling. "She sure is."

"What's she talking about?" she asked, and her eyes narrowed.

"Soul purpose, love, healing," I said, thinking I was covering everything she could worry about.

She shook her head. "What about God?"

I was puzzled. "What about God?" I asked.

"Does she know Him?"

"Of course," I said. "She says she's from God, the Light."

"Does she know the Blessed Mother?" she asked.

"She knows *about* her," I said. "I never thought to ask if she knows her personally."

"Well, ask," she said.

"Why?" I asked her. "What do you want to know?"

She hesitated. Then she admitted, "From the time I was young, I've seen the Blessed Mother. But I never understand what she's trying to tell me."

"I'll ask," I said.

My father must have been listening, because as soon as my mother went to talk to Barbara, my father called me in to the living room.

"Baby?" he said, and he patted the couch next to him.

I sat down. "Yes, Dad?"

"You've made tapes of this angel who speaks through Teri?" he asked.

"Yes," I said. "Lots."

"Do you happen to have any handy that I could borrow?" he asked.

I laughed. "Handy, Dad? I thought you'd never ask."

My father looked thoughtful. "We've always shared what we've found of value," he said, "haven't we?" I nodded. "I want to see if this has any merit. I'm not promising anything. But I want to listen. I want to draw my own conclusions."

"Fair enough," I said. "Janith always says she wants her words to be listened to with an open mind, not an empty one."

"I know, Teri," he said. "I know how she thinks. I'll know if this is something different."

I went into my study and grabbed a handful of tapes. When I brought them out to him, he chose two. "This will be enough for now," he said. He kissed me good-bye before he went over to Barbara's side to get my mother.

Ashley didn't learn to talk as quickly as Jessica. She stayed much more a baby. She didn't have as many opinions or complaints as

Jessie. She loved the trees and the grass and was intoxicated with the smell of flowers and the colors of the sky.

Then one day when Jessie was five years old and Ashley was almost a year and a half, I was over at Teri's house, having lunch with her. The kids were playing together in the playroom. From the kitchen we could hear Jessie talking to Ashley. She sounded excited. And Ashley was chattering back.

Teri and I got up from the table and went to sit in the den so we could watch them through the doorway. From there we could see as well as hear them.

Jessica had gotten quite tall and so she looked older than she was. Her blond hair was pulled back in a ponytail and her jeans showed how long her legs had gotten. Ashley, on the other hand, was still chubby, with fat cheeks and loads of curly, dark locks.

Jessie had found a book she loved, so she sat Ashley down on the floor beside her and began to read it to her. Jessica had learned to read early, and well. But each time Jessie pointed at a picture, Ashley grabbed her finger and began to play with it.

Jessica was very serious about learning, so she kept repeating, "Ashley, look at this." Ashley laughed again. Still, Jessica read some more. Finally, when she had finished the book, she got up and began to rummage through her toy chest. Suddenly she squealed with excitement.

"Look, Ashley," she said. "Look what Jessie has!"

Teri and I could see she was holding a photograph, a still taken from the video of Greggy.

Jessie sat down on the floor next to Ashley again, and this time her voice, though excited, was quiet. "Look, Ashley, it's Gregory Thomas," she said. "Wasn't he a cute baby?"

Ashley reached up to touch Jessie's face and laughed again.

But Jessie was very serious when she said, "Ashley, look what Jessie's doing." She kissed the photo. Then she held it over Ashley's lips. "Kiss the baby, Ashley. Kiss Gregory Thomas."

Ashley kissed the picture and then she looked up at Jessie.

"Ashley," Jessie said, looking straight into her eyes. "Say 'brother,' Ashley. . . . Say 'brother. . . .' "

Chapter Fourteen

T he day after my father listened to his first Janith tapes, he came over to my house in the afternoon, alone.

He reached into his jacket pocket and pulled out the tapes. "I put them on my Walkman," he said, "and listened to them as I was walking through the preserve today."

"What did you think?" I asked.

He looked puzzled. "I tried to keep an open mind," he said. "I listened to its content, which, as you said, was creative, kind, and loving enough . . ."

"But?" I asked, because there seemed to be a but.

"I don't recognize our Teri here," he said, pointing to the tape. "I mean, Teri is an intelligent girl, we've always known that, and she's certainly bright enough, but let's face it, baby, she's not a philosopher. And this is philosophy. Where is it coming from?"

"Some higher realm, I imagine," I said. "Some realm of consciousness that interacts with our own."

My father looked at me intently. "She told you she was an angel?" he asked.

I didn't dare tell him yet that I had seen her. "Actually, she said she was the High Spirit of Creative Communications from the Core Group of Healers closest to the One or All-Knowledge," I explained.

"So why do you call her an angel?" he asked.

"She said it was the nearest metaphor," I told him. "To help us envision her. Calling herself an angel is probably some upper-realm shorthand. For us on earth it comes with associations we can trust."

"I never remember Teri talking about love, God, or angels," he said. He wasn't looking at me; he seemed deep in thought. "Teri was always so rational, she liked to have a good time. This isn't the Teri I know."

"That's because it isn't Teri," I said.

He nodded, and I could see he was trying to digest what he had heard on the tapes, trying to integrate it and fit it into his store of knowledge and his already-existent belief system. He smiled when he said sheepishly, "Well, even Jesus had to deal with doubting Thomas. . . ." He held out his hand and pointed to the palm. "Until he saw the marks from the nails of the crucifixion, he didn't believe."

Now I laughed, because I remembered Janith telling us in one of the early sessions that as Jesus took on doubting Thomas, she would take on doubting Theresa, Teri.

"If you come up with anything I haven't thought to ask her, let me know," I said.

As my father was ready to walk out the door, he turned to me and said, "I'll take a few more of those tapes, baby."

During the next few weeks I had several dreams. One night I woke and found myself chanting something I didn't recognize. I thought I was losing it, so I didn't say anything to Teri. I didn't want to make her nervous. But that morning she called to tell me that she'd had a dream too . . . about the burned Native American village. She wanted to know what I thought it was.

"Maybe it's past life stuff surfacing," I said. "Next time you do Janith, I'll ask."

So the next session I again asked Janith about our karma; what had happened in our past life that had a direct effect on our present life? I told her about the dreams we'd been having and I explained that Teri's having another baby who was healthy wasn't enough to make us feel that Gregory's death had a purpose. We wanted to understand more. "When are we going to know what we're really doing?" I asked her.

To my surprise, Janith said, *"It is time."*

She asked Teri and me if we would sit together in meditation, holding within our hearts and minds the intention of finding the past life that was important to work on in this life. She didn't give us any other instructions except to protect ourselves with red and then white light, and to call to our higher Spirits and see what would unfold.

I was curious to see what would happen, and though Teri was a little more tentative about it, she decided to give it a try. So we went into my study and put on the soft music of Pachelbel's Canon. Then we sat on the floor opposite each other, lit a candle, and closed our eyes. We began to meditate. Almost immediately, in full panoramic color, a story unfolded for me.

Grandfather Running Elk was almost seven feet tall. A ruddy, dark-skinned, imposing Indian chief. His wife was Marigold Woman. His son, Running Deer, was a shaman, the medicine man of their tribe. He and his wife, Hummingbird Woman, had three children. The oldest boy, a gifted scout, was called Little Running Elk after his grandfather. Another son, a gentle huntsman, was called Little Red Arrow. But it was their young daughter, Morningstar, who was Running Deer's favorite child.

Now, Morningstar was off one day, running through the fields gathering herbs, when she came across a young brave who'd been injured in a fall while hunting. He was from another tribe, she knew that from his markings, and so she was afraid. She hid behind a tree. But the young brave had seen her, and called to her to help him. Timidly she approached. When she saw the blood streaming from his leg, she kneeled and stanched the flow by placing medicinal leaves over his wound, and then helped him fashion a crutch from some branches she had found. When he asked her name, she told him, and without her asking, he told his. White Eagle. Now Morningstar knew who he was. The son of Chief Red Cloud, her father Running Deer's sworn enemy.

There were only a few meetings of those two young lovers. But soon Morningstar knew she was with child. She tried to hide it at first, then refused to speak about it to anyone except her brother Little Red Arrow.

When the babies were born, and there were two, Running Deer quickly took those children from her. One was a perfect baby boy, the other had a harelip. They were children of darkness, Running Deer swore. That very night he buried them alive beneath the dark red clay of the earth. He trapped their souls.

Morningstar was heartbroken. As soon as she could walk, she wandered away from the campsite, hid herself in a cave, and starved herself to death.

It was Little Red Arrow who rode his pony to the neighboring tribe. It was Little Red Arrow, crazy with grief, who brought the news of the death of Morningstar and the burying of the babies to the son of Chief Red Cloud.

That night Little Red Arrow ran the raid on his own father, Running Deer, with White Eagle.

The young brave White Eagle didn't have to struggle with Running Deer as he sat cross-legged around the campfire. White Eagle approached, challenged him, then hit him just once with his flying tomahawk. When Running Deer gave himself over to Great Spirit, it was with gratitude, for his guilt and shame was already too much to bear.

The warriors from White Eagle's tribe, along with Little Red Arrow, chanted and danced their mourning around that same campfire. Then they set fire to the village. But only the body of Running Deer was left to burn.

For early that morning Chief Running Elk had moved his tribe. After he had banished his son Running Deer and forbade him to return to the tribe ever again.

Teri looked puzzled as I told her what I had seen.

"That was exactly what I saw," she said. She shuddered.

My emotions were mixed. That story had come to life more clearly than any movie I had ever seen, complete with the kind of understanding and emotions that I'd experienced only in my most vivid dreams. "Maybe we should check with Janith and see what happens next," I suggested. I had no idea where to take it.

Teri agreed.

I turned on the tape to record the session.

When Janith came in this time, I asked, "Can you please tell us who we were in that past life?"

Janith answered, *"Within the soul mind of each is knowledge of past lives. Each soul knows its part."*

My eyes filled. I nodded. "I feel I was Running Deer, Janith," I told her.

She acknowledged my answer. *"Teri will also know her part,"* Janith said. And then she added, *"Janith will return once you have spoken to this little one."*

"Who were we?" Teri asked when she opened her eyes.

"Janith said you'd know," I told her.

Teri lowered her head. "I was Morningstar," she said. And when she lifted her head, her eyes glistened too. "It's strange, Mom, but she was familiar—the girl on the beach in Malibu."

"That's where I know *him* from," I said to Teri, the pieces falling into place. "Running Deer. Of course, he was the Indian in my dreams. He was the Indian behind the tepee on the beach in Malibu."

"Mom," Teri said. "I'm getting nervous. This is too strange. What can it have to do with us now?"

"I don't know," I said. "I'll ask Janith."

"How important is exploring past lives?" I asked her.

Janith answered, *"How important are your eyes to see?"*

Janith instructed us to meditate again. To go inside ourselves and let the story unfold. I thought of the psychodramas we had seen as a form of therapy while I was still in nursing school. I had no idea where I even got the next question, but I found myself asking, "Now is it the tribunal court of the Indian nation? And should we ask for Running Elk or would you like to give us some suggestions?"

Janith explained. *"You are doing quite well . . . I may say—listen carefully to what Father Running Elk speaks of. He is a wise man. And he also must forgive his son, and acknowledge that justice is done in a bigger way than earthly justice."*

"Thank you, Janith," I said. And then I asked, "Will you come back again after the next session?"

Janith's voice was filled with compassion when she answered, *"Of course."*

Teri closed her eyes again and we both began to meditate. We began to go deeper and deeper. Suddenly I heard Teri speak, but it wasn't her voice and it wasn't Janith's. This time it was a deep, strong male voice which announced, *"I am here."*

I heard myself speak, but it was without thought or volition now. *"Father Running Elk,"* I said, and suddenly my voice was filled with deep sorrow. *"How is it, then, that any son makes up to his father what it is that I have done?"*

"You have," he said, his voice equally pained. *"I see that this test of sincerity has almost reached a conclusion . . . and you have fared well, my son."*

The feeling in my body began to change. I felt my shoulders broaden and then sag with the weight of my pain. The cry in my voice was a cry from the soul. *"Did you ever know how much I loved those children, all of those children? Did you understand that* by taking those small things who I saw as evil that it was my attempt to protect those children and that wife that I loved so well?"

Father Running Elk answered, his voice hoarse. "I was ashamed that my son thought that evil was higher than the good."

Running Deer explained in a voice still racked with pain. "It was the physical that fooled me. And when I buried those children, and when my own child died, I buried with it everything physical I'd ever known. I swore never to look again with physical eyes. I swore never to allow anything physical to touch me. And I have suffered. I have never seen the green of a tree, I have never seen the red of a sky, I have never seen the brown of the earth. . . . I have never really touched or been touched since."

"I feel that you are ready to be awakened," Running Elk said. "I must also say that in the giving back of this child, you are giving your eyes back to yourself."

"How may I best do that?" Running Deer asked.

"You must ungrave this child," Father Running Elk said. "You must reach deep within your soul, dig deep into that brown earth, for in the touching you will receive your nature's eye back. You must also lift this child high into the air and give its soul back to its mother to be released. Morningstar, you must release this soul. And in doing so you will reclaim your own."

Running Deer asked, "When may we begin?"

With great compassion Father Running Elk said, "Running Deer, it has been far too long that you have sat with this burden. Begin as you will."

I felt myself bend over, I felt my hands bigger than they were, I saw the ground beneath me now. . . . And then I saw an incredible sight. . . . Brilliant, glowing light in the shape of a tiny baby . . . Crying so much I was almost unable to speak, Running Deer could say only, "Oh . . . oh . . . this thing I thought so ugly when I buried it is the most beautiful Star Child of All." Running Deer's sobs filled the room as he continued in a voice filled with wonder. "It is Star Sun, and Star Water, and Star Earth, and Star Mountain, and Star Tree and Star Flower, and Star All That There Is. And from the bottom of everything that is me, I give you back this Star Child to be free. . . ."

Running Deer raised the Star Child and handed him to Morningstar. She could barely speak as she raised him toward the heavens. "Oh, God, look at him," she said. "He is to be with the All. He has waited too long for this, for he is of the highest good."

Teri coughed and blew her nose before she could speak again for Running Elk. But when he spoke, he said, *"He has found his place among the stars—for you have met the Elk. . . . And I give you now, Star Water . . . for you are ready."*

Teri cleared her throat again, and I saw her gestures change as Janith began to speak. *"I may say hooray! This is a wonderful homecoming. Thank you for letting me be so much a part—"* She paused for only a moment before she added, *"I wish to tell you that the test is not over. Yet it has already been decided that final outcome will be best outcome."*

By the time Teri and I got back to ordinary consciousness, we were both stunned. "I'm not sure I even get it," she said.

"Even for me, this was a stretch," I admitted.

Teri laughed. "Well, thank God for that," she said. "They've finally taken you to your edges."

"True," I said. "True." I shut off the tape recorder and began to put it away. My mind was still so muddled, all I knew was I really wanted a cup of tea.

Teri was getting up, stretching again, when she suddenly stopped. "Mom?" she asked. "Do you think that baby was Greggy?"

"I'll bet it was," I said.

"That's probably why we couldn't bury him in this lifetime," she said. "That's probably why we had to throw his ashes onto the wind . . . we had to give him back to the Light."

"Makes a certain sort of sense," I said as I rubbed my eyes. I was trying to focus, trying to ground myself. Something had happened to my vision and everything was looking clearer and more dimensional.

"That would be creative," Teri said. "And it sure would be justice. Letting us have him again for long enough to give him back."

I thought of the scene at Tobay. I thought of the way Teri swung around and threw Greggy's ashes . . . freeing his soul.

Suddenly, just as Teri was walking out of my study, she stopped short and turned around toward me. "Mom," she said. "Mom, did Running Deer dig up one baby or two?"

"How should I know?" I asked.

Teri looked frustrated. "Mom," she said impatiently, "think about it. What did you see?"

I thought about it. "I think I only saw one. . . ."

Teri shook her head. "I don't believe this," she said, "I really don't believe this."

"What?" I asked.

"Mom," she said, "Running Deer buried twins. If we gave Greggy back, what happened to the other baby, Mom? Where's Greggy's brother?"

I covered my eyes with my hands. "Honey, I don't even want to think about it. Not now. Not after all we've learned today."

"What did you learn?" she asked.

I put up the tea kettle and turned on the gas. Then, as I reached into the cabinet to get two cups, I told her, "I learned that there's no percentage in burying babies, no matter what you think about them. And I swear, no matter how many lifetimes I live, I'll never do it again."

"Mom," Teri said, laughing. "You're so nuts!"

"Admittedly," I said. "And the test isn't over." I teased. But what I was really thinking was *Where is Greggy's brother?*

Teri went home after the session to talk to Gordon and I took a walk around the block. I was amazed to find that the way I saw the world had truly changed. All my life when I looked at nature, everything seemed to blur together. Even when I put my glasses on, nature had always been like an Impressionist painting to me. Except for rare times like those in Malibu, Venice, and the pyramids of Mexico. But now, every tree, every rock, every flower, and each blade of grass seemed to be outlined in black Magic Marker. I felt as though I were on drugs. I kept rubbing my eyes and shaking my head to clear it. Why did I say "the red of a sky," I asked myself. I know skies are blue. That wasn't the kind of language I used. And how could Running Deer's getting his nature's eye back have affected my sight so profoundly? What had really happened in my study?

That night Danny came over to visit. He wanted to talk about starting his own business. He had been working for others for years and as long as he still loved printing, he wanted to begin to build his future with a shop of his own.

We were sitting in my study. I was at my desk and he was sitting on the couch.

"What do you think, Mom?" he asked. "Is there any way you can help me with this? Any advice how I can do it?"

I was still distracted from the afternoon's session, so all I said was "Get some prices on printing presses and other equipment. Check out some locations. Then I'll try to help you figure out how to do it."

He looked thrilled. "Mom, I know this is what I'm supposed to do. It's been my dream for years," he said. "I want this more than I've ever wanted anything in my life."

"Have you talked to Poppy about it?" I asked. "He's pretty good at this stuff. And he's been working in business forever."

Danny laughed. "The only thing Poppy and I have been talking about is going hunting together this fall," he said. "Gordon's coming too. Poppy said he wants to make it a yearly thing. Just the guys. He wants us to know the way of the woods and he wants us to spend time together."

"Sounds great," I said.

My father hadn't hunted for the past several years since his own brother Tony had died. Going back into the woods without him had been just too painful. I was glad he was going with the boys now. It seemed to be a step toward healing.

Danny pushed his hair off his forehead and sat back on the couch. "What's going on with Teri lately?" he asked. "I haven't talked to her in a couple of weeks. And Gordon's been working his butt off, so I haven't been able to talk to him either."

"Janith did a past-life thing with us today," I said.

Danny shook his head. "Ma, what has that got to do with anything?"

"You don't believe in past lives?" I asked him.

"Sure I believe in them," he said. "But I think the past should stay in the past. All that spirit stuff isn't what I'm doing this life. This life I'm a printer. This life, I want to be rich."

"Ah," I said. "Material values are fleeting things; they're not enduring."

"But," he said, "they'll make my life a hell of a lot easier while I'm here."

"Don't you even want to hear what we found out?" I asked him.

"Not really," he said, "but if you want to tell me, I'll listen."

"Good," I said. And so I told him the story.

When I was finished, Danny laughed. "Gordon was probably White Eagle in that life," he said. "And now to pay him back for killing Running Deer, he gets to marry Morningstar and live happily ever after with all her children. That's his punishment."

"Give it a break," I said. "That's his *reward.*"

"It depends on how you look at it," he said, still laughing.

"Who do you think you were?" I asked. "Little Running Elk?"

"I don't think like that," he said. "But if I did, I'd be Red Arrow because I like the idea of running a raid on my father and moving Gordon into action."

"It wasn't your father," I explained. "It was me."

Now Danny really laughed. "That's even better, Mom. You better watch yourself."

"Forget it," I said. "Talking to you about this is like talking to Mario. A waste of my precious time."

Danny's eyes sparkled. "Well then, talk to Gordon. He loves this stuff, and he remembers things that nobody else does. Besides," he said, "telling me is no good because this isn't my part in the family."

I made a face. "What exactly is your part?" I asked.

He raised his eyebrows. "Teaching everyone to have no expectations," he said. "And printing. That's my part."

When he left to go back to his apartment, I was still shaking my head and he was still laughing.

Then late that night, while I was watching the eleven o'clock news on TV, Teri called to say, "I told Gordon what happened. He said he was White Eagle. And guess what?"

"I give up," I said.

"Gordon said that Danny was Little Red Arrow, he's sure of that," Teri said.

"Great," I said, "my son and my son-in-law ran the raid to kill me. I buried my grandchildren and that killed my favorite child. . . . Some history."

Teri laughed now. "Another point for Spirit. If we were making this up, you could have chosen to be Cleopatra or Jesus, not Running Deer. You could have been some great hero. Instead, you've got a lot of karmic debt from that life, Mom," she said. "You've got a lot of paying back to do."

"I'm paying, honey" was all I said. "I'm paying. . . ."

Barbara came over to have a cup of coffee with me before she went to bed. I told her the story. And I was sort of stunned when she didn't seem surprised. "Were you in that past life?" I asked her.

"You don't remember?" she asked.

Now I was shocked. She had never mentioned anything like this before. "I didn't know you even believed in past lives," I said.

"Carol," she said. "I was the one who brought home all those tapes on past lives years ago. You really don't remember?"

"I remember you bringing home tapes," I said. "Now. But at the time, I didn't believe in past lives. I thought they were a crock of shit."

Barbara laughed. "I always knew things you didn't," she said. "I just didn't talk about them the way you did."

That was true. "Do you know who you were in that life?" I asked again.

She smiled. And nodded. "Of course," she said.

"Who?" I said. "Tell me. . . ."

She grabbed me by my hand and pulled me toward her side of the house. "Come on," she said. "Let's see if you can figure it out."

Once in her bedroom, she pointed to the pictures on her wall. There were two. Hummingbirds. On the shelf in her kitchen she had a porcelain statue of a flower and a . . . hummingbird. I followed her into her living room. She pointed to her couch and love seat. On the dark green floral background of the upholstery there were scattered birds. Hummingbirds.

I turned and looked at her. My eyes filled. "Hummingbird Woman?" I said, unbelieving. "You were my *wife?*"

She nodded and smiled with self-satisfaction. "And you were always a pain in the ass. Even back then you caused a lot of trouble," she said.

I put my hands up to my head. "I can't believe this," I said. "No wonder we were always so close, no wonder I felt I had to take care of you."

She laughed. "You were always stubborn," she said. "You never listened. But you make better decisions now."

Barbara seemed excited that I finally could see what she had known all along. Before she left she kissed me good night.

By the time I got into bed that night, my head was still spinning. The ripples from a past life could really affect a present life, I understood that fully now, but the way in which karma worked seemed much more creative than I'd ever imagined. Having taken the life of my child as Running Deer, it seemed ultimately sensible to have to give her life again. Having buried her children in that life, it seemed absolutely fair to have to be so much a part of helping them live in this one. The relationships between Barbara and me, between Gordon and Danny and me, seemed to take on another dimension. Barbara had been Teri's mother in that past life, and so the depth of their relationship and Barbara's relationship to Teri's children became even clearer.

But if all of that was true, and if the trapped soul of Greggy's had to be set free, it meant there was still at least one more big debt for us to pay.

That thought forced me to sit bolt upright in bed. I looked over at my altar. Then, like a down payment, I bowed my head in gratitude and thanked the Great Mystery for helping us make right what we had done. When I put my hands together and prayed to the Blessed Mother, I prayed more fervently than ever before.

Please go easy on us this time. Don't make it quite so hard. Please don't take another child of ours. . . . But let us find the other twin. And please help us set him free.

Chapter Fifteen

*M*y father enrolled in college. He registered for two courses, physical anthropology and cultural anthropology, which explored the belief systems of indigenous peoples like the Eskimo and Native American. He went two evenings a week and stopped by my house one night on his way home.

He walked into my study carrying a book. "Baby, look at this," he said. "I think you'll find it interesting."

The book was called *Seven Arrows* and it was written by Hyemey-ohsts Storm, a Native American storyteller. My father flipped it opened and pointed to a line which read "This story is called 'The Star Water.'"

I took the book from his hands and began to read.

"There was once a star, way out in the universe, and it fell to earth. It fell upon the great prairie, and when it did, it shattered into many pieces. Gradually they changed into glowing pools of water, into lakes. These lakes shone like stars.

There was a beautiful young girl who went out to these lakes, and from each one she took a handful of the Star Water. She brought these back to the people. But one man became angry and threw his star water into the fire. He then went to live under the ground in an earth lodge. After this the other people also threw their star water into the fire and also went to live in earth lodges under the ground. Only the girl was left with her Star Water. She remained above the ground in a beautiful painted lodge.

Then one day she took back the Star Water that had been thrown into the fire and returned it to its lakes. She had one piece remaining and at this last lake she made medicine.

A great Elk came to her, told her that the people had forgotten how to live above the ground in painted lodges.

. . . And now if you want to find the Morning Star you have to go to where the Elk is. Then he will give you back the Morning Star Water because it is yours."

"This is very strange," I said to my father. "Teri and I knew nothing about this when we did that past-life session."

My father smiled. "It's a Native American story. History from a Native American view is very different from what I was taught. They're great storytellers."

"Dad?" I said. "Don't you think it's strange? Don't you think it's just a little bit odd that you come across this after we've already discovered a past life very much like it?"

"Where do you draw the line, baby?" he asked.

"Oh," I said. "You mean it's all a little strange?"

He laughed. "I think its safe to say that," he said.

My father sat and talked for another hour, telling me all he was learning. He was surprised and touched that the teacher in his classes as well as the other students seemed to accept him and respect his desire to learn.

"Why would that surprise you, Daddy?" I said. "You're a pretty nice guy."

He shook his head. "It's wonderful, isn't it, Carol, the opportunities we have to grow throughout our life? Whoever imagined life could be so exciting, so rewarding, especially at seventy-two?"

"You're a young seventy-two," I told him. Then I said, "Danny told me you were going to take the boys hunting this year? You're going to climb those hills again and trek through those woods?"

He smiled. "It's my legacy to them. When I'm no longer here, I want them to remember the good times we had together."

"You going someplace?" I asked.

"Baby, as long as I can stay, I will," he said. "Still, there's no reason to believe that death will be any less kind to me than life has been."

I patted his shoulder. "You know I have nothing against death," I said. "But I'd prefer if you'd put it off for as long as you can."

"You have my word, baby," he said.

* * *

Malibu. The sun, the beach, the same house we'd had the year that Greggy died. But this time I was really glad to be there. Mario was doing another screenplay as well as working on his new book, and I was retyping it into my computer because he still used an old manual Olympic typewriter. Our California friends visited often, we went to movie meetings together now, and because we were as busy, those next months just flew by.

That year, besides Mario's kids, my mom and dad came out to spend some time. It was a kick for me to see them there. My father loved the long walks he could take along the beach, he took my mother driving through the canyons and out to lunch, and in the evenings they both cooked often for Mario and his friends.

"This is better food than the best restaurants out here," Mario always said whenever my mother served him something she'd made. And she would just smile proudly.

Late at night, both Mario and my father would go out onto the deck and smoke their cigars. I don't remember seeing my father ever more content, and I never heard Mario talk as much as he did with my father.

One night after we had all gone to bed, Mario was lying next to me, awake.

"What's up?" I asked.

"I never met a happier, more well-adjusted man than your father," he said.

"Why should he not be?" I said, laughing.

"With you two girls for daughters," Mario said, "I can imagine how many nights he and your mother lay awake wondering what they did wrong."

I sat up in bed. "Wrong?" I said. "What are you talking about?"

Now Mario laughed. "They're Italians," he said. "Both of their daughters got divorced, insisted on thinking for themselves, chose lifestyles that weren't exactly conventional. You don't think that's a worry to a father?"

"Why? Would it worry you?" I asked.

"I'd commit suicide," he said.

"I can't believe you," I told him. "I thought you said I was the best thing since sliced bread!"

"I did," he said. "But I'm not your father."

"What's that got to do with it?" I asked.

Mario smiled at me. "Even you have to admit, that *if* you have a flaw, it's that you're a little headstrong. That's difficult for a father to deal with. He wants to see his daughters married so he's no longer responsible for them."

"Nobody has to be responsible for me," I said. "I can take care of myself."

"Still, I admire your father," he said.

I lay down again and tried to fall asleep. I thought how tickled my father would have been to hear what Mario said. But the truth was I admired my father too. It was because of him that I was able to withstand so many of the blows life had dealt me and still manage to be optimistic.

"Mario?" I said as I was drifting off to sleep. "Mario, let's get married?"

He leaned up on his arm "Can't do it."

"Why not?" I asked.

"I can't marry you till I'm ready to get rid of you," he said. "You don't keep husbands. . . ."

Life had gotten back to normal since Ashley had been born. Granted, it was an expanded norm, but still, for our family, things had fallen into place. In the weeks following my return from Malibu, Teri and I decided to transcribe some of Janith's tapes to put into a book, and so we formed a publishing company called Star Water Press. Much of what Janith said seemed valuable, and we felt it could offer important teachings for others.

Teri knew how frightened she had been when her consciousness began expanding and knew that if she hadn't had the support she did, it could have made her really crazy.

Even my mother and father considered Janith part of our family now. Once she had proven herself a good influence, they dropped their prejudice. As long as we all still took care of each other, they accepted everything else. I was grateful and wanted to give something back.

Janith reminded us that she did not wish "followers" and she stressed that the advantage and usefulness of real spirituality was that each seeker could find the truth within themselves. She wanted her teachings to help individuals connect to their own spirit and each "human living" to access their own high guides and angels. That would empower them. She explained that there was no greater authority than the voice of truth within each person, no greater wisdom than the "I" of that person. She told us she would be happy to help with the interpretation of any past-life problems, karmic resolutions, spirit names, and soul-purpose questions.

When we had transcribed the material we thought necessary, Janith helped us choose the colors for the book cover and I hired a wonderful artist, Anabel, who was also very spiritual. When the book was ready to be published, we called it *On Wings of Truth.*

Anabel was also a gifted visionary, and one day while we were all sitting together at the table in the kitchen, Anabel told Teri that she saw her having another baby. "I see twins," she said.

Teri didn't say anything, but I almost had a heart attack.

For three days afterward, Teri struggled with the information. She thought of nothing else as she took her showers, cared for the children, cleaned her house. Finally, when we were sitting together later that week she told me, "I've been considering what Anabel said. It's been a hard decision to make, but I think she's right. I think having another baby is part of my purpose."

I could hardly breathe. I dreaded having to go through another pregnancy with Teri. I didn't think my heart could bear any more worrying. Everything seemed to be going so well, I was terrified that if we pushed our luck, we'd jinx ourselves.

"Teri," I said, "don't be crazy. You've been through enough. You're just getting settled. Ashley's still so young. Three children are too many to take care of."

"How can I give information on tapes and in books about *surrendering* to universal purpose if I'm not willing to do it myself?" she asked. "It feels completely hypocritical."

"But how do you know this is purpose?" I asked, thinking, *Is this karma? Is this the time?* "You don't have to get pregnant now," I said. "You could wait for a while."

Teri looked at me. "Mom," she said, *"waiting* isn't going to solve anything. Whatever we have to go through is already set up, and stalling isn't going to change it."

Every cell in my body was screaming in terror. "If you and Gordon decide not to make a baby, there won't be another," I said, trying to keep my voice even.

Teri laughed. "Mom, you sound so naive," she said. "Besides, Gordon still wants a son."

I made a last-ditch effort. "How do you know Anabel's not reading you wrong?" I asked. "In fact, how do you know she's not crazy? Then you'll be getting yourself in over your head for no reason."

Teri patted my arm. "I'll tell you what, Mom," she said. "I'll give Spirit two weeks. If I don't get pregnant in that time, I'll forget it. How does that sound?"

"It sounds like a compromise," I told her. "But it doesn't feel like one."

That night I locked the door between my side and Barbara's so no one could come in and I sat in my living room, sulking. I was furious at myself for my attitude. After all, I was the one who had encouraged Teri to honor her own truth. I was the one who kept pushing for the understanding of karma. So what the hell was I moaning about? I was even the one who prayed that we could find and free the other baby. What was my problem?

After two hours of getting nowhere by analyzing the situation with my mind, I decided to meditate. I sat for a long time, I went deep within. But I was completely unprepared for what I found out about myself. . . .

I didn't want to do "it" again, whether or not it was karma or soul purpose. I didn't care about freeing anyone else's soul. I just wanted those of us who were alive to keep on breathing. Those of us I loved in the here and now. And though I was the one who spouted the spiritual beliefs, Teri was far more willing to surrender to that Spirit I had fought so hard for her to trust. She was far more willing to sacrifice herself again. But when I completely grasped the problem, I was stunned.

It really had been an arrogance. A *spiritual arrogance.*

Janith told us from the very beginning that the questions we asked were the doors that would open to us. Even though she had given us plenty of time, plenty of choice, I had still asked those questions. Teri didn't. But I thought if there was a price to pay, I would be the one to pay it. It had never occurred to me that she would. Even after my father had warned me. So because of my own curiosity, my own quest for knowledge, I had not been able to hear.

Now from deep within I heard a voice I recognized as Eva's, which asked, *Is it possible that this will be the gift in the tragedy?*

When I opened my eyes, I told myself to stop whining, to shape up and get it together. I took deep breaths to fortify myself and promised I would accept whatever followed.

But then, when Teri told me she was pregnant, I cried. I couldn't cover it up.

"Mom?" she asked. "Couldn't you just try to be happy for me? Couldn't you just once try not to make this any harder?"

"What you're looking at," I told Teri, "is me when I *am* trying."

I blew my nose. I wiped my eyes. *I'm humbled, God, I swear. Please don't take my arrogance out on my kid.*

Chapter Sixteen

Teri was sick from the beginning of her pregnancy. She lost weight, she couldn't eat. She was tired all the time.

When they came out to Malibu that year, it was Gordon who played with the kids on the beach, carried Ashley around Disneyland, and read Jessie and Ashley stories at night. During the days he built sand castles with them and watched them splash in the surf at the water's edge. Teri slept a lot.

I was worried about her. I asked Janith why Teri was so sick. Janith reassured us that this baby's purpose was to be a healer and that the "changes" Teri was feeling was due to the difference in vibration between the baby and herself.

I was uneasy the whole time Teri was in Malibu because she wasn't close enough to Dr. Bures in case anything went wrong. And when they finally left to go home I was grateful my mother was with her so that when Gordon had to go back to work Teri wouldn't be alone.

During that three-month period Mario and I had several projects we were working on. But I spent most of my time talking to Teri on the phone, and even in her fourth month she was still very sick.

"What does Dr. Bures say?" I asked her.

"He says the baby's heart rate is good, my blood pressure is good, but I'm still losing weight. He was a little concerned about that, so he gave me some pills to build up my appetite and keep me from throwing up," she said.

"Did he say when you're due?" I asked.

"July tenth," she said. "This baby and Jessie will both have birthdays in July."

"Is he going to do a sonogram?" I asked her.

"Next month," she said. "He doesn't want to take a chance at disturbing anything right now."

"Good," I said.

When my sister Barbara came out to Malibu that year, she told me she wasn't happy with the way Teri looked. "She's as thin as you are now," she said.

"What does Mommy say?" I asked her.

"She says Teri will be okay," Barbara said. "She's making a novena to St. Teresa."

I laughed. "I don't know whether that's reassuring or not," I said. "Mommy calls in the big guns only when we're in trouble."

"Try not to worry too much," Barbara told me. "There's nothing much we can do now anyway. Except wait."

The week before we were leaving Malibu, we had a formal dinner to go to for the signing of a contract for Mario. Those meetings made me very uncomfortable, so I usually ducked them, but this one was a must. So all day I tried to talk myself into trying to do it with some grace. I even lay on the beach, trying to get some color into my cheeks.

Then I took a long, relaxing bubble bath. I had just gotten out of the tub, when, as I was drying off, I felt a lump on my neck. I walked over to the mirror and looked. Sure enough. A lump. I ran my fingers along my throat from my chin downward. I could feel it clearly. It was hard. And it was on my thyroid gland. Shit! I said aloud. Then I decided to ignore it to see if it would go away.

During that week, several times a day, my hand would unconsciously travel up to my neck . . . the lump was still there. In fact, it was getting bigger. And it was much too hard.

Finally, the day before we left for home, I visited a local doctor. He was a caring family physician and didn't take more than one minute to feel my lump before he said, "This will have to come out, I think. It will have to be biopsied in any case, so you might as well wait to see someone at home."

I didn't want to tell the family. I didn't want them to have anything else to worry about, but a few days after I'd arrived, on the first day

I didn't wear a turtleneck sweater, my sister noticed it. "How long have you had that?" she asked.

"A couple of weeks," I admitted.

"Did you call the doctor?" she asked.

"Not yet," I told her. "I'm waiting a little while."

Barbara frowned. "Don't wait too long," she said.

Teri didn't look too bad to me. She was thinner but her color was still good. When she saw my lump, she asked, "Did you meditate and see what your Spirits have to say?"

"I haven't talked to anyone," I told her. "I'm not sure I want to hear."

Now Teri frowned. "Don't be stupid, Mom," she said. "Whatever it is, you'll still have to deal with it."

The following morning I went to my family doctor. He felt my neck and said, "You should see an endocrinologist. It looks like a thyroid tumor."

I called the endocrinologist and made an appointment.

He felt my neck and said, "Let's put you on some supplementary thyroid medication, maybe that will shrink it."

"How long should I take it?" I asked him.

"One month," he said.

I took the medicine for a month. Nothing happened. The endocrinologist gave me the name of a surgeon. I made an appointment.

The surgeon felt it. "You have to have a sonogram," he said.

I had the sonogram.

"It has to come out," the surgeon said.

That afternoon Teri and Gordon were waiting at my house when I got back from the doctor's office.

"What did he say?" she asked.

"It has to come out," I said.

"Why?"

"Because it could be cancer," I told her. And quickly added, "But don't worry, thyroid cancer has a pretty good prognosis."

"Great," she said, upset, "when do you have to go in?"

"He scheduled me for surgery on May twenty-ninth," I told her.

"But that's over three weeks from now," she protested.

"That's fine," I said. "I'm not in any hurry."

"Why not?" she asked.

"I have to meditate first," I told her.

When Teri and Gordon left, I sat on my couch. I put some soft music on and began to meditate. I tried to see what was going on. Finally I asked my healing Spirit, Eva, what I had to do. *"It must come out,"* I heard her say.

Why? I asked. I knew that healing could be accomplished from higher levels, why did I have to get cut up? It seemed so primitive.

Eva's answer was clear. *"We don't want you to become an alternative medicine fundamentalist,"* she said. *"When one is meant to be healed, one will be healed by whatever means one chooses."*

I thought about it. Though I didn't want surgery, the doctors had said it, and now Eva had said it.

So I asked her, "Am I meant to be healed?"

But before I could hear her answer, the doorbell rang. When I opened the door, Teri was standing there, bent over, hanging on to Gordon's arm.

My heart skipped several beats. "What happened?" I asked as I let them both in.

Teri was crying. "Mom, my water broke."

"Shit, shit, shit," I said. She was only twenty-eight weeks pregnant.

We called Dr. Bures, but he was at County Medical Center, twenty-five minutes away. When I told him what was happening, he wanted to see Teri immediately.

"Hurry," he added, "put her right in the car and come over."

I knew why he was worrying. I had seen babies this small just slip out, and if that happened, Teri would need to be in a hospital with a high-risk neonatal unit in order for the baby to survive.

We met Dr. Bures in the emergency room and he examined Teri. He looked grim when he came out into the waiting room to talk to Gordon and me. "I'll have to admit her," he said. "And I'll have to refer you to a specialist in high-risk pregnancy. I'd feel better after the problems she's had if we could give her an edge."

I didn't like that hospital. County Medical was a big county hospital. I had worked there years before in the burn unit. It was always understaffed, never clean enough, and had too many interns and students who weren't watched carefully enough to make me comfortable. I had fought against that while I worked there, and though they had improved it, I still wasn't comfortable.

Teri was lying on a stretcher when Gordon and I went into the emergency room to see her, and she was crying. "Dr. Bures wants to admit me," she said.

Gordon reached for her hand to comfort her.

"I hate hospitals," Teri said. "How long do I have to stay?"

"Dr. Bures wants you off your feet for a few days," I said. "Maybe if you rest, it will give your amniotic sac a chance to seal up so it will stop leaking fluid."

"But what about the baby?" Gordon asked. "How's the baby?"

Dr. Bures pushed back the curtains around Teri and walked in. "The baby's fine, according to its vital signs right now," he said to Gordon, "but before it has a decent chance of survival, Teri should be at least thirty-two weeks into the pregnancy."

Teri made a face. "I can't stay in this hospital for four weeks," she said. "What about my kids?"

"Don't worry about the girls," I said. "Between Gram, Bibs, and me, we'll work it out. And later tonight I'll come back and bring you some nightgowns . . . and, of course, your favorite quilt."

Dr. Bures's expression was compassionate when he explained, "Right now you don't have much choice. Once the amniotic fluid starts to leak, there's not only a danger of going into labor, there's also the danger of infection. Neither you nor this baby can afford to take that chance."

They moved Teri into a big private room on obstetrics because of the fear of infection, and immediately hooked her up to a fetal monitor.

That evening, Dr. Nina Vee, the specialist in high-risk pregnancy, came to see Teri. "We won't do anything to prevent this delivery," she told Teri, "but we'll try not to do anything to induce it either." She asked if Teri had any questions.

Teri asked, "How long do I have to keep this monitor on?" The constant sound of the baby's heartbeat was making her nervous, and she was even more nervous worrying about hearing no sound.

"For as long as you stay here, the monitor stays," the doctor said. "Remember, the more time we can get, the better off the baby's chances will be."

Each day for the next two weeks my mother and father, Danny, Gordon, and all our friends visited Teri. But as the days went on, Teri was getting frantic. She had long hours each day to do nothing except worry. She had tried to meditate to contact her Spirits but she heard no one. She thought that maybe the constant beeping of the fetal monitor was distracting her.

As the days passed, Teri was getting frustrated by not having her own doctor. Because Dr. Vee was chief of obstetrics, and County Medical was a teaching hospital, Teri had to be seen by many different residents, interns, and medical students each day. She had to be examined too often. Soon she couldn't bear it.

I talked to my nursing friends, Bridie, Maureen, and Wanda, to try to find a solution. Wanda suggested that we move Teri to LIH, a private hospital. I knew how good that hospital was, and Wanda knew a specialist who, as she put it, "has a lousy bedside manner but is really good with high-risk delivery."

I asked Teri about it. She wasn't certain she wanted to go anywhere else except home. But one morning, after a crazy patient had escaped from the psychiatric ward and walked through the wards spilling cold water on many of the patients, Teri agreed to be moved.

It was raining on the day the ambulance came to pick her up. Gordon and I packed Teri's clothes, her flowers, her tapes, and books into my car, and I waved as they put her in the ambulance.

Gordon and I got to LIH right after Teri did, but we couldn't see her for hours because she had to go through the whole admission process all over again.

Teri was fuming when we finally got to her room. "I can't believe this," she kept repeating. "I can't believe they won't just read my history. I've just been transferred and still I have to have all the tests done again. And all the blood work."

That night, when Dr. Fraser came to examine her, he told her she had to spend the night in a different unit, where she would have to sleep in a special bed. The top of that bed would be lowered in order for Teri to build up a pocket of amniotic fluid so the doctor could do an amniocentesis early the following morning. Analyzing the fluid would help him determine the maturity of the baby's lungs. That would tell us whether or not the baby could survive outside her womb.

When I called Teri that night, she admitted, "This hospital is better. And Wanda was right. Dr. Fraser is a creep, but he seems to know what he's doing."

Teri got through the night, though she slept little and woke with a terrible headache. As she put it when I spoke to her the following morning, "It's hard to fall asleep standing on your head."

Gordon and I went to the hospital to be with her when she had the amniocentesis. Dr. Fraser was in the small, darkened room when we arrived. He nodded his greeting and I stood in the corner out of the way. "This won't be too uncomfortable," he told Teri, "but you have to lie very still. This baby is pretty big and you don't have a lot of fluid around her. If you move, the needle could stick her somewhere it shouldn't." I had visions of him sticking the baby in the ear or, worse than that, the eye.

Teri hardly breathed as Dr. Fraser, guided by a sonogram, inserted the long, thin needle into her slightly swelling belly. Teri closed her eyes and tried not to move an inch. But the whole time my heart was in my throat.

When he was finished, he looked at the syringe full of fluid. Then he looked at Gordon. "This should tell us what we need to know," he said. "Say your prayers."

We left to pick up Jessie as soon as Teri was being moved back to her room.

"Thanks for coming, Mom," she said. She kissed Gordon good-bye. "Tell Jessie I'll call to talk to her later."

The nurse who transferred Teri to the obstetrics floor put her in a wheelchair rather than let her walk. "Why?" Teri asked. "I feel okay. I'm not dizzy."

"Sometimes an amnio precipitates labor," she explained. "I don't want you on your feet as well. I think it's a better idea to take it slow for the next few days."

"Slow?" Teri said. "If I take it any slower, I'll barely be breathing on my own."

The nurse put her in a semiprivate room. The other bed was still empty.

"Can I have the bed by the window?" Teri asked her.

The nurse shook her head. "Sorry," she said. "That one's already taken. I can't switch because there's more room on that side and that girl's baby is rooming in."

"You mean there's going to be a baby staying in the room with us?" Teri asked. Normally she would have loved that, but now she was so worried about her own baby that it seemed unbearable.

As the nurse helped Teri get into the bed, she added, "He's a cute little fella. And he's quiet enough to be a good little roommate."

"It's a boy?" Teri asked.

"Yes," the nurse said, smiling. "She has two girls at home, but this time she had a boy. They'll be wheeling her back in soon."

Teri was glad the baby would be far across the room from her. She didn't want to have to worry about him not breathing.

Within minutes the nurse's aides brought the girl in and were moving her from the stretcher to the bed. "Hi," she said to Teri, "my name is Judy. What's yours?"

"Teri," she answered. She was surprised the girl was wide awake.

"I had an epidural," the girl explained. "I wanted to see the delivery."

The nurses left and Judy pulled herself up in bed. "I'm supposed to lie flat for a while, but I've been in the recovery room for hours, waiting to be moved out. And I feel so stiff."

Teri smiled. The girl was sweet. "Where are you from?" Teri asked, noticing her accent.

"Des Moines, Iowa," Judy said.

"What are you doing so far from home?"

The girl looked down at her hands. "It's a long story," she said.

"I'm sorry," Teri said. "Forget I asked."

The girl just smiled.

Ten minutes later the nurses from the newborn nursery wheeled Judy's baby in. When the nurse handed him to her, she looked peaceful and happy. But Teri's own arms ached and her heart felt as though it was cramping in her chest.

When Judy finished feeding the baby, she put him back in the plastic bassinet.

Then she turned again to Teri. "When's your baby due?" she asked.

"July tenth," Teri said. "But it doesn't look as though she's going to wait that long."

"Yours is a girl?" Judy asked.

"That's what the sonogram shows," Teri said. "But the doctor says sonograms aren't a hundred percent accurate."

"Yes," Judy said. "I know. I have two girls at home. The doctors thought that this one was a girl."

Teri smiled. She felt as though she betrayed Gregory when she said, "I have two little girls too."

Judy fell asleep then, and Teri didn't pick up the phone to call home even though she really wanted to talk to Jessie. She didn't want to disturb Judy. So she tried to meditate to reach Janith, to reach Suhamaraan. But again, as it had been since her water broke, there was only silence. *Why are you doing this?* she asked them. But still there was no word.

When Dr. Fraser came to see her that afternoon, he was no comfort. All he said was "I can't let you go yet. The baby needs more time."

Later that night Judy pulled the curtains between the beds. She was getting visitors. Teri saw a couple come in. From the conversation, she realized that Judy was giving them her baby. She was giving away her son.

When the couple left, Judy pulled back the curtains and Teri could see she'd been crying. "I guess you heard us," she said.

Teri admitted she had. "What are your girls going to say when you don't bring the baby home?" Teri asked.

"They don't expect it," she said. "Neither does my boyfriend. They know this baby belongs to someone else."

Teri felt compelled to ask, "Why are you doing this? Do you have to?"

Judy climbed back into bed and confessed, "I wanted to do something for someone else. Something really special. I don't have a lot of education, and I don't have any money. What could I contribute? When I saw the ad in the paper, I knew this couple really wanted a baby. That's why I did it."

Teri couldn't imagine anyone being so brave or so good. "Did they give you enough money that your life and your kids' lives will be easier now?" she asked.

"I didn't ask them for money," Judy said. "I wanted them to have a baby."

Teri leaned back in bed feeling very sad. What kind of world was it where a girl could give away her baby, her only boy? Was this karma too? She tried to ask her Spirits. But again there was no answer.

We'd all been taking turns watching the girls. Ashley was fine, but Jessie was very unhappy. No matter who was with her, she kept asking for her mother.

One night Gordon called to tell me Jessie wouldn't stop crying. She was almost seven years old, and usually she could be reasoned with, but now nothing seemed to comfort her.

Danny took the phone away from Gordon. "Mom," he said, "I'll bring Jess over to your house. She's been crying for hours."

"How's Ashley?" I asked.

"She's fine," Danny said. "She's been sitting on Gordon's lap, playing all night."

"What's wrong with Jess?" I asked. I could hear her screaming in the background.

"She won't tell anybody," he said. "But I've got to get her out of here."

"Fine," I said. "I'm home."

Within five minutes they arrived. Jessie's face was blotchy from crying as Danny carried her in. When Danny handed her over, she didn't struggle. "Good luck, Mom," Danny said. "You've saved a life today."

I looked at Jess. "She doesn't look saved yet," I said.

"I wasn't talking about her," he said. "I was talking about Gordon."

"Where are you going?" I asked him.

"I'm going to take a ride over to see Teri," he said. "I figure if you can cheer up Jessie, I can cheer up Teri."

When he left, I sat Jessie down on the couch in the living room and went inside to get her some tissues. When I came back in, she was still crying, quietly now. I kneeled in front of her. "You feel crummy, huh, Jess?" I asked.

She wouldn't look at me. "Don't be mad at me," I said. "I'm willing to do anything I can to make you feel better."

Jessie looked up at me. "Where's my mommy?" she asked.

"Daddy told you the doctor wants to keep her in the hospital till the baby comes, didn't he?" I asked.

"I'm scared about her," Jessie said. "I want her to come home."

"I know, honey," I said. "Mommy will be okay. But she can't come home yet. The baby in her tummy isn't big enough to be born yet."

Jessie tightened her lips. And then she frowned and folded her arms. "Carol"—she said—she had been calling me Carol for months now—"I'm really mad at that new baby. It's not fair my mommy has to be with her instead of me and Ashley."

"But, Jessie," I said, "that baby can't live without Mommy. You and Ashley can. You're already big."

Jessie shook her head. "I can't live so good without Mommy either," she said firmly. "And me and Ashley aren't *that* big."

I hugged her. "Mommy and the baby will be home soon," I said. "Then you'll be glad to have another baby in your house."

Jessie loosened up a little. She seemed less angry when she said, "They better come home soon or I won't even talk to her when I see her."

"You won't talk to Mommy?" I said. "She'll be crushed. She misses you so much."

"Not Mommy, Carol," Jessie said."That new sister. I won't talk one word to her and then she'll only have Ashley. And Ashley can't even read yet."

"Oh, God," I said. "I'll pray for that new baby even harder now. Not only that she should get big enough to stay alive but also that by the time she comes home you won't be mad at her anymore."

Jessie looked satisfied now. "You better, Carol," she said. "Because I'm not a good person to be mad at you."

"I know that, Jess," I said."And Daddy knows, and Mommy knows and maybe soon the new baby will know."

Jessie knew I was teasing her, so now she smiled at me. We watched TV, she read to me, and I let her sleep with me that night. She tossed and turned and several times I heard her whimper. Poor Jessie, I thought, she really isn't that big to have gone through so much.

Two days before my scheduled surgery, I called the surgeon to ask him if I could postpone it.

"No," he said adamantly, "we've waited long enough. I can't, in good conscience, wait any longer."

"My daughter's in the hospital trying not to go into labor," I argued. "It's a really bad time for me to be in too."

"Carol, let's find out what we're dealing with," he said. "I'll release you in three days if everything goes well."

I struggled with the decision. I didn't want to leave Jessie and Ashley, and if Teri ran into any problems, I wanted to be able to monitor what the doctor was doing.

That afternoon, when I visited Teri and told her, she said, "Mom, get it taken care of. I could be here another month."

The following morning the doctor told Teri her amniotic fluid was building up again, and if he hadn't tested her before, he'd never believe there'd been anything wrong. Dr. Fraser decided to release her.

It was all falling into place. Now I would be able to go into the hospital the following day and not worry.

The day Teri came home, Lois called to say that the SIDS support group was willing to come over to her house for their evening meeting if she wanted them to. That way they'd all be able to visit and talk about what was going on for each of them. Teri was very close to them and really wanted to see them. She'd been locked in a hospital away from real life long enough.

I decided to go over to help her.

Ashley was already asleep, but Jessie wanted to stay up for the meeting. She had gone to several of them over the last three years. And from the time she'd been four years old, she was accustomed to not answering the "FIDS" phone, as she called it, when it rang. She knew that only her mother could answer that phone, and when she heard her mother talk, she always was quiet because she knew there was someone on the other end whose baby had died and her mother was trying to help them feel better.

After the last few weeks of seeing Jessie's misery, I was happy to see her smiling as she opened the door to greet the couples who were arriving.

Lois got there first, and when she hugged Teri, I thought she was going to squeeze the breath out of her. Teri laughed. Gordon was making coffee, and now Lois helped Teri cut some cake to put out with the cookies that were already on the table.

"Are you sure you're up to this?" she asked Teri. "Though if you say no now, I don't know what we'll do."

Teri laughed. "I'm fine," she said. "In fact, I feel better than I have in months."

"Only one new couple is coming," Lois said, "Eric and Joan, the child psychiatrist and his wife, who was a social worker. The ones you talked to last month."

"How are they doing?" Teri asked. Their situation had touched her deeply.

Eric was upstairs working in his office at the hospital when another doctor called him to tell him that his son had stopped breathing and was in the emergency room. He dropped the phone and ran down the two flights, ran into the ER just in time to see the doctors in their white coats resuscitating his five-month-old son, Ricky. Superimposed on that horrible picture were the faces of all the children with brain damage he had cared for over the years. Viscerally he remembered how hard their lives had been for them, how little life some had. Instinctively he began to fight through the ER staff to try to stop them. If God wanted Ricky, he didn't want him brought back. If he'd lost too much oxygen to his brain, he didn't want his beautiful son to live life vegetating. He fought and screamed for them to stop. He swung at them and tried to force them away.

Suddenly there were police and security guards all around him. They tried to drag him out of the emergency room, but when he refused, they handcuffed him to a wheelchair and forced him to watch from the corner of the room.

Lois had taken a gift from her pocketbook and was trying to hand it to Teri. "Teri?" she asked. "Are you okay?"

Teri's mind snapped back to the present and she reached for the package that Lois held out to her. "What is it?"

"A present for your new baby," Lois said. "And all my wishes for the best of luck and a very long life for her."

That night Rita came, still pale and thin. But she explained she was taking fertility drugs to try to get pregnant again.

Pam and Johnny came, hugged Teri and Gordon, and then sat on the couch holding hands. They'd had two subsequent sons since I'd seen them last. Pam had stopped working and Johnny had opened an office in the house as a base for his business. They looked happy.

When Maria and Pete came in and hugged everyone, I could see she was pregnant again. He looked both glaringly happy and a little bit afraid. They sat on the other couch.

Eric and Joan arrived next. And Eric looked especially happy to see Teri. "Talking to you really helped that night," he told her. Joan smiled at Teri and asked, "How are you feeling?"

"Good," Teri said. "I feel terrific actually."

They sat on the couch next to Maria and Pete.

Everyone there knew Jessie from the other meetings, so now she walked around greeting them and offering each of them a pack of tissues.

Gordon moved some folding chairs into the den for the rest of us, and finally we all sat waiting for the meeting to begin.

Lois spoke first. "I'm sure I speak for all of us when I say how happy we are that everything is working out so far for Teri and Gordon . . . and all the rest of us."

They smiled and clapped. Then Lois led the group in the introductions again.

Eric was the first one to speak, and when he told his story, everyone nodded in understanding. He said, "I guess when they handcuffed me and I couldn't move, I finally realized that I couldn't interfere, I couldn't control what was happening. As a doctor, I'd been taught to control situations, but in that one moment I knew I had to turn it over to someone or something higher than myself."

Teri said, "I think that's the hardest part and the scariest part of SIDS. In fact, it's the scariest part of life and death. To understand, to recognize that we don't have control. Then we're forced to ask ourselves, who does? God? Destiny? Whatever we call it, we have to build a belief system that can hold it, because each of us has watched our whole life change in just one instant. Each of us has had to realize that we faced situations where we had no decision to make, and no control over the outcome."

Maria spoke then, her hands resting on her belly. "Pete and I go to church ever since Colin died. We find it helps sometimes. And sometimes going to the cemetery helps, because I feel him there."

Lois smiled and admitted, "I always talk to Sean at the cemetery. I've been going for so long that everyone knows me. The caretaker offered me a job last year because I was spending so much time planting flowers."

Gordon had been quieter than usual, but now he said, "It makes you believe there's a spirit that goes on past dying."

Rita chimed in with "I'm still pretty pissed because whoever's controlling my life when I'm not is really doing a screwed-up job." She laughed, but then she added, "Except for Shannon, my oldest girl. She's my grace."

Joan reached for Eric's hand before she admitted, "I felt it when Ricky died. I mean the minute he died. I was doing dishes at the kitchen sink when suddenly the house felt empty. I forced myself to dry my hands before I went up to the baby's room." She began to cry. "That's when I called 911. But before that, I knew. I already knew."

Lois looked at Joan and explained. "Since I've been involved with these meetings, I've heard so many stories from parents who 'knew' or 'felt' something had happened to their babies before they ever found them. Too bad we don't have any scientific studies to monitor that data. Maybe if we did, we'd have more knowledge about SIDS than we do now."

Teri never talked about Janith at these meetings; only Lois knew. But often she used the information Janith had given, put in her own words, in order to comfort them.

Jessie had been standing in the doorway, eating a cookie. Now she smiled at Joan and looked around at everyone else. "I think all these babies are angels who just came to visit. They came to help us remember where we come from and what's really important."

They all nodded. Teri got up to hug Jessie and then she announced, "I think the coffee's ready. Does anyone want some?"

When the meeting was over, everyone kissed Teri and wished her luck again. I helped Gordon clean up the kitchen while Teri sat on the couch next to Jessie, stroking her hair.

Before I left, I went inside to kiss them both good-bye.

"Good luck, Mom," Teri said. "What time do you have to go into the hospital tomorrow?"

"Early," I said. "About six, so I won't be able to call you. But I'll talk to you both as soon as I can."

Chapter Seventeen

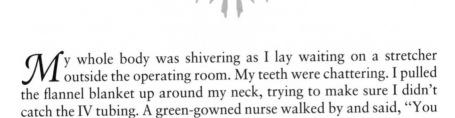

$\mathcal{M}$y whole body was shivering as I lay waiting on a stretcher outside the operating room. My teeth were chattering. I pulled the flannel blanket up around my neck, trying to make sure I didn't catch the IV tubing. A green-gowned nurse walked by and said, "You look like you could use another blanket."

She moved across the hallway and pulled a warm blanket from the heater and placed it over me. It felt good. "How much longer?" I asked her.

"Couple of minutes," she said. "Dr. Weiss is running a little late this morning. He had an emergency surgery between his first and second case."

"How did it go?" I asked her.

She laughed. "Everybody lived."

"That's something," I said.

I felt pretty silly lying there, paper cap over my hair, hardly dressed, as loads of nurses, doctors, and technicians walked past me, not really seeing me. I felt as inanimate as the cardiac crash cart at my feet.

I hated being a patient in a hospital as much as I loved being a nurse. Hospitals are very different places from those different points of view. As a nurse I felt in control, not only competent but fierce in my knowledge, and almost invulnerable. As a patient I felt completely out of control and completely helpless.

And surgery on my neck? My father always told me that when dogs and other wild animals fought, the weaker one would lie down, roll on his back, and expose his neck. His most vulnerable part. It was called posturing. The victor then would consider the fight over. The loser had surrendered.

It had not been so easy for me. New Age theory told that in creation, you had a part and a responsibility. You could return yourself to health by eating healthy food, imaging, reducing stress, making your intention clear, and wanting it badly enough. I didn't for a minute believe that was true. I knew that if your soul purpose, what Janith called "plans once made," included a subclause for physical healing, then you could explore the human potential for such healing. But if instead you'd planned to "teach" or "learn" by sickness and even by dying, then there was nothing you could do but surrender. The media focused on all those who had built-in subclauses. That made it hell for those who hadn't. It made me crazy. And it was as cruel and compassionless a theory as anything in modern medicine.

In the weeks before my surgery I had really struggled in my meditations with whether to pray for healing, do imagery, or otherwise try to interfere with what I'd already "planned." But until I prayed, did imagery, or any of those other things that the alternatives suggested, I would never know whether my spirit had built in a healing subclause. So I did them. But at the same time, I held tight in my heart the knowledge that if it wasn't meant to be, there was nothing I could do about it. And the conscious me, living on earth, promised I wouldn't blame myself if it turned out that my soul had made a plan I didn't agree with now.

I was deep in meditation again, covering myself with purple inner light and talking to my healing guide, Eva, when Dr. Weiss approached me. "How do you feel this morning?" he asked. He looked concerned.

"I'm okay," I asked. "Why?"

"The sonogram showed a cyst, but on closer examination there was also a mass," he said. "I may have to do a complete rather than partial thyroidectomy."

"Do what you have to with my thyroid," I said. "But don't do any head and neck surgery. I'd rather be dead than have no chin."

He nodded. "I hear you," he said.

Dr. Weiss had spooked me. I tried to connect with Eva again and this time I asked fervently, "If you don't mind, would you please ask God if it's not too much trouble, and if it doesn't screw up our plans too much, to give me a break on this one?"

They wheeled me into the OR and slid me onto the table. I closed my eyes. And the last thing I remembered was hearing someone say, "Expose her neck . . ."

Teri's water broke again very early that morning, and she began to have contractions. Dr. Fraser insisted Gordon bring her into LIH immediately. While she sat on her couch, trying to will her pains away, Gordon threw a bathrobe and some slippers into her case. They called Gram and Pop to come over to watch the kids.

Dr. Fraser was waiting for them in one of the labor rooms just outside the delivery room. Once he examined Teri and had the lab draw her bloods, he started an IV to try to stop the contractions. But as soon as he got the results back from the lab, he told Teri that they would have to do a cesarean section and take the baby.

"Why?" she asked. "Is she in trouble?"

"Your white count is going up," the doctor said. "That signals infection."

"Even though I'm in labor, you still have to do a cesarean?" Teri asked.

The doctor frowned. "That baby is small," he said. "Her lungs are underdeveloped. She won't have the strength to fight through a regular delivery." He turned to Gordon and said, "You can come into the operating room and hold her hand during the section."

"That's fine," Teri said. "Just put me out and let's get it over with."

Dr. Fraser hesitated before he told her, "We can't give you anesthesia; it crosses the placental barrier and the baby lungs won't tolerate it. You'll have to be awake, but we can give you a spinal or an epidural so you won't feel anything."

"No way," Teri said. "I'm not going to be awake while you're cutting me open. Besides, if something's wrong with the baby, I don't want to know it right away."

Dr. Fraser's reputation was well deserved. "Dammit," he said, angry now. "I'm trying to get a live baby and a live mother out of this. Stop thinking of yourself and start thinking about your baby."

Gordon held tight to Teri's hand. But then he turned to the doctor and said, "We'll do what we have to."

Teri was crying when Gordon bent down and whispered, "I'll be there with you. I'll take some of the pain. You can hit me, pinch me, do what you have to, but do what he says, and in a little while we'll have our baby."

"Sure," Teri said. "I don't care anymore."

While Gordon gowned and washed in the anteroom of the delivery room, the delivery room nurses were preparing Teri. She tried to call on her Spirits one more time, but by now she had given up the hope that they would answer. She took a deep breath and asked the nurse, "How long will this take?"

"It shouldn't be too long, honey," she said. "Is this your first section?"

"No," Teri said, "but it's the first one I have to stay awake for."

They wheeled her into the delivery room, where the anesthesiologist, Dr. Melen, was waiting. The nurse helped Teri onto the table. It was hard and cold. Then she helped Teri turn on her side so that they could give her the epidural. Teri heard Dr. Melen instruct his assistant as he took the long needle and inserted it between the vertebrae in her spine. She tried to steel herself, but it hurt less than she thought it would.

There was an emergency call and Dr. Melen had to go. But before he left, he reassured Teri, "The hardest part is over. Soon you won't feel anything." Then he turned to his assistant and said, "Just give the medication slowly."

It seemed to take forever as she lay there on her side. The nurses reassured her, told her that in just a few moments she could turn on her back and Dr. Fraser could begin.

She tried to keep her eyes on Gordon. "Talk to me," she said. She was beginning to feel funny. As though she was going to throw up. And she was beginning to have trouble breathing.

"I'm sick," she said as loud as she could, and she struggled to catch her breath. The delivery room nurse took one look at her and ran next door to get the anesthesiologist. By the time he got there, Teri was on her back, throwing up. "I want to sit up," she said. "I can't breathe." Gordon held her head to the side as she spit into the small kidney-shaped basin the nurse held under her chin.

"How the hell much did you give her?" the anesthesiologist asked his assistant.

The assistant told him, "seven or eight."

Dr. Melen sounded upset. "She's too small for that," he said. "I wouldn't give that to a five-foot-eight-inch woman."

Teri's head started spinning. It was true that she could no longer feel her legs, but now everything from her chest down also had no feeling. She was getting panicky. She really couldn't breathe.

"You've paralyzed her diaphragm," Dr. Melen told the assistant.

"You'll have to be more careful about your dosages. Watch her breathing closely, and if she keeps having difficulty, give her oxygen. You shouldn't have to bag her."

Suddenly Teri realized that the young man was an intern. She had to vomit again. She was afraid she was going to choke. But the nurse turned her head to the side as she had before and held the basin. Behind her Gordon looked on helplessly.

"What if I stop breathing?" Teri asked the nurse.

"You'll be okay," the nurse reassured her. "They've put a little something to reverse the effects of the medication into your IV. In a few minutes you'll feel better."

Dr. Fraser came in with a team of pediatricians, who began to warm an incubator for the baby. The room filled with people in green gowns and masks. When the nurse put a strap around Teri's chest, and then strapped down her hands, Teri asked, "Why do you have to do that?"

"If you touch anything, you'll contaminate the field," the nurse told her.

Surrounding her now was a sea of masked people in green. All she could see was their eyes.

Someone turned on the large overhead beam and aimed it at her belly.

"Here we go," Dr. Fraser announced.

She felt him make the first cut. Not the pain of it, but the pressure. She turned toward Gordon, who was sitting alongside. "Talk to me," she said. Looking into his eyes helped. "Tell me something wonderful. Say anything that will help take my mind off what's happening."

She felt pressure again, then more pressure, and she looked at the clock. She felt very dizzy and the hands of the clock seemed to be moving in slow motion. Surrounded now by doctors, nurses, and technicians who were speaking in sort of a hum, Teri moved in and out of consciousness.

"Hold that damn thing aside," she heard Dr. Fraser say in a sharp voice. Then, "Where's the damn suction? I can't see a thing." She heard the slurping of the machine. She looked at Gordon. She could see his lips moving, knew he was saying something, but she couldn't understand him. His eyes looked worried. He looked as frightened as she felt.

Now Dr. Fraser was shouting at the nurses. "Am I working alone here?" he screamed. There was a flurry of activity, and Teri watched as a man in green scrubs approached from the other side. She watched as he lifted his sterile-gloved hands and lowered them into her belly. Again Teri looked at the clock. This seemed to be taking too long.

"Is the baby out yet?" she asked.

Dr. Fraser was gruff when he said, "I'm trying to cut through all the damn adhesions from your other sections. This scar tissue is like a steel plate."

Teri remembered Dr. Bures saying that no one should go in again to make a horizontal cut because of that. He said this would have to be a new cut, a vertical one. She had told Dr. Fraser that, but he had just scoffed at her.

Now there seemed a lot of activity around her again. "Will somebody grab this baby?" he shouted.

Several people moved forward.

Suddenly Teri's consciousness shifted.

Alien creatures, hands inside, pulling something precious from her center. What would they pull forth, what small mortal piece of her own body and soul? Her whole self recoiled. . . . This child is not voluntarily given. This precious piece of being dragged from her body under harsh, glaring lights, with curses and hard words instead of blessings. Don't break it! Be gentle with cold steel tools and hearts frozen in fear. She's fragile! Be careful! Barbaric, this whole thing, she thought. This is hell. I should die now, but let my baby live. I give up . . . it's all too hard. . . . But let my baby live. . . .

She heard a sucking noise and someone held a small, bloody-looking baby toward her for just one minute. "Here she is," the nurse said, but her voice held no sound of victory.

"Is she alive?" Teri whispered. She listened for a baby's cry.

Gordon, with tears in his eyes, kissed her forehead. "Yes," he said.

Teri turned her head in time to watch them put her baby on a high padded table. Someone was sucking the fluid out of her nose and mouth, Teri could hear it.

"Is she okay," Teri asked again. Still, she heard no cry.

"She's okay," one of the nurses said. Then from what seemed like very far away she heard a doctor say, "Let's run this baby down to neonatal and put her on a respirator right away . . . and let's try to warm her up."

Teri was panic-stricken. She turned toward Gordon to say something, but suddenly Dr. Fraser shouted. "Fuck! She's hemorrhaging. I'm going to have to do a hysterectomy."

"What are you saying?" Teri asked. "You're the only surgeon here. You're not allowed to say fuck."

Dr. Fraser turned to Dr. Melen. "Put her out. I can't listen to this." Then he pointed to Gordon. "And get him out of here, will you? We have to stop this bleeding!"

They whisked Gordon away.

Teri was so tired, she didn't care what happened to her, her consciousness ejected. . . .

She saw a limousine, a white, luminous limousine, and holding the door open for her was a tall, thin old man dressed in a flowing white robe. He had a mane of white hair that fell soft as a cloud to his shoulders. She looked at his face. She had seen him before. She hadn't remembered till now. He was the old man she saw with Greggy on the day he first spoke to her. "Are you the Angel of Death?" she asked now.

His face radiated with compassion as he told her, "The Angel of Death and the Angel of Birth are the same. I am called Santori."

She climbed into the limousine and he got in next to her. "Where are you taking me?" she asked.

"To many places," he told her. "There is something I wish for you to remember."

The first place they stopped was a magical blue. The landscape was fuzzy, but coming toward her she saw people she recognized. Love radiated from them and her heart responded. She had been close to each of them and felt tears of homecoming as she greeted each. But before long Santori told her, "We must go on." She felt a certain longing as she got into the limousine again.

The next place they stopped had trees and mountains and lakes . . . all the things she loved. But the colors were like none she'd ever seen before. Again, coming toward her, there were others she recognized, others she'd loved who loved her. She felt safe and warm. And again she felt a certain longing as Santori led her back to the limousine.

Place after place they went, and in each of those places it was the same. Love meeting her, greeting her, the feeling of coming home. Love as strong as she had ever known. "But that means," she told Santori, "that even if we're alone in this life, even if we have no family, as soon as we're out of body again, we return to our loved ones wherever we go."

Santori smiled at her. "That is true. No one is ever alone. . . ."

Teri felt as though she'd been gone a very long time. She wondered what was happening to her new baby. Then she thought about Gordon and the girls. "I should go back," she told Santori.

Teri was in the recovery room. She didn't have a hysterectomy. Dr. Fraser had managed to stop the bleeding. But Gordon had spent the last hours promising himself that he would never let Teri go through anything like this again. If he wanted a son and she still wanted a little boy, they'd have to adopt one. While Teri was still in the operating room, he had gone to see the baby, and though she was on a respirator, he was praying she'd be all right.

He was standing next to Teri, stroking her forehead, when she finally woke up.

"Cut it out," she said. "That's annoying." Everything in her body hurt. "Is the baby still alive?" she asked.

Now he smiled at her. "Yes," he said, "our baby girl is alive. And I have a good feeling about her."

Teri was still sleepy from the anesthesia. "What did my mother say about her?" she asked.

"I called University Hospital," Gordon told her. "But she's not out of surgery yet."

I woke up back in my room. I felt a lot of pressure from the bandage around my neck but my throat didn't hurt much. I reached up and felt my face. At least I still had my chin. I turned to my side and looked around. Aside from a single IV in my arm, I wasn't attached to any machines and I had no drainage bags. I figured the operation must have gone fairly well. There was no clock in the room, so I didn't have any idea what time it was, but there were already flower arrangements on the windowsill. Big ones from my family and Mario.

I picked up the electric bed control and raised the top of the bed. And that's when it started. I was so sick to my stomach, I vomited. I rang for the nurse. I threw up again. And again. And again. The nurse gave me a shot to stop the nausea. It didn't work.

I could hardly catch my breath when my sister came in. She held cold cloths on my head, but still I was sick. "It's the anesthesia," I said.

She nodded. Somewhere in my muddled brain I noticed she was

even quieter than usual. I figured it was because she was worried about me.

"Go home," I told her. "I want to be disgusting in peace. And tell everyone else to stay home."

Mario came up to visit. "Please go home," I gasped.

He left too.

The surgical resident came to see me. He was a young man who looked sincere and intense. "We have to drop a tube to drain your stomach," he said. "We have to stop this vomiting or you'll split your stitches."

"Nobody's dropping any tubes," I gasped. "It doesn't make sense to try to drop a tube down my throat, which will make me gag even more. Just wait a while. The anesthesia will wear off."

Then the chief resident came to see me. She looked a lot cooler than the resident. All she said was "We'll have to put a tube down your throat to try to break the cycle."

"Nobody's dropping a tube down my throat," I repeated. She walked out.

When the resident came back, he had a nurse with him and they were carrying equipment.

"Forget it," I said. "Go away."

The resident tried to explain. "If there's fluid in your stomach, you'll keep vomiting until we can drain it."

"But if it's from the morphine you're giving me for pain and from the anesthesia," I argued, "putting a tube in my stomach isn't going to stop it."

"It's procedure," he said as he started to lay out his sterile gloves.

I sat up straight. "Look," I said. "My head is spinning. When it stops spinning, I'll stop throwing up. Can't you see what I'm saying?"

He didn't. He turned to the nurse. "Do you have the jelly to lubricate the tube?" he asked her.

Now I was a maniac. The problem with being sick in a hospital is that you need all your faculties to defend yourself, and usually the very fact that you're in the hospital means you're not in top form. "Get out of here," I shouted. "I'm refusing treatment. Write on the damn chart 'Patient refuses,' and leave me alone."

They looked at each other. "She's refusing treatment," the nurse said.

"I hear her," the doctor said. "Put it on the chart." Then he turned to me, and threatened, "Well, we can't give you any more pain medication. No morphine now."

"Thank God," I said. And lay back down.

I finally remembered Janith telling me that the key to my success in this operation was to trust the universe, not the medical profession.

The following morning, when Dr. Weiss came in, he told me that the tumor was benign. He had done a partial thyroidectomy and he was very pleased that it went so well.

"Sign me out?" I asked him. "Release me this morning?"

"You really have to stay another day," he said. "I don't want to take the chance of your neck swelling and compromising your breathing. We should watch you for at least another twenty-four hours."

Barbara called to tell me that Teri had the baby. She said she was going up to see Teri first and then she'd come to see me.

"Are they all right?" I asked.

"Teri's in a lot of pain right now," she admitted. "And the baby's on a respirator in the preemie nursery."

"How much did she weigh?" I asked.

"Three pounds ten ounces," she said.

"That's not so little for a preemie," I said. "What do the doctors say? And how are Teri and Gordon?"

"The doctor says it will be some time before they'll know," Barbara said. "Gordon seems fine. He thinks the baby will be okay. But Teri doesn't believe anything anyone is saying."

"Maybe tomorrow morning, when you come to pick me up, we can stop at the hospital and see them on our way home," I told Barbara. "That way I'll be able to reassure her."

"And me," Barbara said, worried.

Once they took the IV out, I got out of bed and paced around the room. I felt fine except when I had to cough. Then my neck killed me. I was glad my surgery was over, but I was wary about the next crisis.

When the phone rang, I thought it would be Mario, but as soon as I picked it up, I heard Teri. "You should see what they're doing to her, Mom," she said, crying into the phone. "I'm helpless and you're not here and so no one can stop them. They can do anything to her."

"Shh, shh, baby," I said. "Have you seen her yet?"

"Not since she left the delivery room," Teri said. "But they've got her on a respirator. And you know how we hate respirators. . . ."

"Wait a minute," I said to her. "Listen to me. We hate respirators to prolong a life that's over. We hate doctors to put terminal people who could never have a normal life on them. We don't hate respirators that help until someone can breathe on their own. That's a completely different story."

"Mom," Teri said, still crying. "I know they're not telling me the truth."

"Why would they lie, honey?" I asked.

"You should see how tiny she is," Teri said. "And her lungs aren't fully developed. How can I believe she'll live?"

"Preemie babies much smaller go home."

"When are you getting out?" she asked.

"In the morning," I told her.

"Come here first?" she asked. "Can you? Can you look at her and tell me what you see?"

"Yes," I said. "Of course."

"Are you okay, Mom?" she asked then. "I mean, was the surgery awful?"

"No, honey, it wasn't," I said. "How was yours?"

"I can't talk about it," she said, her voice cracking. "If you had been here, you never would have let them do it to me."

"Are you still in pain?"

"Yes," she said, and I could tell by her breathing it was true. "Nothing they're giving me seems to help."

"Have you gotten out of bed yet?" I asked.

"They won't let me," she said. "I have too many tubes still in. I even have a bag coming out of my scar."

The lump in my throat from the tears that were trapped was pressing on my incision. I felt bad I hadn't been with her. And I wondered why Spirit had scooped me out of the way. I knew it wasn't an accident that it happened this way. "Honey," I said, "I can't talk anymore. I'll get released as early as I can, and I promise I'll see you tomorrow."

Mario came to see me and so did Barbara and several of my friends, but I was surprised that my mother and father didn't come. That wasn't like them. They were going to see Teri and the baby first and then ride over to see me; when they didn't come, I knew something was up.

The next morning, when Barbara came to pick me up, she explained. "Daddy couldn't come. Once he saw the baby, he was so upset, all he did was cry. They didn't want to upset you. I didn't even see them last night because Mommy couldn't get him to come out of the house. This morning he still isn't right."

"What did you think when you saw the baby?" I asked.

Barbara looked down. "I didn't see her. I don't want to see her until she's walking, talking, and eating," she admitted. "Besides, I wouldn't be a good judge. I'll get too crazy."

Dr. Weiss visited that morning while Barbara made several trips downstairs to drag my bags and flowers into the car.

He looked pleased when he told me, "I knew you'd do well."

"Thank you," I said. "You must have been gentle, because the incision doesn't really hurt that bad."

"Just take it easy for about a week or two, and I'm sure it will be fine," he said. "Use this time to pamper yourself, to take care of yourself, to give yourself a break."

It was a beautiful spring day, and the sun on my body felt wonderful. I sat quietly, not talking too much to Barbara, just hoping that nothing was wrong with the baby: that she hadn't suffered any loss of oxygen during delivery so she wasn't brain damaged. I knew she wouldn't be able to take a bottle for a while because her sucking reflex wasn't well enough developed. I tried not to focus on all that could be wrong. I tried to be hopeful. I forced myself to remember that very early on, Janith had said this baby's purpose was to be a healer. I just hoped she had a different specialty than Greggy.

Once we arrived at LIH, I went right up to check the baby while Barbara went to visit Teri. The curtain was drawn across the window of the preemie nursery, so I knocked on the door. "I want to see the Griswold baby," I told the nurse. "I'm her grandmother, and I haven't seen her yet."

The nurse smiled. "The baby's doing well," she told me. "But you'll have to wait a few minutes to see her. The doctor's with her. We want to try to take her off the respirator and see if she can tolerate it."

I smiled. "Great," I said, praying that nothing would go wrong while I was standing outside that door.

I began to pace. I walked up and down the long hall, looking through the nursery windows at all the other preemie babies. They were quite a sorry lot, I must admit. Most of them were surrounded by so much medical equipment that they looked like bionic babies.

I knew that Teri would be horrified if she came down to the nursery alone.

I heard someone call. I turned. "Come on," the nurse said. "She's off."

I got into the yellow paper isolation gown she handed me, scrubbed in the small anteroom, and walked into the nursery. I began scouting for our baby while looking at all the others. In the background, respirators hissed as their bellows rose and fell, monitors beat in a cacophony of different rhythms, and oxygen bubbled while I circled the room.

There in a little covered plastic incubator was a small pink baby, her eyes covered with black patches, an oxygen tube coming out of her mouth, a Velcro monitor belt around her belly, electrodes from the cardiac monitor covering her chest. I walked closer to the incubator. Stood alongside it. Watched the rhythm of her chest going up and down with her even respirations. She didn't look very small to me. As I twirled open the vents on the side of the incubator to touch the baby, I crooned, "Hey, baby, welcome to the world. I'm glad you came. I'm glad to see you."

Suddenly her legs started to kick and her head started to shake and I watched her chest rise and fall in quick, short starts. Without hearing a sound, without being able to see her eyes, I knew she was crying.

"Shh . . . shh . . ." I comforted. "It will be okay. This is only temporary. You're going to grow to be a big girl, and everyone is going to love you." I ran my fingers over her small chest, soothing, comforting with words, with strokes, with love. Soon her breathing eased again. "I love you," I said again. "I'll be back to see you soon." Just as I started to pull my hand back out of the incubator, the baby grabbed my finger. And held tight. Really tight. My eyes filled. "I'll make you a deal, baby," I told her. "We'll be partners. Stay alive, you'll live in love. I'll teach you everything I know. My grandmother touched my life, but died. I'll live and stay with you."

When that baby let go of my finger, I knew the deal was sealed.

I walked quickly over to see Teri. It was a long walk through many corridors. I had to take an elevator up to get to the sixth floor, and when I finally got to Teri's room, I was almost breathless.

Barbara got up from the chair next to the bed and said, "I'm going down to get Teri a malted." But she warned with her eyes that things were not good.

Teri was lying in bed, her face lined with pain, her eyes filled with suffering. There was an IV running into her arm, which was black and blue from too many IVs. She was pale and teary. She looked too thin. "Did you see her?" she asked me.

I bent down and kissed her forehead. "She looks great," I said. "She's off the respirator. She only has oxygen on now, but she's strong, Teri, and alert. She grabbed my finger and wouldn't let it go."

Teri frowned. "She doesn't sound like the same baby I saw in the picture that Gordon took," she said.

"Where is it?" I asked.

She turned her head toward her nightstand and said, "In the top drawer."

I picked up the picture and looked at it. She looked the same to me. "She doesn't look bad," I said.

"You were a nurse for too long," Teri said impatiently. "You don't even see what normal people do. This baby does not look okay. She looks like shit!"

"Honey," I said. "You're in pain. You've been through a terrible time. But I think the worst is over. Remember Janith said she was meant to be a healer."

Teri's eyes looked sharp and black as coal as she said, "Don't talk to me about Janith or Spirits. Where were they when I needed them?"

"Okay. Have you seen the baby in person yet?" I asked.

"No," Teri said. "They won't let me go in a wheelchair, and I'm in too much pain to walk that far. Besides, I'm not ready yet."

"What did you decide to name her?" I asked.

Teri hesitated. "Sharilyn," she said. "Jessie was too upset . . ."

For weeks now Teri and Jessie had been fighting over the new baby's name. Teri liked the name Cheyenne, but Jessie thought it was awful.

"All the little kids will tease her," Jessie had said. "That's a weird name."

"I like that name, Jessie," Teri objected.

"Mommy, listen to this," Jessie argued. "Cheyenne Griswold? Mom, she not an Indian baby. Not in this life. She's a Griswold baby. Her name should be Sarah or Sandra or something like that."

They eventually agreed on Sharilyn.

Teri was restless now, she couldn't get comfortable in the bed. She rang for a nurse. "Can't I have more pain medicine?" she asked.

The nurse looked sympathetic when she said, "You just had it two hours ago. I can't give you anything else yet."

"Where's your pain?" I asked Teri then. "What's making you so uncomfortable, is it your section scar?"

Teri began to cry. "You don't know what they did to me, Mom. You can't imagine how horrible it was. All those people with their hands inside me, pulling my baby out. . . ."

I held her hand. I couldn't say anything. And I was getting weak and dizzy myself. I didn't want to pass out in front of her.

When Barbara came back a few minutes later, I told Teri, "I have to go, honey. I'll call you later. And I'll see you again tomorrow."

Back at my house I drew the shades. I crawled into bed, crawled under my own cool sheets, and tried to take a nap. *I can't do this if it's going to be too hard,* I told whoever was listening. *We can't keep going from one tragedy to another without a break. On earth humans need to catch their breath. Or they lose hope . . .*

I fell into a deep sleep and slept for hours. And just on the edge of waking up I heard Eva's voice say, *Don't be fooled again by the physical. This is truly a gift.*

That night my mother and father came over. They had just come from visiting Teri, but only my father had visited the baby again. I was lying on the couch in my living room, leaning my head back on a pillow. My mother sat next to me, patting my feet, but my father sat in the chair opposite. "How did the baby look, Dad?" I asked.

My father put his handkerchief over his eyes and tried to push back the tears. He tried to manage some control, but his voice was hoarse when he explained. "I can't believe that tiny baby will survive."

"Why?" I asked. "Is she worse than this morning?"

He shook his head. "No," he said. "The nurse said she was better."

"She looked okay to me," I said. "Small babies do live now. That's the advantage of all our medical technology."

He wasn't hearing me. "I can't believe she'll have a chance at a normal life if she does survive," he said.

"I think she'll be fine," I said. "She has great muscle tone. She seems alert. She breathed on her own and she's keeping her formula down."

"They keep taking blood from that small baby," he said helplessly.

"They're trying to monitor her oxygen levels, I'm sure," I said. "And if she wasn't doing well, she would have been put back on the respirator. That she managed to breathe on her own is a good sign."

My father shook his head. "If this little baby survives and comes out of this whole, then I'll believe in miracles. I'll believe in angels."

"What about you, Mom?" I asked. "What did you feel?"

She had been sitting quietly, not saying anything. "I lit a candle," she said.

"Mom," I said, "that's not an answer."

My mother sat up straight. "It *is* an answer," she said. "Maybe not your kind of answer, but it's an answer."

"Translate please," I said.

"It means without the help of God, Mary, St. Teresa, and all the angels, I don't think—" she began, but then she stopped. She looked over at my father. "I feel like your father about it," she said.

"That's not good news," I said.

But something held tight within me insisted that that baby, Sharilyn Griswold, would certainly survive. And more than that, she would live.

Teri stayed in bed the next two days; she didn't feel well enough to get up. Everyone went to see Shari. Each night my father visited her in the preemie nursery and then came home and cried. But Gordon stayed each night for hours, talking to her, touching her; in fact, he held her before Teri even got to see her.

On Teri's fourth day I went to see them again. This time Teri seemed a little better. Her IV was out and she was walking around. Not well yet, but it was something. "Do you want to walk over to the nursery and see the baby?" I asked. "I can come with you. Maybe that would help."

Teri thought about it, and then she agreed. "I have to walk slowly," she told me, "because this drain keeps bouncing against my incision if I don't."

It must have taken at least twenty minutes for us to navigate the corridors. Finally we arrived. I noticed that Teri kept her head down, didn't look through the windows at the other babies. "Look," I said. "Most of these babies are so much smaller than Shari."

She looked at me. "Mom," she said. "It feels like I'm caught in some kind of Frankenstein movie," she said. "All this tampering with life and death . . . all this pain for such new babies."

The pediatric nurse taking care of Shari was pleased when she saw us. "Shari's doing great," she said. "She's taking another ounce every two hours. And her oxygen levels are holding, so her lungs are doing well."

"She's taking a bottle?" Teri asked.

The nurse shook her head. "No," she said, "we're still tube-feeding her, but soon her sucking and her gag reflex will kick in, I'm sure."

Teri just looked at her. Once we had gowned, the nurse took us into the nursery and showed Teri the baby. She looked great to me, had even gotten stronger, I thought, but when I looked at Teri's face, I knew we were seeing different things.

The nurse got Teri a chair.

"How long do these babies usually last?" Teri asked her.

The nurse looked surprised. "Most of them will go home."

Teri said, "I had a perfectly healthy baby who died at fourteen pounds of SIDS, so how can you tell me this baby will live?"

"I can't guarantee it," the nurse said kindly. "All I can say is that most of these babies go home and most of them don't go on to die of SIDS."

Teri sat in the chair. I saw her eyes scan the jumping lines on the cardiac monitor, look at the belt across her new baby's chest from the apnea monitor which she had fought hard for Ashley not to wear. I watched as she stared at the long, twisted oxygen tubing extending from her baby's face like a transparent plastic trunk of a small elephant. And the dark black patches over her baby's eyes. "How can I see my baby under all that stuff?" she asked.

"Would you like to hold her?" the nurse asked. "I can take her out for a few minutes."

Teri looked startled. "Hold her?" she repeated. I could see she was frightened to death.

The nurse walked over and lifted the top of the plastic incubator. She carefully wrapped the baby in a blanket—tubes, leads, and all—and put her gently into Teri's arms. But Teri was stiff with terror. The nurse looked at her, and then with compassion said, "I'll take her patches off, then you can see her eyes. Maybe that will make you feel better."

The nurse kneeled down in front of Teri. She turned to me and said, "Here, hold this," as she took the oxygen tubing off the baby's face. "Hold it close to her nose. I just want her mother to get a look at her without all the gadgets on."

Once the oxygen was off, I could see she had a tiny little nose. "Look how cute," I said to Teri. She said nothing.

When the nurse removed the patches, Shari's eyes were closed. But without a doubt, she was a gorgeous baby. She looked unreal. Porcelain skin. Tiny nose, fat cheeks, full lips. She was beautiful.

Teri touched her cheek. Ran her fingers gently over the baby's forehead and down her nose. Touched her little lips. "Hi, Shari," Teri said, but she sounded guarded. Then Shari opened her eyes and Teri was so startled, she almost dropped her. "Mom," she said, "Mom, look at her eyes. They're blue eyes, Mom, they're crystal blue."

I looked. Sure enough. Crystal-blue eyes. Big blue eyes, clear blue eyes. Just like Greggy's.

"Take her back," Teri said to the nurse. "Hurry, put her back in. I have to go back. I feel sick."

We left the nursery quickly. Teri couldn't wait to get away. "I can't do this, Mom," she said, crying. "I know I can't do this."

"Teri, stop," I said. "She'll be okay. Really. I feel it."

She was very quiet after that, even once she got back into bed. She hardly said a word to me. Until I said, "Your Spirits wouldn't do that to you again."

She laughed at me. Then she said, her voice angry now, "How do you know what they'd do? Look what they've done so far. That's your idea of fair play? Angelic blessings and all?"

"Teri," I said, "you're acting as though none of this would have happened if you hadn't been involved with Spirit. People live very hard lives every day across this whole planet. Your Spirits just help explain the lessons you're learning, the reasons for your pain. You act as though you wouldn't have to suffer if it weren't for them. And that just isn't true."

Now Teri's eyes filled again. "I trusted them, especially Janith, but this whole time, where were they? I tried to reach them every time I got afraid. I tried to hear what they would say. But time after time I got no answer."

"I'm sure Janith has an explanation," I said. "When you feel well enough, we'll just have to ask her."

Teri put her head down. "You better tell them, Mom, if anything happens to this baby, I'll die myself. I'll be no good to them at all because I'll be a raving lunatic. It would mean that the first time I trusted them enough, trusted the universe enough, they betrayed me. And I could never trust them again after that."

Later, after he visited Teri and the baby, Gordon stopped by to see me.

He looked tired but happy that night.

"How's Shari?" I asked.

"Great, I think," Gordon said.

I offered him some steak and salad. When he sat down to eat, he said, "The first time I saw her in the nursery, I was worried, Carol, because it seemed to take too long a time before she breathed in the delivery room. I was scared until I saw her."

"Do the machines bother you?" I asked him.

"No," he said. "I hardly notice them. Except for that little red light on her toe. Because when I watch it blink, I know she's breathing and it reassures me.

"I think she's going to be fine," he said. "It was so cool knowing that I was the first one in the family to touch her. I told her that we'd be here for her, that we'd wait until she got strong enough to come home. I reassured her that we all loved her, and that she was perfectly safe."

"So she felt good to you?" I asked, smiling.

"Her skin is so soft," he said. "I love to touch her."

"Teri doesn't trust her yet," I said.

Gordon nodded. "I know," he said. "And maybe it's better if she gives herself some time. When the baby comes home, she'll catch up. In the meantime, she's dealing with it as well as she can."

"She doesn't really like to visit the baby," I said.

Gordon nodded. "I know. But I can keep going. Every night on my way home, I can stop and see Shari. It will give us special time together."

"That's important to you?" I asked.

"It was a good feeling to be first this time," Gordon explained. "Usually a mother gets to hold a baby first. The mother is the first one the baby connects to, but with Shari it was different. It was me who touched her first." He laughed then. "I welcomed her and asked her if she remembered me. She grabbed my finger and held on. I'm sure I know her, Carol. I can feel it."

After Gordon left that night, I felt better. Now at least there was another person who felt the way I did about the baby.

Three days later Teri was discharged from the hospital, but she had to leave without Shari. Though the baby had begun to suck, she still tired too easily to be fed only by bottle, and her weight had dropped a few ounces. Before we left, Teri went to see her again in the preemie nursery. She held Shari that day and kissed her. But some part of her still held back. "How much longer does she have to stay?" Teri asked the pediatrician.

"If all goes well, just until she reaches five pounds," he said.

"How long will that take?"

"About a month," he said, "excluding any setbacks."

Teri stood in the hall a long time that day just hugging her pillow before she agreed to leave. She desperately wanted to see the girls, but she hated leaving her baby.

"She'll be fine," I said. "You can come visit her."

But Dr. Fraser disagreed. Before he discharged Teri, he told her that he didn't want her riding in a car for at least two weeks. Her body had gone through too much trauma and needed time to heal.

Jessie and Ashley were thrilled that their mother was back home. Several times each day Teri called the nursery to see how her baby was doing. Once the baby had started drinking from a bottle instead of being fed through her tube, Teri pinned a big chart on the wall to monitor Shari's weight, and she and Jessie recorded every ounce that Shari drank.

My mother and father visited the baby at the hospital several times. When I wasn't helping Teri with the girls, I visited too. So did most of our friends and the rest of the family. Because in order to enter the preemie nursery one had to be related to the baby, each was a cousin, an uncle, or an aunt. Only Barbara wouldn't go. She stood firm. Until Shari was home, Barbara didn't want to see her.

Gordon was transferred to another store farther out on Long Island, but still he drove the hour into the hospital each night to visit Shari. To talk to her, to reassure her, to hold and hug her. Every night when he got home, he reported her progress to Teri. So far she'd had no setbacks.

Teri was soon feeling almost well enough to drive. In just a few days she'd be able to see Shari. I was at her house, helping her pack some things for the baby, when she explained again how betrayed she felt by her Spirits. It was then, sitting at her kitchen table, after my mother took the kids outside to play, that Teri showed me the list of questions she had written for me to ask Janith. In all the years she'd channeled, she'd hardly ever asked any.

"As long as Gram has the kids," Teri said, "maybe we can do a session now and I can see if Janith shows up."

I agreed, and we went inside her den to meditate. We set up the tape recorder and turned it on. Then we put on some soft music and

I began to pray, but even before I was finished I felt myself surfacing and felt Janith around.

Teri seemed to slip into trance much more quickly than she ever had, and it seemed a smoother transition from her voice to Janith's. When Janith began to speak, I felt enormous relief.

I greeted her, told her how glad I was to be able to speak to her again, and then I asked, "Janith, can you explain why Teri wasn't able to reach Spirit from the time her water broke?"

Janith answered, *"With the death of her son, Gregory, this one called Teri also died, and with the birth of her daughter, Shari, this one was also born."*

Some part of me understood what she meant, but a bigger part didn't. So I said, "That's not clear enough for my mind to grasp. Can you help clarify it for me?"

Janith's voice was filled with compassion when she answered. *"The birth process is one of separation. It is coming from the collective into the individual. You feel alone, you feel taken from the whole. It is not so much that spirit is not there, it is that you must not hear us or feel us in order for you to hear and feel your own individual soul. It is the birth experience we are speaking of."*

"Is this Teri we're speaking of, or Shari?" I asked.

"It is both. Let us say a child comes into a soul, into the womb of its mother. In that time there are plans being made. The soul is acclimating to its new environment. Spirit must stay quiet so that the soul is not confused by the All, and by the vibratory level of All There Is. It is coming into its own vibratory level. That space must be protected as a cocoon, as an egg, if you will."

The answers Janith had given covered all the questions Teri had written. I didn't know whether that would comfort Teri, but I thanked Janith, and in seconds Teri blinked her eyes and was back.

"What did she say?" Teri asked.

I played the tape and Teri's eyes filled. Her whole expression signaled understanding, but even more, an acceptance. "When I gave birth to Jessica, it felt like I gave birth to a baby. When I had Greggy and Ashley, I was asleep. Later, when they handed me those babies, it felt like I gave birth to them. But with Shari, it was all very different."

"How?" I asked.

"When I was awake on the table in that operating room, it didn't feel like I was giving birth to a baby. It didn't feel like it was only a baby they were taking; it felt like a part of me. They were pulling my insides out. The baby was part of it, sure, but I myself was no longer intact. Later, when Santori took me to all those places, I felt like I was up in spirit again. With the unconditional love and Light and peacefulness that a baby feels before it comes to earth. I felt no separation, no harsh reality of earth. By the time I made the decision, when I asked to come back, I had been changed. Both Shari and I had been delivered. Shari came from the depths of my being, from my soul. That day they pulled a part of me out into the world."

"I think that what's called death and rebirth in all the Eastern religions," I told her.

"I didn't know they were being literal," Teri said.

New studies showed that when preemie babies were cared for with love, when they were touched a lot, their stay in the hospital was shortened and they grew more quickly than the babies who were not cared for in that way.

So Teri went almost every day to stay with Shari, while my mother or my sister or Jennifer watched Jessie and Ashley. By the time I went again with Teri, the only equipment left on Shari was one IV in a vein in her head. They'd shaved her hair into a mohawk and she really looked like a little Indian. Even the nurses called her "The Little Mohican." Teri hugged her and kissed her and fed her all day long.

"I knew I should have called her Cheyenne," Teri said to me that day. And her eyes were alive with happiness.

"Are you feeling more secure about her?" I asked. "Do you trust her yet?"

Teri smiled a big, broad smile. "I'm getting close," she admitted.

During those days when Teri visited Shari at the hospital, her whole state of mind began to change, and even more important, her heart softened and she began to see her life in a whole new way.

The first few days she felt sorry for herself. Felt bad that her whole family had to suffer again because of another baby. She felt bad for Shari too, felt bad about all the pain and discomfort her new baby had to endure. But when the doctors were examining Shari, or the nurses had to change her leads or monitor her bloods, Teri was sent outside the nursery to wait.

It began on the first day she was there. She walked downstairs to go outside to get a breath of air. On her way through the children's hospital, she noticed that many of the children were bald. She knew that meant chemotherapy. Those children had cancer. She also watched the children who walked with canes, those in wheelchairs, those who because of the strain on their hearts could hardly move.

Outside, she saw the same people day after day. Most of them were parents too. But when she heard their stories, she knew many of them were waiting for their children to have treatments for terminal diseases. Many of them had children who would die.

Only the mothers who were there for the babies in the neonatal nursery were helping to grow their children toward life. She would eventually leave with her baby. Many of these parents would leave the hospital alone. It was then she resolved to stop feeling bad for herself. It was then she began to feel grateful.

She stopped by my house on the way home one day to give me an update on the baby. We sat as usual to have our tea, and then she asked if I had a pair of scissors.

"For what?" I asked.

She held her arm out toward me. Bent her hand at the wrist. "The bracelet, Mom," she said. "Greggy's bracelet. I think it's time to cut it off."

"Really?" I said. "You're ready for that?"

Teri smiled. "Greggy is etched in my soul, Mom," she said. "I don't need it anymore. I want to be happy with what I've got. I don't want to focus on what I've lost."

I took the scissors and placed it under the cotton macramé, which was now more gray than white. "Here goes," I said, looking at her to be certain. But she didn't flinch. It fell to the table. "Do you want to save it?" I asked.

She picked it up and put it in her pocketbook. "Just a little while longer," she said.

When Gordon had his next day off, they took the girls up to see the baby. Ashley was two and a half, and so for her it was like having a baby to play with, but for Jessie it was something else.

The next time she saw me she said, "Did you see Sharilyn? Did you see her eyes?"

I smiled at her. "I did," I said.

Jessie put her hand over her mouth and giggled. Then she whispered, "Carol, I *know* those eyes. . . ."

Chapter Eighteen

S hari came home from the hospital on the first of July, ten days
earlier than the day she was due to. She had just been impatient,
in a hurry to get here. Though she weighed a little under five pounds,
the doctors had released her because she had no setbacks and all she
needed was some extra care. Teri was more than happy to give it to
her.

Teri and Gordon took Jessica and Ashley when they went to pick
the baby up from the hospital. All of us were waiting for them when
they got home.

Barbara cried when she saw Shari for the first time. "She looks
like Jessie," Barbara said. From the moment she picked her up, she
hugged her and kissed her and never put her down.

Teri's friends came to visit, and Anabel brought a present.

When Teri saw her, she said, "Well, you were half right. I did
have a baby, but she wasn't twins."

Anabel smiled at her. "That's the problem with being a visionary.
I hear twins, I think they mean twins. But the zodiac symbol for May
is Gemini—the twins. So there you have it. Accurate information,
an error in interpretation."

My mother was in her element again, sterilizing bottles, washing
baby clothes, and helping Teri with the girls. And my father . . . well,
my father was on top of the world.

"What did we do to deserve such a blessing?" he asked.

"What didn't we do?" Teri answered.

My father laughed. "It's a wonderful day," he said with gratitude. "In order to be any happier, I'd have to die and go to heaven."

"Don't cause trouble," I said.

Ashley ran over to my father. He lifted her high in the air. "Want to go for a walk, Ash?"

Without a word, she went to get her shoes.

"Want to come, Jessie?" my father asked.

"No thanks, Poppy," Jessie said. "I want to stay with Mommy and the baby."

The days went well and Teri said the nights went even better. Each time she had to get up to feed Shari, as she sat in her rocker, just the two of them alone, she found herself filled with wonder at this miracle that was her own sweet baby girl.

Summer passed quickly and life was on the upswing again. Teri, Gordon, and the girls were happy. Spirit had been right. Teri's daughters would fill the hole that her son had left. My father and mother spent so much time with them that I also began to be able to see that those three little girls, Jessie, Ashley, and Shari, were part of the miracle of Greggy's message to our family. Having survived the bad times, the good times seemed even more precious.

One afternoon that fall Teri brought the girls over to my house. We all went outside to play. Teri and I built a big pile of leaves in the middle of the yard and Ashley and Jessie were throwing themselves in and climbing out of it. Jennifer was watching Shari inside the house, playing with her. But when Teri heard the baby cry, she went inside to see if Jennifer needed her. Ashley kept jumping into the leaves, but Jessie walked over and stood next to me, watching her.

Ashley, with her dark curls bouncing, was jumping so high her feet hardly touched the ground. She was laughing out loud, having a glorious time. Each time she emerged from the mountain of leaves, she wrinkled her nose and brushed them from her hair, but then she ran around in circles and jumped again.

"Isn't she adorable?" Jessie asked me. She looked very grown-up.

"She's pretty cute," I admitted.

Jessie looked thoughtful now. Then she asked me, "Do you remember my brother Gregory Thomas's music box?"

"I sure do," I said.

"Well, remember how whenever I listened to it, it made me cry?" she asked.

"I didn't know, Jessie," I said.

"Well, guess what, Carol?" she asked, her brown eyes shining. "I took it out of the crystal case last week and listened to it again. And it didn't make my heart hurt anymore. I didn't even cry."

I hugged her. "I'm happy about that, Jessie," I said. "I really am."

Jessie reached for my rake. Then she saw Teri carrying Shari toward us. She laughed. "Do you know my sister Shari makes little music notes come right out of my heart?" She looked at me, her face upturned, and added, "Gramma Carol, I think the best thing in the world is watching a baby grow."

In the following months Teri moved from being president of the SIDS Foundation chapter to parent contact director. Now she could help train parents of SIDS babies to counsel new parents. There was less paperwork and more service.

Right after that change Teri had a dream that she and Gordon bought a house.

The following morning at breakfast she told Gordon.

He laughed and said, "You take your nickel and I'll take mine and we'll see who will sell us their house."

Teri shrugged and said, "If it's supposed to happen, it will."

It took only another week for Teri to find a house she loved.

The owner, Mr. Capallini, was willing to sell it with no money down once he had spoken to Teri, and even hold a second mortgage for the down payment. So that weekend she took Gordon to see it.

Mr. Capallini explained to them that he'd built the house himself. He'd lived there with his wife and his dog almost all his life. Now that his wife had died, he felt too lonely and so he wanted to live with his daughter. To do that, he had to sell his house.

Gordon felt at home the moment he walked in. Within a few weeks they went to contract. At the closing, when Mr. Capallini congratulated them, he also mentioned that he had to have his dog, Ginger, put away. His daughter had no room. Gordon looked at Teri, Teri smiled back. That day Teri and Gordon left the lawyer's office with both a new house and an old dog.

* * *

Their new house was almost an hour's drive from my house. But Teri felt safer now, felt comfortable being away. The girls were getting older and they needed a backyard to play in.

Danny helped Gordon move all their furniture. Teri, my mother, Barbara, and I bought curtains and shades to cover the windows. When everything was moved in and put in place, the house looked like a dollhouse. Teri and Gordon were excited. Everything was perfect.

When Shari was six months old, Jessie asked Teri if she could have a session with Janith. Jessie had never asked to talk to Janith before and Teri wanted to know why. "Sorry, Mommy," Jessie said. "I can't tell you, it's a secret."

The next time she saw me, she asked, "Will you come in to sit with me? Mommy says I'm too little to go anywhere alone."

"Sure," I said. "What's up?"

"You'll hear when I ask," she told me in her no-nonsense voice.

"But why do you have to ask Janith?" I asked. "Why can't you ask one of us?"

"Because it's an answer that only an angel knows," Jessie said.

The next time everyone was at my house, Barbara watched Ashley and the baby while Jessie, Teri, and I went into my study. I dimmed the lights, put on soft music, and Teri and I began to meditate. Jessie was so quiet, I could hardly hear her breathing.

Finally Teri's voice changed and Janith began to speak.

"Welcome, Jessica. There is a question of great importance that you wish to ask Janith?"

Jessie's voice was strong when she asked, "Janith, I want to know if my sister Sharilyn is really my brother Gregory Thomas. Because even though she looks like me, and Ashley looks like he did, there's something in her eyes."

Janith answered, *"Your sister is your sister at this time. But the essence of these two beings is very similar. That is what you are feeling. That is what you know."*

Jessie looked thoughtful for a minute and then she asked, "Janith, does similar mean more the same or different?"

Janith answered, *"The same."*

Jessie clapped her hands, her eyes alight. "I knew it," she said. "I knew it from the first time I saw her."

I thanked Janith and told her we had no other questions.

When Teri blinked and came back to her own consciousness, she saw Jessie's expression and asked, "What did you ask? What did Janith say?"

Jessie smiled. "She said Shari and Gregory Thomas are the same."

Teri looked thoughtful. "I felt that too," she said. "Funny, we never talked about it before."

I ruffled Jessie's hair. "What would you have said if she told you they weren't the same?" I asked her.

Jessica looked at me and frowned. "I wouldn't have believed her for a minute."

In November my father took the boys hunting again. They spent a week in the woods where my father had always gone with his brother. They stayed at a lodge with other hunters and, as my father said, "We roughed it." He climbed hills and walked miles each day. Both Gordon and Danny marveled at his endurance and agility. They both tired before he did.

When my father shot a buck with a big rack, he called the boys from their stations in the woods to show them how to clean it. Then they all carried it back to the lodge, where the other hunters admired it.

Gordon shot a doe that year, and my father made him gut it.

But when Danny's deer showed up, he had his safety on, and the click it made when he released it gave that deer time to run.

"I was kind of glad," Danny said. "He looked straight into my eyes . . . and he looked as scared as me."

It was a rite of passage for Gordon. Still, he wanted a buck. My father made them leave one deer at the lodge so that it would be eaten. He never took more than he needed.

At home the boys carried the deer downstairs to my father's basement so that he could teach them how to butcher it. But before they did, my father bowed his head in gratitude, thanked the Lord, and thanked the deer. Then they toasted him with a special drink of my father's aged Pinch scotch. It was a ritual, that whole thing, and my father insisted it remain one.

"You never kill another living thing," he told the boys, "without awareness of your responsibility to treat it with respect."

Both Gordon and my father had the skins tanned. From those skins Gordon sewed small medicine pouches by hand. It took him months to stitch and bead them. Once they were finished, in each of them he placed a special crystal. Those were the gifts he gave to everyone at Christmas.

That winter Mario and I went to Malibu again. This time it was a bigger house, closer to the beach, but also right next to the highway patrol station. I liked that house. It also had one big room upstairs surrounded by windows, but only one large bathroom. Mario and I had to share. Still, we both had plenty of space to keep long tables so that we each could write on opposite sides of the bedroom.

From California that year, Mario and I went to England, to Cannes for the film festival, and then on to Venice. It was a year of freedom for me, a year of beauty, a year of healing.

By the time we got back home, it was only a few months till my mother and father's fiftieth anniversary. The family, and Mario too, wanted to give them a big party.

Barbara and I had decided not to hire a hall. We wanted it to be more personal, so we opted to do it ourselves. But we did get a local caterer to help.

As Barbara wrote out the invitations at my dining room table, she asked, "Do you think we have enough room in the backyard if everyone comes?"

"Never does everyone come," I said.

But they did. All of them. They came in cars, on planes, on foot. Every last one of the people we invited.

When the big day finally arrived, it was raining. Barbara and I just looked at each other. We were in big trouble.

My mother called. "Are the tents up?" she asked.

"Yes," I told her. "But the dance floor will be pretty wet and slippery if it keeps raining. And the yard will be muddy."

"It won't keep raining," she said. "I just went to church, lit a candle, and said a prayer."

"Thank God you know people in high places," I teased her.

"Laugh," she said. "But watch . . ."

My mother, of course, was right. The rain stopped and the sun broke through the clouds to shine mightily on my backyard. Barbara and I covered the twelve round tables with bright floral table-cloths and put a small dish of gardenias in the center of each table. Danny and Chris put the liquor on the standing bar and unloaded several cases of champagne. After we set up the glasses, Barbara and

I looked around. With the lanterns hung from the tall shade trees, and the bright yellow tents, everything looked very festive.

Barbara and I watched as the house and the yard began to fill. Then Teri, Gordon, and the girls arrived. My cousin Rosemarie and Aunt Josie flew up from Florida. Friends of my parents' I'd known all my life came, as well as friends I'd never seen. Then Mario and his family came, including his brothers and sisters.

The band started to play "Here Comes the Bride" as my parents walked in. They were all dressed up. Dad looked sharp in his light blue linen suit and my mother had bought a cream-colored linen dress with cotton lace appliqués for the occasion.

When I asked if they had any requests, my mother and father said they wanted to renew their vows. So Barbara called the priest.

"We've been so happy," my father explained to the group that stood around him, "I can't take a chance she'll get away."

My mother smiled shyly and said, "He always says the silliest things."

When the priest arrived, the whole rowdy group quieted down.

As he began the ceremony, my mother and father smiled at each other. Then they looked around at all of us. Their family, their struggles, their victories, their whole life together shone in their eyes that day.

Their original best man raised his glass and made a toast. And everyone clapped. Then the boys poured the champagne.

But my father couldn't stand not making a joke about it.

"God forbid, another fifty years . . ." he gasped. He grabbed his head and held it. He got soft and serious again when he looked at my mother. He raised his own glass and said, "I can't wish my two daughters a marriage like my own, but"—he held his glass toward Gordon and Teri—"I can wish it for my granddaughter and grandson. May you both be as happy for as long as Grandma and I." He bent over and kissed my mother. "To my lotus blossom," he said. "I thank you for all your years of belief in me, for all the years you've trusted and supported me. And for helping me raise such a wonderful family. You've made me a happy man."

Ashley, Shari, and Christopher were running through the yard, playing. Shari had made up for her beginnings, she was now a chubby toddler. I took Jessica around to introduce her to everyone who didn't know her.

The dance floor cleared for my father when he asked to dance with each of his daughters. He danced the polka, first with me and then with Barbara. Teri walked over to him next, cut in, and danced with him. Then Jennifer. Then all the little girls. Jessie danced on her own feet, but both Ashley and Shari danced with their feet on my father's, just as Teri, Barbara, Jen, and I had when we were young.

Gordon danced with my mother. And Danny danced with her until Christopher cut in. Then my mother and father danced a waltz. God knows what he whispered in her ear on the dance floor that day, because suddenly her face was all red. Imagine being married for fifty years, I thought, and still being able to blush?

It was my father who wanted photographs.

"Why, Dad?" I asked. "Don't you see enough of us?"

He patted me on the cheek. "Baby," he said. "A man likes to look at his dynasty. It makes him feel important. I was poor, from an immigrant family, when my mother brought me to America. And now, as I look around, I see how rich I am. I have a family who loves me in spite of my shortcomings, and a lot of good friends. I want pictures because I always want to be able to see how we all looked on the happiest day of my life."

Chapter Nineteen

*T*eri had a dream. . . .
    A woman with twelve children came knocking at the doors of all the houses in a small neighborhood. But when each door was opened, this woman announced apologetically, "Before I come in, you should know I have twelve children."
    Each door slammed shut. No one would let her in.
    Teri watched for a long time.
    Finally the woman knocked at her door. And she said to Teri apologetically, "Before I come in, you should know I have twelve children."
    Teri said, "It's okay, come in anyway. I'm sure the older ones will look after the younger ones."
    The woman seemed very grateful. But the moment she came into the house, Teri woke up.

The next morning was a Saturday, so all Teri's kids were home. She was sitting at her kitchen table, drinking her coffee and leafing through the local paper. Shari was playing house with Ashley in the living room, Jessie was lying on her bed in her room, reading.

A small ad caught Teri's eye. It was an ad for donations of clothing and money for the orphaned children in Romania. Teri knew she wasn't going to have any more children, and she still had cartons of almost-new clothes and toys packed away. She'd been wanting to give them away to a child who could use them.

She picked up the phone and dialed the number. When a woman

answered, Teri offered her all the girls' baby clothes. On impulse she also offered what she had left of Greggy's.

Liz Hammil was the woman's name. She said, "By the way, there are a lot of healthy children in Romania who need parents. Children who need to be adopted."

Teri laughed and said, "I was calling to donate clothes and toys."

As though she hadn't heard Teri, Liz continued. "We're having a meeting tonight at my house for all prospective parents. Would you like to come?"

Teri thought about it for a moment. Gordon would be home, it was his early night, so she said, "Let me see if I can find a baby-sitter. What's your address?"

Liz gave her address and then said, "By the way, I have twelve children."

Teri was so excited. She could hardly talk when she told me what had happened. She knew it was a sign from Spirit. I couldn't believe it. I had seen a *People* magazine earlier that year, with a picture of a beautiful Romanian baby on the cover. I bought it, read it, and then hid it, hoping Teri hadn't seen it. The night of the *20/20* broadcast on the terrible conditions of the Romanian orphanages, I had chosen not to mention it to Teri. I had avoided talking about it. Because from the moment I saw that magazine, it touched me so deeply that my heart knew if Teri got wind of it, we were getting another baby.

Still, in spite of my attempt at sabotage, Teri had come across the same things on her own. The iridescent arrows of fate were aimed straight at their target.

That night Jennifer offered to baby-sit. Gordon and Teri went to Liz's house. It was in a cul de sac and there were cars as far as they could see. They parked, got out, and walked down the long driveway to the front door.

Inside there were rows of folding chairs filled with couples.

Liz and her husband handed Gordon and Teri a large manila envelope before they sat down. Teri opened the envelope and on the first page, she saw, "Approximate cost: $9000."

Gordon went ballistic. He turned to Teri and whispered, "Where do you think we're going to get $9000?"

"You said we couldn't get a house," Teri said, smiling, "but we did."

Liz began to explain the deplorable conditions in Romania, and why there were so many children available for adoption. The dictator, Nicolae Ceausescu, a Communist, had ruled with an iron fist for twenty-four years. Ceausescu dreamed of building a master race just like Hitler had wanted to. He had forced the women into having children. He forbade abortion, made any woman of childbearing age take periodic pregnancy tests, punished women he believed were practicing birth control. He swore to provide for the children. Yet the people in Romania didn't have enough food; most of what was grown was exported to bring in money for the country. The people were starving, their children were starving, and mothers could no longer afford to keep their babies. Instead of taking care of them as Ceausescu had promised, the state warehoused them in huge orphan-ages—cold, barren buildings filled with white metal cribs and infested with bugs and disease.

But finally in late 1989 his government fell and on Christmas Day Ceausescu and his wife were executed by a firing squad. Then the country opened up to visitors from other countries. When the journal-ists and camera crews arrived, the condition of the country was brought to the attention of the rest of the world. Romania had too many children locked away in orphanages. Children who needed parents who could feed and clothe them.

Liz explained she was a facilitator. She'd been working with a lawyer in Romania. The parents would have to do all the paperwork. Or they could hire a lawyer in the States, but it would cost another $3000.

She explained that foreign adoptions were easier than domestic ones because the rules weren't as stringent as in the United States. In fact Romania had no regulations as far as age, marital status, or how many children were already present in the home. Another big advantage was that once the adoption was final in Romania, and the child came to America, that child could never be taken away. But every opportunity was given to the adoptive parents if they wanted to change their minds before the adoptions became final. In Romania there was no right to repeal or rescind the adoption. Once you got your baby, he or she was yours.

There was a lot of anticipation, nervousness, and excitement in the room. Most of these were skeptical New Yorkers who were wary of this woman who told them that she needed $2000 up front, in cash. And that there was no guarantee they would get a baby. She also told them that the country was open at the moment, but it was a country at war with itself, and they could close it down at any time. In that case all their money would be lost.

That night Teri saw the children Liz had adopted from Romania, a five-month-old girl and a six-month-old boy. Teri fell in love with them immediately.

As they left the house, Gordon turned to Teri and said, "Our son is there. I know it. We're going to do this. I don't know how, but I know we are."

In bed later, Teri remembered Greggy's voice as clearly as on the day he first spoke to her and said, "I have to make room for my brother. He needs you more than I."

Before she fell asleep, lying in her soft warm bed with her children sleeping peacefully in theirs, she thought about that other baby. Her baby who was out there. Cold, hungry, alone . . .

The following day Teri filled out the application. In the box where they asked boy or girl, Teri checked "boy." When they asked the age preferred, Teri wrote "Fifteen months or older."

Then she drove to my house to ask for my support. I had always tried very hard not to say no to my children. I tried always to understand their needs, and to help. Even when I disagreed. But this time I couldn't. This time my whole body contracted in fear.

"I can't be part of this, honey," I said. "If anything goes wrong, I'll never be able to live with myself."

"I thought you believed in adoption," Teri said. "You always said if you had stayed married longer, you would have adopted a baby yourself, because you believed we should care for the children of the world."

"I do," I said. "But the children of Romania have been so abused, they've been deprived of so many basic needs from such an early age, I'm afraid that any parent who adopts them will have to spend an enormous amount of time fixing what went wrong. And so I worry— not only about you and Gordon—and the energy you'll have to expend, but also about the toll it will take on the girls."

"This family is big enough and loving enough to fill even the biggest need. If we can't do it, who can?"

I thought about it, tried to be as honest as I could. "Teri," I said. "A lot of those kids have AIDS."

Teri's eyes opened wide. "I can't believe you're saying that. I can't believe that you of all people would be afraid of a baby with AIDS."

I shook my head. "I'm not afraid of a baby with AIDS. I'm afraid for you and Gordon and the girls. Once a baby comes and you all learn to love it again, how will any of you survive if that baby dies? I thought you couldn't go through it again."

Teri's voice was filled with resolve when she said, "Mom, what about surrendering to the universe? What about karmic debt? Mom, what about freeing a soul? Even if you don't believe this is it, you have to acknowledge that any child we get will be saved from a terrible life. *I* need a baby who needs Gordon and me as parents as much as we need him. I gave a child to death—now I want to help a child through life."

"I understand," I said, "I really do. But I can't surrender in this case. I really can't."

"Well, you'll have to at one time or another," Teri warned. "If it's not in this way, Spirit will come up with another."

"I'll take my chances," I said. "I just know I can't do this."

That night when my father and mother came over to visit, Teri was there. Once they sat down to have coffee, Teri began. "Poppy, have you seen anything about those babies in Romania? The ones in the orphanages?"

My father looked straight at her. "I know what that bastard Ceausescu did to his people," he said. "Why?"

"Poppy," she said, and her voice quavered, "Gordon and I want to adopt one of those babies."

My mother sat silently.

I just shook my head. "There are so many of them," I said softly.

My father stood up and began to pace. He always did when he was struggling to clarify his thoughts. Now he was standing still, staring far out into the dark night sky through my dining room window. Slowly he repeated what I had said. "There are so many of them . . ." and then he added, as though in trance, "but if each of us could light one small candle . . ." He shook his head as though to clear it and smiled at Teri. "What's your question, baby? What can Poppy do for you?"

Her eyes filled. "Poppy, we need two thousand dollars to start the application. We don't have it. Mommy can't give it to us. Can you? Would you be willing to?"

My father nodded his head and smiled again at her. Then he repeated a poem we'd all heard since we were kids.

"Give to the needy, sweet charity's breath
For giving is living, the angel said
But must I keep giving again and again
Without ever stopping?
No, said the angel, to your own self be true
Just give till the Lord stops giving to you."

It was then that my mother finally spoke up. "Sure," she said, looking from one of us to the other, and finally focusing on Teri. "Sure, that's all Gordon and you need, another mouth to feed."

"Wheezy," my father said, "this is their life, not ours. And you can't fault them for their intention."

"Whose talking about faults?" she said. "I'm talking about trying to take care of another baby. Gordon works too hard as it is, and Teri has enough to do already."

"Gram," Teri said, getting up and walking over to kiss her on the cheek, "you can come out to my house and help me. It's a baby, Gram—one who won't have a chance to live if we don't get him out of that country. They have no clothes, no food. . . ."

My mother shook her head. "People shouldn't have children if they can't take care of them."

Even I couldn't listen to that. "Ma," I said, "he was a dictator. He made them do it. They had no choice."

My mother looked at all of us again. "Do we?" she asked.

Teri hugged her, and then hugged my father. "Thank you so much," she said. "I knew you'd help me."

When Teri dropped the application off at Liz's, she stressed again that they didn't want an infant, they wanted a toddler. Liz explained that the first thing they needed to do was get a private home study done. She gave Teri a list of adoption consultants who were licensed by the state to do home studies. Then Liz asked for a donation of formula, diapers, and cigarettes. She explained that if she was to continue to get the babies out of Romania, she needed to send gifts to the doctors and nurses there.

When I talked to Barbara that night, she was teary-eyed. "You don't want her to get the baby either?" I asked her.

"Why would you think that?" she asked.

"Because you look so sad," I said.

"I'm not thinking about the baby who's coming, Carol," she said. "That's fine. We always have more than enough to eat. I'm thinking of those poor children who we're *leaving* there."

Mario didn't want to give Gordon and Teri the money to adopt because he was superstitious. If the child wound up to be a serial killer and hurt anyone in the family, he'd feel responsible. But the next time he saw Teri, he bet her that she wouldn't get a baby out of the country within six months; if she did, he'd pay her $1000 and she'd win the bet. He said he wasn't helping, he was gambling.

My cousin Rosemarie heard about the baby and sent Teri a thousand dollars. By the time I lent them another two thousand dollars as an advance against their tax refund, they had enough money to go on to the next step.

That year my father and the boys again went hunting. Gordon shot a buck and cleaned it himself. Danny finally shot a doe and then the next day shot a buck. He couldn't gut either of them, so my father and Gordon did. My father didn't shoot at all. They'd killed three deer, they had enough. My father helped them mount their racks. They had a drink and gave thanks again. But when they came home, I noticed they didn't talk as much, they didn't seem as excited, and I wondered why.

By that winter Danny pitched the idea for his print shop to the family. Mario and I gave him a down payment to buy a printing press and he leased the other equipment.

"Thanks, Mom," he said the following month as he kissed my cheek at the gala opening of his shop. Then he shook Mario's hand. "Thanks for making my dream come true."

Mario laughed and said, "More tears are shed over answered prayers than unanswered prayers. You're a businessman now. Congratulations!"

My father and mother bought him a huge potted plant. He bent over and kissed my mother and then hugged my father. "Thank you," he said, "I'll keep this for as long as it lives."

Everyone laughed. Another new beginning.

Another gift for Teri and Gordon: the home study was done by an experienced social worker and he approved it with flying colors. No matter how much information Teri and Gordon had about SIDS there was still some small part of them that felt society had stolen something from them—their role as good parents. Now they had an official paper stating that they could provide a safe home for any child. Somehow that document gave them back their parental reputation.

When she brought the home study over to Liz's, she also brought pictures of her house, the girls, herself, Gordon, and the dog. Liz told her she was going to Romania to meet with the lawyers who searched the orphanages, and was going to get releases for the adoptions from the biological parents. She told Teri she would be gone over the Christmas holidays and would return the first week in January. "Hopefully with some good news," she added.

On Christmas Eve, Danny and I stood in my living room and looked at the big scotch pine we'd bought. It was picture perfect. All the lights were blinking and even the tinsel was hanging straight as icicles. The luminous halo on the angel was touching the ceiling, making a rainbow circle of light.

Danny began to bring up more presents from the basement. I'd wrapped each person's in different paper to make it easier to sort and hand out later.

"Poppy's going to have a fit," I told Danny, "when he sees I've gone overboard again."

"Maybe not," Danny said. "Maybe he'll just accept it and enjoy it."

"I got them tickets to Malibu again," I told him. "And Vegas, Gram will like that."

Danny was quiet.

"Do you feel bad that you can't go this year?" I asked him.

"I'm building my dream," he said, smiling. "Even dreams cost something."

Now Danny stood back and looked around. "I think we're done," he said. "Now we just sit and wait for the troops."

I grabbed a cup of tea and sat down beside him. "How are you, really?" I asked.

"I'm okay, Mom," he said. "I'm fine."

"But you look like something's bothering you," I said.

"It's nothing," Danny said.

Barbara came in with Jennifer and Christopher, who had grown into a stocky thirteen-year-old. Then Teri and Gordon arrived with the kids. We put Christmas music on and dimmed the lights. Then I gave each of the kids a present I'd bought them. They went to play with Jenny and Chris.

When Mario came, he sat on the couch next to my father and they began to talk, my father's hands flying with expression, his voice charged with emotion. At one point I turned around and saw him shift his body, and there was a certain kind of stiffness in his movements that I was unaccustomed to seeing. But when my mother called to me, I turned back to the stove, forgot it, and put the sausages in the frying pan.

My mother was cutting the lettuce for salad, Barbara brought in the appetizers, and I cut up the long loaves of Italian bread.

"Is Barbara making her famous meatballs?" Mario called into the kitchen.

"Would we have a Christmas Eve without them?" Barbara called back.

Then Gordon went out to the car to bring in the presents they had brought from home to put under the tree. Teri piled them high on one side and pushed several of them underneath to leave some room for Barbara's. Christopher, his brown hair in a punk cut, carried the presents in from Barbara's side and piled them next to Teri's. Now the presents were almost as high as the tree.

Danny walked over to my father, and I saw my father hand him the keys to his car. "Where're you going, Dan?" I asked.

"Just to get the presents out of Poppy's car," he said.

"Dad, you're slipping," I said. "Where's the usual Christmas Eve speech of gratitude and guilt?"

My father smiled at me. "Everything's wonderful, baby," he said.

Then he turned to Teri and asked, "What do we hear about our baby? Any news yet?"

Teri shook her head. "Liz is over there now, Poppy," she said. "She's looking for him right now."

"My thoughts are with him on this special night," my father said.

At the stroke of midnight we opened all the presents. Wrapping paper, like confetti, flew across my living room. Everyone walked around showing each other their presents and chattering with excitement.

"Everything's ready," I said.

"Then let's eat," Danny said. I watched him walk over to my father again. Then he walked into the kitchen to fill a plate. He carried it back into the living room and handed it to my father.

Now I was concerned. My father never sat in one place for this long. Even scarier, Danny never waited on anyone.

"Mom?" I said as I walked back into the kitchen. "Is Daddy all right?"

She looked over at him sitting on the couch. "He looks all right," she said. "His arthritis has been bothering him a little."

"Arthritis, Mom?" I said. "I didn't know he had arthritis."

"Well, now you know," she said.

It was two o'clock in the morning by the time we finished eating. Gordon and Teri had packed their car, and then carried out Shari and Ashley, who had fallen asleep. But Jessica was still wide awake. "Bye, Jessie," I said, kissing her. "See you tomorrow."

I was cleaning up, taking the plates off the coffee table, when I noticed Danny reach for my father's elbow and help him off the couch.

"Are you okay, Daddy?" I asked.

"It's the arthritis, I told you that," my mother said.

I kissed them both good night. And then I watched from the doorway as Danny helped my father into his car.

When Danny came back, I asked, "What's going on?"

"It's nothing, Mom," Danny said. "Pop's just having a little trouble walking."

"Since when?" I asked.

"Since we went hunting," he said.

"Why?" I asked. "Did he fall or something?"

Danny shook his head. "Mom," he said. "Pop hardly left the lodge this year."

When everyone except Mario had gone, I dimmed all the lamps again, put some more music on, and sat next to him on the couch, watching the blinking of the tree lights.

"It was a wonderful Christmas, Carol," Mario said. "You did a wonderful job."

"Thanks," I said, leaning against his shoulder.

"Every time I see your father, I'm more impressed," he said. "How did he learn to enjoy life so much?"

"Practice," I told Mario. "He's lived with moderation in all things for as long as I can remember. Plus he still works, hasn't missed a day in at least fifty years. Likes the food my mother cooks, reads, learns, and loves us all. He contributes to his world, and always says, what else can a man want?"

"You inherited your good genes from him," Mario said. "That's why you're so cheerful all the time."

"Maybe," I said. Then I asked, "How did my father look to you tonight?"

"He looked good," Mario said. "Why?"

"Did you see the way he moved?" I asked.

Mario patted my head. "He's a seventy-five-year-old man," he said. "No matter how good the shape he's in, he's still not going to move like Danny or Gordon."

"Mario," I said. "I'm going to tell you something, but don't say anything?"

Mario smiled. "I won't even remember it," he said.

"I think we're in big trouble," I said. "I think my father's sick."

Mario frowned. "What are you talking about? It's a little arthritis, your mother said."

I looked over at him. "Mario, when I watched him move tonight, I got that pain in my stomach. The pain I've gotten whenever something awful was going to happen. I get that pain only when somebody's going to—"

Mario put his finger over my lips. "Don't say any more, Carol," he told me. "It sounds crazy. He's only moving a little more slowly."

I looked up at him. "I didn't tell my father, I didn't say it to my mother, I didn't say it to any of them. Who can I tell what I'm feeling if I can't tell you?"

"About this kind of thing? Especially about your father?" he said. "Tell Bridie," he said, "or Wanda, or Maureen or any of your nursing friends. But please don't tell me."

We sat a while longer, talking, when the phone rang. My heart almost stopped. It was three o'clock in the morning. Who could be calling? I held my breath as I answered it.

It was Teri. "Mom," she said, crying and laughing at the same time, "they found our baby! They found our son. He's in an orphanage in Babadag. And he's fourteen months old."

"Congratulations, honey," I said. "I'm really happy for you both. What's the baby's name?"

"I won't know anything till Liz gets back. Our phone was ringing when we got home. But it was voice mail and all it said was 'We found your son!'" Teri took a deep breath and said, "Mom, I can't talk now. I have to call Poppy!"

Chapter Twenty

*T*raveling to California that year was even more uncomfortable than usual. Something was shifting in my inner worlds, but I didn't yet know what it was. The house in Malibu was familiar now, so that wasn't it. And the sound of the waves on the shore brought me comfort . . . but there was still something that nagged at me.

As I drove down the Pacific Coast Highway, I found an ashram. The grounds were beautiful and they had a peaceful path that cut through a Japanese garden dotted with colorful flowers. Over a clear lake there was a small wooden bridge. I felt myself drawn to that place.

I began to drive there every day to walk around. Sometimes in the afternoons I visited the sparse dark wooden chapel. I had long hours alone to think and meditate as I sat on the hard wooden pew and stared at the pictures of the masters on the altar. I wondered what drove each of them. What inner blueprint moved them to seek and then to teach?

During those quiet hours I also reviewed the past several years and tried to understand how the family had been changed by our life's experiences. It was easy to see the changes in Teri and Gordon, and the change in Jessie. Even my niece Jennifer had grown through all that happened since Greggy. She was in college now, taking anthropology, studying tribal cultures, but her first research paper had been done on the loss of a child.

Danny? I wasn't sure about him, he played it close to the vest. He knew his truth, he knew his spirituality, he just never spoke it and often laughed at Teri and me when we tried. Just before I'd left this time, we'd had a talk.

"You think you can teach people this stuff?" he said. And then he laughed as though it was absurd.

"You don't think so?" I asked.

"People either know or don't know," he said.

"Fine," I'd said, "but what happens to those who know but just don't remember?"

"Okay," he conceded, "that's one way to look at it. But that's for you and Teri. That isn't my purpose. It isn't my part." He insisted he knew his part and we'd know it in time.

My mother? Her goodness had been a constant in our ever-changing equation. My father had always been open to new ideas, but now he had expanded his boundaries. After Shari, he even believed in miracles.

I thought about Barbara now. I didn't know any more about how she had changed than I did about Danny. Because they never spoke much, they remained a mystery to me.

And how had I been changed? In ways too numerous to mention. I certainly had been humbled. And I did trust my God and the universe more since Janith, since Ashley, since Shari. I even trusted myself more. But not as much as Teri did. I couldn't surrender as willingly as she had with Shari. Or with the adoption. There was something about it that terrified me. I thought about what she had said; "You're going to have to surrender completely sometime, Mom. . . ." And I knew she was right. But I could not even imagine how I would be called upon to live my deeper truth.

I phoned my parents several times, and though my father sounded all right, my mother told me his "arthritis" was still acting up.

"Have you gone to the doctor?" I asked him.

"Don't worry, baby," he said, "I have an appointment tomorrow. Don't think about me. Have a good time."

At least he was going to see a doctor.

When I talked to Barbara the following night, she sounded upset. "Something's wrong, Carol. Daddy's having a lot of pain," she said. "I've been giving him Darvocet, but he's limping now."

"Is it that same limp he had at Christmas?" I asked, thinking, *that damn limp.*

"It's the same leg," she said.

"Did the doctor order any tests?" I asked her.

"No," she said, "Dr. Kerlin gave him some anti-inflammatory medication and told him to see how it worked. But it *didn't* work." Barbara told me she had been spending a lot of time running between her house and theirs the last week.

I asked to talk to Danny.

"Poppy's walking with a cane now," he said. "It's an old mahogany cane, so he thinks he's cool."

"How does he look to you?" I asked, concerned.

He didn't answer me. "I'm driving them to the doctor's again tomorrow" was all he said.

"Poppy can't drive?" I asked, but the ringing in my ears kept me from hearing. I had to ask him to repeat what he had said.

"Not right now, Mom," he said again, and his voice was controlled.

When I talked to my mother, I asked, "Ma? What do you *feel* is going on?"

"I think you're spending too much time on the phone," she said. "Go have a good time and stop worrying about what's going on back home."

Teri was excited when she called to tell me the latest news. "Liz's back from Romania. She said the baby's name is Petre. He was a preemie so he's in the Children's Orphanage for Premature and Dystrophic Children. She says he's very cute."

"Is he all right?" I asked. "I mean, is his brain all right?"

"I'm sure he's all right."

"Why are you sure he's all right?" I asked.

"Because . . ." she said.

"That's great, honey," I said, handing it over to fate. "What happens next?"

"We have to get a release from his parents," Teri said. "Then we can start the formal adoption."

"Where *are* his parents?" I asked.

"Liz says that's anybody's guess," Teri explained.

"Who has to track them down?"

"The lawyer," she said.

"Are you sure we're going to wind up with a baby?" I asked.

"I'm sure," she said with certainty.

Ashley had gone into kindergarten and told everyone she was

going to have a baby brother. "The teacher congratulated me because she thought I was pregnant," Teri said.

"That must have been funny," I said. "Can I talk to Ash?"

Ashley got on the phone. She had a sweet and funny voice. "Hi, Gramma Carol," she said. "Did you heard I'm getting a brother?"

"I did," I said. "That's great."

"I can't wait," she said anxiously. "I can't wait to see my brother's face. I've been waiting so long."

I asked to talk to Jessie next. "Are you excited about the baby?" I asked her.

"It's a boy, Carol," she said with eight-year-old sincerity. "And he's nobody's baby. A baby needs parents."

Late the following afternoon I was sitting upstairs on the bed, reading. The doors to the balcony were open and a warm breeze was blowing. In the background I could hear the sea gulls. From the stereo the soft strains of the music of "Fairy Ring" played. I felt good.

When the phone rang, I picked it up absently. "Hi," I said.

It was Barbara. "Carol, we just got back from seeing the doctor. Daddy had a CT scan. He has cancer." She said it all at once, without taking a breath.

The bottom dropped out of my world. Suddenly I was spinning through space. From far away I could hear my own voice asking calmly, "What kind of cancer? Where?"

"Cancer of the spine, metastatic bone cancer spreading from someplace else, Dr. Kerlin doesn't know the primary site yet," she said.

A part of me was walking through the sky high above myself, walking through the clouds. But then I heard myself ask to speak to my mother.

When she got on the phone, she said softly, "I knew it all along, I just didn't want to worry you." *She knew it? And didn't want to worry me?*

"Are you all right?" I asked her.

"How can I be?" she asked. Thank God for my mother, I thought.

My sister got back on the phone. "Do you want me to come home?" I asked her.

"For what?" Barbara asked.

"So you don't have to go through this alone," I said.

"I'm not alone," she said. "Danny's been perfect. He's been here with Mommy and Daddy for weeks. He's taken them everywhere they had to go, and in the daytime he's even been taking Mom shopping so Daddy can rest."

Danny's crisis behavior was very different from his ordinary behavior. He'd been like that from the day he was born. Whenever something special was required of him, something special was received. Simple enough.

"If you need anything, you'll let me know?" I said.

Barbara said, "Dad's going for a bone scan on Monday. We'll know more then."

"Is Danny taking them again?" I asked. "Or are you?"

"Mommy wants both Gordon and Danny to go," she told me. "She said Gordon will talk enough to keep Daddy's mind off what's happening."

From the time they injected my father with radioactive dye until the time they snapped the pictures would take three hours. It would travel through his bones and light them up like glow sticks. Three hours is a long time to wait to find out if your cancer's growing. I hoped Gordon really would be able to talk enough.

In the background I heard my dad ask to speak to me.

"Hi, Daddy," I said. "The one time in your life you get sick, and it's the big one?" I tried to keep it light, he would hate it any other way.

My father's voice sounded pensive when he repeated, "The big C . . ." But then he seemed to reach inside himself and pull out something strong. "I want you to promise me something, baby," he said.

"Anything," I answered.

"No theatrics, no heroics," he said simply.

I knew what he was saying. He and I had spoken often about his choices—about the way, when the time came, he wanted to die. "You'll never hear the hiss of a respirator," I promised.

"Thank you," he said softly.

"I'll catch a plane home right away."

There was silence first. Then he cleared his throat before he said, "Don't come home now, Carol. There's no reason to."

His voice wasn't sharp, but still I could read the measured meter of his voice. I could feel the harness pulling me back. I had been presumptuous. He was "The Chief" in the family. He wanted to let me know that he was coming into a time of weakness. But he wasn't that weak yet. I wasn't needed yet. He'd called just to put me on alert.

I walked downstairs to tell Mario. He kept wiping his eyes, but then he said, "Your father's tough. He'll beat this thing. They haven't even found out what kind of cancer it is, right? He'll be okay. . . ."

I sat on the bed. "Mario, listen to me. My father never takes his hat off when he visits. He also never cries wolf."

"What does that mean?" Mario asked.

"He won't hang around, Mario, I know him," I said. "He wouldn't want to be a burden."

"How can you give up so quickly?"

"I'm not giving up," I said. "I'm just changing my hope. Now I'm hoping this won't be too hard for him . . . for any of us. Especially for my mother."

"Carol," Mario said, "you're jumping to conclusions. You've been a nurse for too many years. A lot of people live with cancer for a long time."

Teri called that day. She told me she had just talked to my father. She said, "Poppy told me, 'I've made my peace with God.'" And she was upset. "Why would he tell me that?" she asked. "I didn't even ask how he was. I just called to say hello."

"He figures talking to you is like talking to me, I guess, because of the spirit stuff," I said. "Besides, he's got grace under pressure. You know, nobility and courage. Dignity, I think it's called."

"Well, if he's going to do a death-with-dignity thing, I'm not ready for it," she said. "If he's going to die, I want him to die screaming and yelling and fighting all the way."

"Why in God's name would you want that?" I asked her. "As a spiritual counselor, you teach others how to accept death, how to surrender to God's will unconditionally."

"That's when I'm being a spiritual counselor," she said, "not when I'm being a granddaughter. Then, I want to hear that he's fighting like hell to live, or something about the miracles of healing."

"What do you feel is going on?" I asked her, trying not to give myself away.

Teri hesitated, and then she said very softly, "I feel like Gordon and I better hurry up and get this baby here while Poppy can still enjoy him."

I tried to call Danny several times, but could never reach him at home. Finally one morning very early, he picked up the phone.

"Hi," I said. "Are you all right?"

"I'm fine, Mom," he said. But he offered nothing more.

"How's work been going?" I asked, trying to ease in gently.

"I haven't been going to work, Mom, you know that," he said. "I've been with Poppy and Gram."

"Do you want me to come home?" I asked.

"No," he said simply. "We're doing okay."

"But I thought making your business work was your dream," I said. "If I don't come home, how can you keep it going?"

Danny took a deep breath. "Dreams can be replaced, Mom," he said. "Grandfathers can't. I want to spend every minute I can with him."

"It won't help if I'm there?" I asked him.

"If you need to come home, then come," he said. But he sounded reluctant. "It won't change what I do. I still have to do my part."

I was crying when I hung up. Nothing else had made me cry. Not talking to my father, my sister, my mother, or Teri. It was talking to Danny. It was knowing how hard it was going to be for him.

The following day I called my parents. My father answered.

"Hi, baby," he said. But I could hear the pain in his voice. When I asked him about it, he whispered into the phone so no one else could hear, "This is a killing pain, baby. Don't let anyone tell you different. This is not the kind of pain a man could have and still live."

"I believe you, Daddy," I said, tears filling my eyes. "I'd like to come home."

"I can't keep you away," he said, but again there was the warning in his voice.

"Okay, Daddy," I said. "I'll wait till you ask." I had respected my father's decisions for all of my life; it made no sense to stop respecting them now. I hesitated before I added, "Is there anything you want to say to me that you haven't?"

"Baby," he said softly, "we're like Siamese twins. I've never had a thought you didn't know . . . and I like to think that I know that much about you. What's left to say?"

"I love you, Daddy," I said.

"I love you too," he said. "You've grown to be more than I ever hoped for, more than I had any right to expect."

"What about Mommy?" I said. "Do you need me there for her?"

"Your mother is fine," he said. "Danny's here. He's good with her."

"Bye, Dad," I said. And I tried to sound strong.

"Baby?" he said before he hung up. "Don't spend your time being sad. Remember what your dad taught you. Make every precious moment count. Walk on the beach, go up into the mountains. Enjoy yourself. I've had a perfectly happy life. I've always said that I'd have to die and go to heaven to have it any better."

The days weren't as bad as the nights. That's when I got fidgety. That's when I wanted to be home to help, that's when I felt guilty about being away. Lying in bed, I asked myself, *Do I need to go home? Even if no one needs me yet? Did I have any unfinished business with my father?*

I didn't think so. All through the forty-nine years he'd been my father, I hadn't left any business between us unfinished. Each time I uncovered anything he'd done that hurt my feelings, I immediately called him, set up a meeting, and confronted him with it. And he always met with me, talked to me, stood for what he'd done, but he never apologized. He just listened to me and then stated his case as he saw it. Over the years, we'd always come to terms with each other.

"Anything special you want to talk about?" Mario interrupted my thoughts.

"I was just thinking," I said. "My father was the first one to ever clap for me. And he never stopped. I wonder if I'll be able to stand the silence."

Mario reached over and hugged me.

Teri went over to see Poppy.

"Any word on our new baby?" he asked her. He was afraid the baby was hungry; he worried that he wasn't warm enough.

"Not yet, Poppy," she said. "We're working on it."

"You have a beautiful family," he told her. And on that day, for the first time, he asked Teri if he could ask Janith a question.

"What's the difference between a soul and a Spirit?" he asked.

A Spirit soars; a soul discovers. A Spirit is free, a soul is burdened. The difference between them is one of our plane and yours. It is one of what must remain individual to touch down into a physical body. A soul is a human soul. We, as Spirits, do not have a soul. Therefore there is, as ones have said, a silver cord not only between soul and physical body, but between physical body, soul, and Spirit.

My father liked Janith's explanation. So he asked another, "What is freedom?"

Flying as a dove flies is freedom. Crying as a baby does is freedom. Loving as a mother does is freedom; working as a father does is freedom; dying as a grandfather does is freedom; trying as a brother does is freedom. Every time a lesson is learned, freedom for the soul is a little closer.

My father laughed suddenly.

"What's funny?" Teri asked.

"I didn't believe there were angels because I couldn't see them," he said. "And those doctors couldn't believe I had cancer even when I told them, until they could see it. Isn't that crazy?"

When Teri called me that night to talk, she told me my father had said that he couldn't have planned his life any better if he'd planned it himself. He was cheerful that day, she said, and seemed to be having less pain.

She brought him over some healing tapes of Louise Hay, Ram Dass, and her favorite guru, Amrit Desai. Her grandfather told her he hadn't planned to stay in long enough to watch them all.

"In your body or in the house?" Teri asked him.

He just smiled at her and winked.

Families are funny constellations, and I felt like a lost star.

I walked on the beach that day. I watched the water break again and again as I dragged my bare feet along the water's edge. And I talked to myself.

I *must* have known this day would come. I knew humans didn't vaporize into thin air to get out of this world. They *died*. Even special men. Even fathers. Seventy-five was a pretty decent age to die. He stayed around long enough to help us grow. Gregory was just a baby when he died and yet he left a hole in the tapestry of our family that everyone could feel. What kind of a hole would my father leave?

That night, when I went upstairs to bed, I told Mario, "I have to go home. No matter how much I try to talk myself out of it, no matter what my father asks, I still have to go."

"I think you should," he said. "After all, you're the one who knows about sickness. You're the nurse."

"I don't think my father needs a nurse," I said. "But maybe there's something I can do."

"Don't give up," Mario said. "See what the doctors say."

"I won't believe them anyway," I told him.

Early the next morning I called my father to let him know I was coming.

His voice sounded sad when he said, "Come, then, baby, if you think you should. I'd love to see you."

Something in his voice, a certain poignancy, woke me right up, made me see something clearly I hadn't been able to see before. Finally I understood why no one wanted me to come home: Usually, I wasn't called in until someone was terminal. As a nurse or a friend, I had a reputation. So it was natural; for as long as I stayed away, everyone could believe that my father would get well. But as soon as I arrived, my family would know in their hearts why I'd come.

Chapter Twenty-One

I stopped at my house long enough to dump my suitcases and change my clothes. Then I drove right over to my parents' house.

I took a deep breath, got out of the car, and walked up to the door. I knocked. But no one answered. Finally I opened the door and walked into the kitchen.

"Hey," I hollered. "Where is everyone?"

I met Danny coming down the hall. He bent down to kiss me. "They're in the TV room, Mom," he said. "Aunt Barbara's there too."

I walked into the den. There, sitting in his recliner, as though nothing was wrong, was my father. He looked fine, and now I felt crazy. I walked over to kiss him hello.

"Hi, Dad," I said. "How are you doing?"

"Well, I haven't been playing golf," he said, smiling.

My sister and mother were sitting on the couch. I kissed them both. But they were watching the end of a movie and so they didn't move. "How was your trip?" my mother asked as she waved her hand to get me out of the way of the TV. "It's just another five minutes," she said. "Sit down."

I sat on the chair across from them. I looked over at my father. He smiled again at me. He looked pretty good. I knew he wasn't talking because he didn't want to interrupt my mother's program. So I got up and walked out into the kitchen to sit with Danny.

"Aunt Barbara just gave Poppy his medicine," Danny explained. "He'll be okay for a few hours now."

"Good," I said. "How are you holding up?"

"I'm okay. When Pop's not in pain I feel pretty good," Danny said. "Tomorrow the doctor wants to see him again."

Now my mother came into the kitchen with my sister. Barbara had started working part-time in a doctor's office as a doctor's assistant about six months before. She was an X-ray technician and a lab technician too. "How's work going?" I asked her.

"Good," she said. "I only have a few weeks left before I get a raise."

My father walked in then, slowly. And when he was standing I could see the dark lines of his pain around his mouth, but he tried to cover it. He smiled, and I thought how I loved his funny face. He was a good-looking man, though short. Still more height could never have given him more stature. I think I was at least twenty-eight before I realized he wasn't eight feet tall.

"I'm going with you guys to the center tomorrow," I said.

"It's good you're coming," my mother said. "You can talk to the doctors."

That night, when Barbara and I got home, we sat at my table and talked.

"We've set up a schedule," she said in a matter-of-fact way. "I go over in the mornings and have breakfast with Daddy and give him his pills. Then I go to work, and Danny comes over to keep Mommy company and help Daddy. It's been working out pretty good."

"How sick is he really, Barbara?" I asked.

Her body stiffened. "He'll do okay," she said. "You know Daddy, he doesn't complain."

"Do you think he's going to get well?" I asked.

She frowned at me. A warning. "I would never allow myself to think about him *not* getting well," she said. "I spend my whole day concentrating on how to help him feel better. From the minute I get up in the morning I start thinking about what I'll make for his supper, what pills will make him most comfortable, things like that."

"It must be hard for you," I said.

She looked at me as though I was crazy. "Carol," she said, "I wouldn't have it any other way. I would never allow anyone else to take care of him."

* * *

Danny supported my father as he walked toward the doctor's examining rooms. I walked behind them. They put us all in a small examining room. Once Danny had helped my father up onto the table, he felt uncomfortable. He said, "I'll wait outside. Call me when the doctor's finished and Poppy's ready to go."

I nodded. My father was lying quietly, shifting his body now and then to try to get comfortable. My mother was sitting in a chair in the corner of the room. After a few minutes my father motioned me over to him. "Baby," he said, "stand by me on this. I don't want a lot of treatment if it's not going to help. I'll do what I have to for all of you. But I don't want to spend the little time I have left in hospitals and doctors' offices."

"Okay," I said.

The doctor came in then. She was a small woman. By her features and her accent I knew she had originally come from India. She had one of those small red dots in the middle of her forehead. A third eye would be good now, I thought.

"I'm Dr. Nella," she said as she walked toward my father. "Dr. Kerlin told me much about you."

"Good things I hope?" my father said, smiling.

"Very good things," she said.

Once she examined him, she said, "I'd like you in my office to speak about a few things?"

I called Danny from the waiting room. He helped my father finish dressing and then walked him into the doctor's office.

My mother and I were already sitting across from Dr. Nella when my father walked in. I stood up, but he said, "Stay, Carol. I can't sit anyway."

He stood by the door.

Dr. Nella addressed him first. "I want to do a few more tests. I want to try to find the primary site of your cancer," she said.

"Does that matter?" my father asked. "My legs are bothering me. What difference does it make where the cancer started?"

"In order to prescribe the proper treatment, we have to know the kind of cell," she explained. "Then we can give the appropriate chemotherapy."

My father smiled kindly. "Dr. Nella," he said. "I know you'll try your best to help me, but I don't think it really matters."

Dr. Nella sat up straight. "Mr. Gino," she said. "It certainly matters for proper treatment to know what we're dealing with. I want to admit you to the hospital and just do a few tests."

"I've already had a test for my prostate, a barium enema, and several blood tests," he said. "What else is necessary?"

"I'd like you to have a colonoscopy to make sure the primary is not in your colon and I'd also like you to have another CT scan. Of the chest this time."

"Why do I have to go into the hospital for that?" he asked.

"The colonoscopy needs a preparation," she said. "And the testing will be more efficient in the hospital."

We took my father straight over to the hospital. They admitted him immediately. My mother and I waited outside the room while Danny helped him undress and get into bed. When Danny came out to tell us he was ready, my mother and I went in.

It was a four-bed room. Two of the patients in the room were very old men, one confused, the other on a respirator.

My father's bed was by the window. Out of his clothes, in a hospital gown, he looked smaller and thinner, somehow frailer than only moments before. And the look in his eyes was pure fear. I had seen that look in the eyes of patients I'd taken care of, but it was so unfamiliar to me on the face of my father, it threw me off balance.

"What's wrong, Dad?" I asked.

"I can't stay here," he said. "I want to go home."

My mother walked over, soothed him as though he were a child. "Stay, just for the tests. We'll come and get you as soon as they're done."

He looked as though he was in pain. "Do you want me to ask for your pain medicine?" I asked.

"Did you ask your sister what she's been giving me?"

"I know what it is," I said. "I'll tell them."

But when I told the nurse I needed two Percocet and three Advil to give my father, she said, "The Percocet is ordered so I can bring that right in."

"What about the Advil?" I asked. "My sister's been taking care of him at home and she says if he doesn't get the Advil, it doesn't work as well."

The nurse looked doubtful but she said, "I'll call the doctor."

"Don't take too long," I said, but I didn't say it with the authority

I normally would have. I tried to pull myself together. "If his pain gets hold of him, it's harder to control."

She looked at me. "I know that," she said defensively.

An hour later she brought in the Percocet. "Where's the Advil?" I asked.

"The doctor didn't call back yet," she said.

When she handed my father the paper medicine cup with the Percocet, he looked at it and said, "Where's my Advil? It won't work without the Advil."

By now if he were my patient and I was his nurse, I would have been a raving lunatic. But he was my father and I wore no uniform. "It's an over-the-counter medicine," I told her. "Can't you just give it to him and ask the doctor later? He's been taking it like that at home for weeks."

She shook her head. "I have to have an order," she said.

My head felt as though it were full of cobwebs. When she left the room, I turned to my mother. "Do you have any Advil in your pocketbook?" I asked.

She did. I poured out three and gave them to my father. As soon as he swallowed them he looked relieved. But then he asked, "What will I do when you go home?"

We put the bottle of Advil in his bedside stand. "Take it when you need it," I said.

When visiting hours were over and we were about to leave, I kissed my father good-bye and left my mother and Danny with him while I walked out to the nurses' station. "Did you get the order for the Advil yet?" I asked the nurse.

"Nobody called back," she said.

"Well, call them again," I said, feeling a little stronger. "Or call another doctor."

She huffed. "I don't know why you're making such a fuss about three little Advil," she said.

My voice was raised when I said, "Because it helps keep my father's pain controlled. Because he's got cancer. And because three little Advil don't seem like too much to ask for."

The nurse stared at me. "Look," she said finally, "I know you're upset, but he's having tests tomorrow anyway. And tonight he's going to be given a laxative but he's not going to be allowed anything by mouth. They'll give him injections for his pain, that will work better."

* * *

But it didn't work better. By the time my sister went back to the hospital the following morning, he was in so much pain that he was curled in the fetal position in bed, unable to speak.

Barbara was devastated. She called me at home. "Carol," she said, "you have to do something. We have to get Daddy out of here. He's a mess."

I was in a fury.

I jumped into the car and drove over to the hospital. Instead of waiting for the elevator, I scaled the stairs up to my father's room.

He was still curled up, lying on his side in bed. I had never seen him like this, never. My mother was standing at the foot of the bed, and Barbara was wiping my father's forehead with a cold rag.

"Dad?" I said, walking over to the bed, but as soon as he saw me, he waved me away.

I ran out to the nurses' station in a rage. "Where's Dr. Nella?" I asked.

The ward receptionist said, "She's in the hospital, but she hasn't been on the floor yet."

"Page her," I said, not even trying to be polite.

She picked up the phone. After a few moments she said weakly, "She's tied up on the second floor. She'll be up in fifteen minutes."

I couldn't wait. As I passed my father's room again, I saw my sister propping some pillows behind my father's head. He was limp and listless.

I ran down to the second floor just in time to stop Dr. Nella before she walked off the ward. "I want to take my father home," I told her.

Dr. Nella shook her head. "You can't to that," she said. "Your father is very sick. He needs care—"

"Well, he's not getting it here," I said sharply. "And this isn't a discussion. I just want to take him home."

"We have to do more tests," she explained, trying to placate me. "The colonoscopy showed no tumor in the colon. But the chest CT scan showed a shadow behind the heart."

"What does that mean?" I asked.

"Possible tumor on his lung," she said. "But we're not sure yet."

"You can do the other tests on an outpatient basis," I told her. "I know that and you know that. You don't have to keep him here."

"We have to regulate his medications so that he has better pain control," she said, trying to bargain with me.

"His pain medication *was* regulated," I said, my hands flying in the air as I spoke. "My sister and he had worked it out. His pain was bearable at home. And it's completely unbearable for him here."

"But he can't keep taking five pills every three hours," she said.

"Why?" I asked.

"Because his stomach won't tolerate it for long," she said. "It will cause an ulcer."

"Dr. Nella," I said. "Don't do this to me. The combination of pills he's been taking is working for him. It will keep working for a while without giving him an ulcer. And by then he won't need any pain medicine."

She looked at me as though I was confused. "You don't understand," she said. "Your father's cancer won't be gone in a few months."

I took a deep breath. And with a voice sharp as steel I said, "But my father will be gone."

She stepped back, looking shocked. "You're wrong. I feel your father has a few years yet . . . with proper treatment."

"Look," I said impatiently, "just release him. You can order whatever tests you need. And if he agrees, whatever treatment."

"He may need injections for his pain," she said. "He can't get that at home."

"Yes, he can," I said stubbornly. "I've been a nurse for years. I'll give them to him."

"I can't take the responsibility for sending him home in this condition," she said then. "Your mother is not a young woman."

I took a deep breath. "It's not your responsibility," I said. "It's mine. It's my family's. And if my mother concerns you, don't send him home, send him to my house."

Finally she softened. "Okay," she said, "I'll release him. But he must have a lung biopsy next week."

"I'll bring him back," I told her. If he wants to come, I thought.

"Try some morphine," she suggested. "I'll give him pills to start. See how it works."

"Okay," I said. "But we're taking him home right now. Not an hour from now, right now. . . ."

My mother was upstairs with Danny by the time I got back to my father's room. Danny looked like a caged animal, he was pacing so fast, and my mother was just sitting next to my father, holding his hand, crying.

My sister was on the other side of the bed, talking softly to my father, whose eyes were shut tight.

I walked over to the bed and stood next to my sister. "We've sprung you," I said to my father.

He opened his eyes but he looked like he didn't understand.

Barbara repeated, "Daddy, we got you out of the hospital."

He turned and looked at me, tears in his eyes. "Really, baby?" he said.

"You have to come back for one more test," I said, "and I want you to come to my house for now."

My mother said, "He'll never go to your house. You know your father always sleeps in his own bed."

"Well, tonight he's got to sleep in mine," I said.

Barbara took his hand. "Is that okay, Daddy? You'll come home with us? You'll stay on Carol's side so we can all be together? That way Mommy can rest. And I can give you your pain medicine when you need it."

My father looked at my sister, and then he looked at me. "Of course. No problem. I'll go wherever you want, as long as I can get the hell out of here."

The first few days at my house were a little chaotic while everyone got settled. I moved into the study to sleep on the couch so my parents could have my bedroom. My father seemed to be able to lie flat there and my mattress was firm enough to be comfortable for him. By the third day, everything was running smoothly.

On the days my sister went to work, before she left she'd put all my father's pills in little cups, mark them with the time, and put them on a shelf in the kitchen for him to take. He trusted that she could take his pain away in ways no one else could.

Danny came over each day and stayed late into the night. He showed Poppy videos of their hunting trips together and then they'd relive them for hours.

My father seemed to recover with amazing speed once he was home and felt safe. One day when my mother was cooking dinner in the kitchen and I was helping her, she said, "Your father was just too afraid there. He's never been in a hospital except to have his gallbladder out. He thinks that they're places to die."

"Mom," I said, "do you know how sick he is?"

She frowned and said sharply, "Not even the doctors know yet, so how can I know till they finish with their tests?"

I wanted to help prepare her. "Mom," I said, "he's really sicker than he's acting."

She looked at me. A long, deep look. "Carol," she said, and she patted me on the cheek, "don't say anything before we know. Go, talk to your father. He likes to hear you talk."

Every afternoon when my sister was at work, my mother went home to her house. To get the mail, to dust a little, to keep herself from going crazy. He would get well, of course, she couldn't allow herself another thought. She'd been married to him for far too long to think of life without him. Since she'd been a young girl she lived for him and her children. He talked too much, for sure, and sometimes he told awful jokes, but he was kind, a good man, and she knew how much he loved her. She told herself, as she vacuumed her house and washed her floors, we'll come home together soon. Things will work out. And then she said a prayer. . . .

One afternoon when my sister was at work and my mother had gone out for a few hours with Danny, my father and I were alone. He was sitting in the recliner watching footage of the Gulf War on CNN. "Silly bastards," he said, and I was surprised because he seldom cursed.

"Who?" I asked.

"Anybody who is killing anyone else," he said. "It's just a stupid thing to do when life is so precious."

"I couldn't agree with you more," I said, sitting down on my couch.

"Carol," he said, "do you remember telling me at one time that some of the Eastern masters could just drop their bodies when it was time?"

"Yep," I said. "That's what I've read."

He looked thoughtful. "How?" he asked.

"I think they just keep meditating until they finally can slip their consciousness out of their sagital suture," I said. "Then their individual consciousness expands and joins the consciousness of All There Is. Or God."

He laughed. "Where's that suture?"

I walked over and patted the top of his head. "Right here," I said. "It's your spirit connection."

"We should try it," he said.

"Try what? Slipping out?" I said. "Dad, I've never heard anything about them slipping back in. It's not a round trip ticket."

"How exactly do they do it?" he pressed me.

"I think you have to clear a path through consciousness in the same way you'd use a machete to carve a path through the woods to get to a clearing," I said.

"What's the machete?"

"Attention, I guess," I said. "Single pointed focused attention. That's the machete."

"I should learn how to meditate," he said. "You should teach me."

"I have some tapes that might help," I said.

"Find them for me," he said. "And then have Dan get me a Walkman. I'll start right away."

"That sounds good, Dad," I said.

He looked at me then and smiled. "Carol?" he asked. "Don't tell your mother or your sister just yet."

"Okay, Dad," I said.

From that day on, each afternoon I watched my father put on his headphones, close his eyes, and begin to sharpen his machete.

Chapter Twenty-Two

T eri brought the kids over to see Poppy. They had missed his visits, had been asking for him. The day they came over, it was snowing. The trees were covered with white, the roads were slick and wet. My father had watched from the window until he saw Teri pull up. When the kids in their colorful snowsuits got out of the car, he called to my mother. "Look, Wheezy," he said. "The kids are here. Open the door."

I watched as Jessie picked up a handful of snow and threw it at Ashley. But when it hit, Ashley just laughed. Shari was struggling, falling as Teri kept scooping her up. They were laughing as my mother opened the door.

They piled in through the front door.

My father was smiling as he greeted them. "Jessica, you've gotten so tall," he said. She took off her jacket, put it down, and walked over to kiss him.

Then, "Ashley?" he called. "Come give Poppy a kiss."

Ashley ran over to him but Teri warned, "Careful, Ash, remember Poppy's sick. Don't jump." Ashley kissed him gently.

"Shari, my baby," he called to her.

Shari walked over too. She tried to climb on his lap, but when she saw him wince, she stepped away. "You sick, Poppy?"

"No honey," he said. "Just old."

Jessica laughed. "Pop, you want to hear my new song. I brought my flute."

Jessie played her flute for him. My mother cried but my father said, "You know where she gets her talent from?"

Teri laughed now. "From you, right, Pop?"

"Smart girl," he said.

My mother made soup for lunch, and later colored with Shari while Jessica was reading. But Ashley kept walking over to my father. Touching him, holding his hand. Finally she said, "Let's go for a walk, Poppy, and let's build a snowman like last time."

My father touched her hair. "Ashes, your poppy isn't really only old. He's a little sick. His legs don't work right now."

Ashley smiled. "Next time?" she asked, and when he hesitated, she said, "It's okay, I don't really like snowmen."

My father's lung biopsy came back positive. My father had cancer of the lung. Dr. Nella wanted to talk to us. Danny took my father, mother, and me to the center.

When we saw the doctor this time, she didn't even offer my father a chair.

She looked upset when she told him, "I believe the lung tumor is the primary site. We don't have too much to offer you at this point. This kind of cancer cell doesn't respond well to chemotherapy."

My father looked at her, trying to digest what she had said. Finally he said, "So there's nothing you can do for me?"

"Oh, yes," she said. "There's radiation. That will help take the pain away."

My father smiled and shook her hand. "That's all I want you to do."

I was waiting on Barbara's side of the house when she came home from work that day. I wanted to tell her what the doctor had said before she went inside to see my mother and father.

"I knew it," she said, and she was still very calm. "In my heart I just knew it came from his lungs."

"Why didn't you say anything?"

"I often don't say what I know."

When she went in to greet my father, she was in complete control. She didn't even look weepy. She ran over to the recliner and hugged him. "Tell me about it, Dad," she said.

"First get me my medicine, baby," he said to her.

He couldn't swallow his pills with anything but the syrup from canned peaches now. So Barbara opened the can of peaches, and began to pour the light syrup out like holy water. When she handed it to him, he looked at her and smiled.

"Thank you" was all he said.

But I heard so much more.

Teri came over to see her grandfather.

"Have we heard anything about our little immigrant yet?" was the first thing he asked. Each time he saw Teri now, he seemed focused on the baby.

"We have pictures," Teri said, her eyes alive with happiness.

"Let me see," my father asked. "Wheezy, get my glasses?"

He held the picture up, looked at it, and smiled. "He looks like a nice baby."

I walked over and looked at the picture. The baby was very cute. He had big dark eyes and a head of curly hair. But he was much too thin and he was lying in a chipped white metal crib without a sheet . . . the only comfort for me was that he looked nothing like an angel.

"Wheezy?" my father asked. "Who does this baby look like? I know he looks like someone."

My mother came over to look. She picked up the picture. She stared, then she frowned, then she swatted my father's shoulder and laughed. "He looks like you did when you were a baby, in the pictures that Josie has."

"His father signed the papers of the release," Teri told her grandfather. "But his mother has to show up in court. She missed the last court date. But we have another one this week."

My father looked at my mother. "Wheezy, honey. Go to church for this baby. Light a candle."

"I'm already lighting too many candles," she said. "We have to leave some for the other people."

"Wheezy?" he said, and he gave her *the look*, "light one more, honey?"

"You're a pain in the ass," she said. But I knew she'd light that candle.

"Did you ask Janith about it?" my father asked Teri. "Can't she put in a good word?"

"I asked," Teri said. "All she's willing to say is he's coming soon."

My father smiled. "Not a bad trade, one Tommy for another." But before any of us could say anything, he added, "How are my girls? How's my Ashley?"

Teri pulled a sheet of yellow construction paper out of her pocket-book. It was a drawing of trees and birds, the sun and a big snowman. She handed it to Poppy. "From Ashley," she said.

That night, after my mother and father went to bed, Danny came into my study to talk to me. He looked older somehow, and even his hair seemed darker.

"Is Poppy going to die?" he asked me.

"I think so," I said.

"How soon?" he asked.

"I can't tell you that," I said. "Nobody can."

"Can you take a guess?" he asked.

I nodded. "But you wouldn't want to hear it."

"Mom," he said, "you've got it all wrong. I'm the one who asked, which means I do want to hear it. You keep trying to tell Aunt Barbara and Gram. They don't ask and they don't want to hear it."

"Okay," I said. I closed my eyes. Then I opened them again. "My guess is pretty soon."

Danny's breath came fast, as though someone had punched him in the stomach. "I thought we'd have more time," he said.

"Don't get crazy yet, honey" I told him. "It's only a guess."

"Don't be modest, Mom," he said with a wistful smile. "There are a lot of things I might not give you credit for, but knowing about dying isn't one of them."

"I could be wrong," I said. "Sometimes treatment helps."

"Then I'll have more time than I expect," Danny said. "But I'm going to live as though you're right. Because then every minute I spend with Poppy from now on will be even more important. Every memory I have is a memory I can keep. No matter what happens then, no one can take those away from me."

My father spent long hours each afternoon meditating, first with guided meditations and then, when he got familiar with the landscape of his soul, his consciousness, with just soft music. He was very excited the first day he broke through.

He was in a valley, a beautiful green valley with a clear bubbling brook running through it. On the distant shore there stood a magnificent pear tree, alongside it, a peach tree filled with juicy peaches, and then another tree, an orange tree with ripe, hanging oranges just waiting to be picked. The sky was clear, an azure blue, and cloudless. Doves cooed, birds flew in flocks overhead, they seemed to greet him.

He kneeled on the bank, dipped his hand in the water. It was cool, so cool, and he was sure it was sweet. He made a cup of his hands, filled it with water, brought it up to his lips. But no. It wasn't time. He had to wait. He'd drink from that brook soon enough. He'd taste those pears, spill the juice from the peaches, and pick handfuls of oranges . . . soon enough.

When he opened his eyes that day, his face was completely serene and peaceful. "Baby," he said, his voice filled with awe. "You should have seen the size of those pears. I've never seen pears like them. And the colors, baby, the colors! I've never seen them before."

"The machete's getting sharper, I see," I teased.

"How much longer do you think it will be?" he asked.

"Till?"

"You know what I'm saying."

"Have you talked to Mommy yet?"

"And said what?"

"Told her you're changing your address," I said.

"She doesn't want to hear it, baby."

I'd spent years helping people share their dying with their families. Now I really believed my father should share his with my mother. "A conspiracy of silence makes a person who's dying feel alone," I said. "According to everything I've read and experienced."

My father smiled and patted my hand. "I don't feel alone. In fact," he said, and he laughed, "I've never felt less lonely."

"Daddy," I said. "Sharing what is happening in your life with the people you love is important. And, Daddy, dying is the most important thing you'll ever do."

He smiled kindly at me. "No, it isn't," he said softly. "Living was as important. Dying is just another thing I'm doing."

"Okay," I said. "But maybe Mommy has something she needs to say even if you don't. I think you should tell her. Give her a chance to prepare."

"Carol," he said, and spoke as though I were very young, "your mother and I have been together for almost our whole life. How can I give her a chance to prepare? If I haven't done that in all our years together, I won't be able to do it now."

"Just give it a shot. See what she says."

He raised his eyebrows. "Okay, for you, I'll give it a shot."

Late that afternoon, when my mother got back and was sitting on the couch, I heard my father say, "Wheezy? Do you know where you put the will that we made? I don't really think I'm getting any better and I want to be sure everything is in order."

She put her cup down on the coffee table with a bang. "Why are you talking stupid?" she scolded him. "What are you trying to do, give me a heart attack?"

My father looked over at the doorway where I was standing. He couldn't hide his satisfaction. He winked at me. "Don't get upset, Wheezy," he said. "Carol and I were just talking this afternoon, and the business about the will came up."

My mother didn't even look at me. She just said to my father, "Both you and your daughter talk too much."

Two days later, when my father was meditating, Gordon called. I whispered into the phone, "He's meditating, Gord, call him back?"

But my father heard me. He wanted the phone. When I gave it to him, he talked without opening his eyes. He said, "You wouldn't believe where I was, son. I was in this place with all my friends."

I couldn't hear Gordon, but I assumed he must have asked, "Which friends?"

Because my father answered, "In this place you're all One, so you don't need names."

When he hung up, he opened his eyes, looked at me, and said, "We're such a lucky family." Then closed his eyes again and went back to his friends.

Later that week, Teri, Gordon, and the kids came for dinner. Suddenly Ashley pointed to the pastel painting of Janith that Anabel had done for me. It hung on my dining room wall. She turned to Jessie then and said, "Jessica? Remember that angel?"

Jessie frowned at her. "From where?" she asked.

"From before we got here to Mommy. She was the one who was calling . . . *Ashley* . . . *Ashley Griswold*? She was the one who came. And remember I said, '*I'm Ashley Griswold*'? and she nodded. She told me my mother was waiting for me . . . remember?"

Jessie shook her head. "Ashes," she said. "I wasn't there. I was already born." Then she turned to me and whispered, "She's a little crazy, don't you think?"

But Ashley heard her and said, "Why, 'cause you can't remember, I'm crazy? I just remember."

My father had been sitting in the recliner in the living room, and he heard what was going on. "Ashley," he called to her, "Ashley, come tell Poppy more about what you remember. I want to hear."

I watched for the next hour as Ashley and my father talked. He smiled when she told her stories. And she laughed when he told his. Both of them were completely enchanted by each other.

Later, before Ashley left, she came over to say, "Gramma Carol, Poppy saw the magic peach trees. Isn't that great?" She had the same excitement in her eyes that I must have had at her age.

My father loved food that was served beautifully. And Mother had always cooked and served in a way that pleased him. Eating was one of his great joys. So it was with tremendous sadness that my father relinquished sitting at the head of the table.

"A man should be able to sit to eat," he said.

But because he was in such pain, he no longer could.

Soon afterward, my father lost his appetite. My mother cooked anything he wanted, but he never could eat more than a few bites. She worried because she was afraid it would make him even weaker. I saw it as another symptom of his illness, but now my sister wouldn't accept that. She began to cook for him.

One night Barbara made him a special dinner.

"Don't put too much on my plate," he instructed.

She made a small cluster of steamed carrots, squeezed three tiny florets of mashed potatoes from a pastry bag, and placed three pea pods beneath them to look like a stem. She cut one small lamb chop to put alongside. Barbara decorated the plate with parsley before she served it to him on a white linen place mat.

My father stood at the counter, looked at her, and then looked at the plate. He swallowed hard. "It's beautiful, baby" he said to her.

And then he spent the next two hours taking small bites, until he got it all down.

One of the big turning points came on a night everything seemed the same as usual. We were all sitting around the living room, watching TV, when my father began having trouble breathing.

I walked over to his chair, saw him struggle for breath, watched him grab his side, heard him moan. My sister went over to him and I ran inside to get my stethoscope.

By the time I got back, Danny had my father lying on the couch. He was really struggling. And his color was lousy. I listened to his lungs. On one side I heard no breath sounds, no air going in or out.

"The lung they biopsied collapsed," I said aloud. I turned to Barbara. "We have to take him to the hospital. They'll put a tube in and reinflate his lung."

Barbara shook her head and pulled me back away from the couch, away from my father.

His whole body began to shake.

Danny kneeled on the floor and put his arms under my father. Leaned over him, pulled him close. "Hold on to me, Poppy," he said. "Let me take some of the pain."

"We have to get him to a hospital," I said to Barbara.

"No," she said, "they'll keep him."

I turned to look at her, her jaw was set. "Bibs, his lung is collapsed," I repeated, thinking she didn't understand.

"They'll never let him come home," she said. "He doesn't want to be in the hospital."

"You can't just leave him here," I said, switching into my nurse mode. "This man needs treatment."

Barbara looked at me steely-eyed now. "This *man* is my father and he's not going to the hospital. I promised him, Carol. I won't break that promise. Not even for you."

Her resolve brought me back to reality.

Danny was still kneeling next to the couch, holding his grandfather, rocking him in his arms. Barbara went over, lifted his head, and gave him some pills for the pain he was having. Then she kneeled down next to Danny. They whispered soft words, and healings.

I stood back and watched them, amazed. Barbara, Danny, and my father, together. Something was going on with them that I wasn't part of. They were able to be strong for him but loving. I watched them with admiration.

Soon my father stopped shaking and the moaning stopped. I walked over with my stethoscope and listened to his lungs again. "Well, it is collapsed," I said. "No question about it."

My father was no longer struggling but his skin was deathly white. "Can a man live with one lung?" he asked me breathlessly.

"Yes," I said. "He can."

"Then I don't want to go to the hospital, Carol," he said weakly. "I'd rather bear the pain."

For the next few hours his body went into spasms and he shook violently. He was cold and afraid. Barbara and Danny took turns holding him, warming him, soothing him until he finally fell asleep.

I was upset about what had happened and even more upset with myself. What had possessed me? Why did I want to treat the situation as though it was an emergency? My sister saw it much more clearly. What good did I think inflating his lung would do? Once my father was in the hospital, we would never get him home again.

Then suddenly something pulled my attention and I looked across the room. My mother. She was sitting in a chair in the corner the entire time. She had never said a word, she hadn't moved at all, and the look in her eyes wasn't shock, it was surrender.

Later that night, sitting in my study by myself, I tried again to analyze why I had reacted as I did. And finally I began to see one of the truths of my relationship with my father that I had never considered before. . . .

We lived and loved in rich and magical mythic realms, my father and I. That was the place we hung out together, that was the place we spent time. In thought, in theory, in history, or on Olympus with the Titans and Greek gods and goddesses.

But Greek gods never died. They were immortal. So for me, my father was immortal.

And I understood why the people my father wanted with him now were those in the family who had never bought into any of the myths. Those who lived on Earth, not on Olympus. Those who were most human. Those in our family who didn't compete, didn't control, who just lived their lives, stayed themselves, and loved him. Surrounded by them, the *man* who was my father could die a safe and warm human death.

Somehow my father's body adjusted to breathing with only one lung. He seemed to stabilize. My sister's combination of pills kept him fairly comfortable and each day that she went to work and my mother went to the house, he'd meditate again.

One afternoon, after a particularly pleasant meditation, my father returned, his face flush with excitement.

"You wouldn't believe where I was," he said. "I was looking through the eyes of a condor from the top of the Pyrennes Mountains over a small conclave of peasants. Beautiful women dressed in colored sackcloth carried earthen jugs on their heads filled with deep red wine, others ground grain on big rocks to make fresh bread. A large oxen was being roasted on a spit in time for a big celebration."

I laughed. "Daddy," I said, "did you recognize that part of you that was looking through the eyes of that condor?"

"Yes," he said. "It was me."

"Well, that's the part of you that I believe will survive the death of your body. That's consciousness."

He smiled at me. "Well, baby, if what you say is true, I hope I get there in time for that celebration."

"Dad," I said, laughing, "I swear, you've been taking so many trips lately, we should sign you up for frequent flyer miles."

This time with my father was very precious to me. We talked again, told myths again, shared stories—and now he was eager to have me teach him all the things that I had learned—just as he taught me all those years before.

Later, when my sister came home, he told her the story of the condor.

She wasn't happy about it. In fact, it frightened her to death.

In the kitchen when she was cooking for my father and I was standing alongside the stove, watching her, she said, "I hate when he trips like that. It annoys me that you make him do it."

"Barbara," I said, "I don't *make* him do it."

"Still," she said, "if it wasn't for you, he wouldn't be doing it. And I just want you to know I don't like it."

The following day my father tired more quickly. So in the afternoon I helped him get into bed. I saw his eyes fill, so I asked, "What's up, Dad?"

"I was feeling so grateful," he said. "I was wondering what I had done in my life to deserve such kindness."

I sat down next to him on the bed. "Daddy," I said, "I for one can point out a few things you did for me. You picked me and the kids up when I was scared and had no place to go, you let me live back home. You helped raise them. You taught me hope and read me fairy tales . . . you let me know all things were possible. I could go on and on. But every one of us in the family has stories to tell of how you helped us."

He shook his head with disbelief. "Who could have imagined that all those little kindnesses would have added up to such a bankroll?"

"What did you think," I asked, "when over the years you watched us help others, some of them strangers? You told us that a hundred-pound log was heavy for one but easy to carry for ten. Why would you think it could be any different when the time came for you?"

His eyes filled again. "While I was helping too, I was standing on the edge of the circle. Now, when everyone's caring for me, I'm on the inside. I wasn't prepared for how full of love that would feel."

That night in bed, when I couldn't sleep again, I began thinking about how often I'd heard people with cancer say the same thing. How often I'd heard that having cancer brings with it the knowledge of how much others love you. A gift of sorts.

When I told my sister about it the following day, she made a funny face and said, "If we knew Daddy needed to learn that, we could have just thrown him a big party."

Gordon often stopped by the house on his way home from work. He told Poppy everything that was happening at work, told him how often all his friends asked about him.

"Tell them to stop over," my father said. "Tell them to come by."

So they started coming to the house to offer their condolences. To cheer him up. All of them. I sat and listened as time after time, one friend or another repeated stories my father had told that impressed them, or in some way changed their lives.

During those visits my father laughed a lot, made light of his pain, had no fear of dying. Before each friend left, my father told them he loved them, and how love was the only thing that really mattered.

Though his friends came to comfort him, they left feeling comforted. Still, they brought with them a special gift. My father was getting a panoramic view of his life—before he died.

Over the next week my father's legs got weaker. So we got him a wheelchair and a walker to help him get around. But often he held the walker up in front of him, playing with it, dancing. Every morning he began to watch the mass on TV. And we sat and watched it with him. But, of course, no one but him understood it, because it was in Spanish. During that time he memorized the mass. By the third week he could chant and sing along with the TV priest.

It was on a Sunday when my mother was off having coffee with Barbara and my father was walking around my living room with his walker that I asked him to help me sum up the dynamics of our relationship. He liked questions like that. Dialectics got his mind off his pain.

"You and I?" he said. "We've always stretched each other to the limit, tested each other, forced each other to be as much as we were capable of being. We were warriors, both of us. I know I was never disappointed with you. Were you with me?"

"Never," I said. "Sometimes it was hard for me to be all you thought I could be."

He shook his head and said, "Your mother tried to tell me. She knew. I was too hard on you."

"It worked whatever way you did it," I said. "I learned a lot."

He looked wistful when he said, "But we'll never know how much it cost you, or how much you lost. . . ." And then he seemed to straighten up, to come to terms with it. "A man makes mistakes with his first child," he said. "He has to learn too."

"What about Barbara?" I asked. "How is that different?"

He smiled in deep remembering. Then he let go of his walker and put his hand in his pocket to demonstrate. "Your sister is like a gold coin I always carry in my pocket. Whenever I'm not at my best, whenever I'm frightened, or weak, I just reach into my pocket and I feel her there. She asks nothing of me, loves me however I am, doesn't test me, just accepts me. Barbara brings me comfort and reassurance."

Chapter Twenty-Three

My father had to go for the radiation consultation. He had been scheduled for over a week, but the morning Danny came over to get him, he was having an especially difficult time standing.

"Daddy," I said, "let's take the wheelchair."

"Baby," he said, "I can walk. I just need a little more time to get some strength."

I watched him try to muster all his inner power, I watched him try to stand again, but his legs were unsteady. He was too weak. Danny stood by helplessly, but my mother finally said, "Honey, just this once. We don't want to make the doctor wait. He's a busy man."

My mother's appeal to my father's sense of responsibility convinced him. "Okay," he said. "Just this once."

He lay on the backseat with his head in my mother's lap as Danny drove to the radiologist. As Danny got my father out of the car and we put him in the wheelchair, it was very cold outside. He asked my mother to get his hat. Still, he began to shiver. Danny took his jacket off and put it over his grandfather's legs. Then he wheeled him down the long paved driveway into the building. We passed several people along the way, and each time someone glanced my father's way, he tipped his hat, and said, "Good morning."

We didn't have to wait long once we reached the waiting room. The radiologist himself came out to greet us. He shook my father's hand."I'm Dr. Erani," he said. "And you are Thomas Gino?"

"I am," my father said. "Not in the best shape, but still . . ."

"Come into my office," he said warmly.

We all went inside with him. "We'd like to begin the treatments next Monday morning," the doctor said. "It will certainly relieve some of your pain."

My father looked thoughtful. "Is that all it will do?"

The doctor looked at him compassionately. "Our skill as physicians is limited in many cases," he said. "Once there's this much deterioration of the spinal column, there is no way to repair it."

"I'm not sure I fully understand what you're saying," my father said to him. "Do you have any pictures you can show me so I can get a better understanding of my condition?"

"The results of your CT scan are hanging in the other room. A wheelchair will not fit," the doctor explained, "so I'm afraid I can't show them to you. They need to hang against a light board."

My father turned toward Danny. "Help Poppy up, son," he said.

Dr. Erani moved quickly toward him. "I don't think it's wise to try to stand," he said. He looked worried.

"I've been standing for my whole life," he said. "That's what a man does."

With Danny supporting my father, he managed to walk into the small office behind the doctor's larger one. There hanging along the long row of light boards were several X-rays.

Dr. Erani moved toward one of them. My father and Danny walked up beside him. I stood back a little with my mother. The doctor raised a pointer he'd taken off his desk. "Here," he said, "is the problem."

He was pointing to the lower spine, to a space where I knew the vertebrae of my father's spine should be. But I saw nothing.

My father looked at the picture of the scan more closely. The doctor was quiet, giving him time to digest what he was seeing. "Excuse me, doc," my father said, frowning. "I'm aware of the anatomy of animals because I'm a hunter. But maybe a man is different. Still, I don't see something here that I believe should be here. Am I wrong?" He pointed to the space.

"That is exactly the problem," Dr. Erani said, and he spoke to my father as though to a colleague. "The lower vertebrae have completely disintegrated. There is no support in this spinal column. It should be impossible for this man to stand upright. There may be a line of bone left here," he said as he moved his pointer to a white line thin as a thread, "but a man should not be able to walk without the lower vertebrae. It would seem to be impossible."

My father turned to call me, but the doctor warned, "Move carefully, please. Or you could be immediately paralyzed."

I walked up to where he was standing. "Look at this," he said, showing me the space. "I have no bone left here. I shouldn't be able to stand or walk. You see, baby, I was right. That's why I had that pain."

"I see, Dad," I said. "I see. . . ."

At that moment the space in my chest where my heart was matched the space in his spine.

Danny's face was ashen and my mother's eyes were red. All of me had turned to stone. But my father's voice was calm when he asked the doctor, "After the treatments . . . I still won't be able to hunt, to play golf?"

The doctor shook his head. "I'm sorry," he said.

My father patted his arm. "Doc, you have nothing to be sorry about. You've done a fine job. Don't feel bad. I've had a wonderful life." His voice was calm as Danny helped him walk back to his wheelchair. Once he was sitting again, he turned to Dr. Erani and asked in a pensive voice, "This means I won't be able to drive anymore, am I right?"

The doctor lowered his head.

"Okay, doc," my father said. "Thanks for everything."

"We'll see you on Monday" was the only thing my mother said.

But as Danny wheeled my father back out into the car, I knew by my father's expression that he had already made his decision.

The days after we went to the radiologist my father was very quiet. He meditated still, but he talked a lot less. I was sitting next to him on the couch, reading, when he asked, "Have you considered what you are going to do with your mother?"

"Have you got a suggestion?" I asked.

"Yes. She'll have a little money, she knows the stockbroker's name," he told me, "and I think you should sell her house. Move her in here with your sister, it's a nice place to live. She shouldn't have to be alone."

"Where will I go, Daddy?" I asked, teasing him. "You've just sold Mommy's house and thrown me out of mine?"

"You travel a lot," he said simply. "You spend a lot of time with Mario. Your mother needs a family to take care of. We have to leave her that."

"Okay," I told him. "Don't worry about anything. I'll take care of it."

He patted my hand. "I know, baby. I know."

That night my father, my mother, Danny, Barbara, and I watched *Field of Dreams* together. Afterward, my father asked to be helped into bed. My mother was relaxing on the couch, Barbara had gone inside to shower, and Danny had gone home, so I offered to tuck him in.

Once in the bedroom, my father held on to my arm as he lay down in bed. Then he looked at me. "Danny was such a help again today," he said sincerely. "He doesn't do things the way I would, but still, he's very special. I had no idea how much he loved his Poppy until now. Isn't that crazy? And your sister, she has so much to give."

"We all love you, Dad," I said.

"You know, baby," he said, and his eyes filled. "A general trains his troops for a long time. He teaches them strategies, maps their positions, he assesses their strengths and weaknesses. But no matter how good the general is, he doesn't know whether he's succeeded or failed until the day his troops go into battle. Then he knows who he is, he sees what he's done. His merit rests on them."

"And?" I asked, paying close attention now.

He frowned. "I've overlooked some of my best soldiers. I've underestimated their strengths. And I was lax in my praise of those whose strengths weren't my own." He smiled and touched my cheek, but he hesitated before he added, "Baby, you've been in the front lines for much too long. I want you to go back to California."

"I can't leave now, Dad. Not now," I said, my first reaction shock.

He smiled gently, his eyes compassionate, when he said, "Carol, listen to your dad. It's time for me to move my reserve regiment up front. They're strong and capable. And they need to be recognized."

I nodded. I tried to process what he was saying, I tried to hear what he meant. I wanted to honor his wishes, but how could I leave him when death was so close?

He saw my reaction and reached out to take my hand. "I want you to do this one last thing for me. I want you to take what little joy I've given you out into the world. I want you to live, really live."

"I can't, Dad, not yet," I told him.

"Carol, the time I have left I want to spend with your mother, my favorite girl, and my grandson," he said. And it hit me like a blow.

His *favorite* girl? His *reserve regiment?* I never heard my father say that either Barbara or I was his *favorite*. But secretly, all my life I thought *I* was. He spent time with me, he talked more to me, and trained me as a Spartan youth. To stand in his place. And in order to please him, I had tried so hard and learned it all so well. Could that be what kept us apart as he lay dying?

His voice was strong when he said, "I want to see you walk away."

Something in his tone brought me back to when I was a child of eight.

I had just gotten my first two-wheeler. My mother wanted to buy me one with training wheels. But my father refused. Instead, he got me a sleek, fast English racer. He lifted me onto the seat and placed my feet on the wooden blocks he'd nailed on the pedals so I could reach them. Then he held tight to the back of my seat. When I first started to ride, he talked to me constantly in a soft and reassuring voice, letting me know he was there, so I wouldn't be frightened.

As I began to pick up speed, my father ran alongside me. He laughed when he got out of breath. He kept pushing himself and me. But every time I tried to ride alone, I fell.

Finally I really started to pedal. I felt the wind in my hair and I had such a sense of freedom that I pedaled faster and faster down that street. My heart was racing, I was thrilled with myself, with the speed, with my own sense of mastery.

I turned to tell my father, but he had let go more than a block before.

I saw him waving and I heard him yell, "Look ahead. Keep your eyes on the target. Don't look back," but it was too late. I was already falling onto the hard asphalt pavement. I cut my knees and hit my head.

My father came running down the street.

And I accused, "*You* let go. . . . *You* let me fall. . . ."

He picked me up, brushed me off, and stood me straight in front of him. He pulled out his clean white handkerchief, wiped my tears, and looked into my eyes. "You didn't fall because I let go. You fell because you were afraid. You fell because you took your eyes off the target. Don't ever look back."

* * *

Now I took a deep breath and stood up. My father was watching me, to see what I would do. But sharing someone's dying was a real intimacy. One had to be invited.

"Okay, Daddy," I said, trying to smile, "I'll take the torch and carry it for you."

He nodded his thanks.

I pulled the covers up around his neck to tuck him in. And I bent down to kiss his forehead as I'd always kissed my kids before they went to sleep. Pictures of all the times we had together flooded my mind . . . the early morning fishing, singing on the car trips, dancing the polka, talking with excitement over new ideas. All the times he helped me when I was scared and confused.

"Daddy?" I said as I stood by the side of his bed. "Just one more thing."

He looked tired. "What, baby?"

I tried to say it evenly, without too much emotion. "I just want to thank you."

He opened his eyes and looked at me, puzzled. "For *what*, baby? For *what*?"

"I want to thank you . . . for my whole life," I said. "Yes, for my whole life."

"It was my pleasure," he said softly. And then he watched me walk away.

That night, when I walked out of my father's room, my sister was standing in the hallway right outside the room, listening.

"Thank you?" she said accusingly. "Thank you for my whole life?"

I nodded.

Barbara said, "You're not going to listen to him, are you? You're not going to leave *now*?"

"Daddy says he wants to be with *you*. He doesn't want me here."

"But what will *I* do?" she asked.

"Everything right," I said. "You'll be fine. There's nothing you can do wrong. He trusts you. And that's powerful medicine."

She began to cry then, and I put my arms around her. "Shh . . . shh . . ." I crooned, stroking her hair. "Danny's here. He'll help."

She pulled away from me, tears falling freely. "But don't you see what this means?" she asked. "Can't you see what he's doing?"

I shook my head. "What?" I asked her.

"Carol," she said, "this is the hardest thing I've ever done in my whole life. If I can do this without you, then I can do *anything* without you."

I heard the rip of the cord that bound us from the time we were children, and my eyes filled. "Another gift he's giving," I said.

My mother was standing in the kitchen, washing some dishes.

I told her, "Daddy wants me to leave. He wants me to go back to California."

She kept washing the dishes. "He's still your father. If he wants you to go, then go."

His whole family was still listening, in spite of the fact that this made no sense to any of us. Humility, obedience, trust. He was still "The Chief."

But what did I want? Not as my father's daughter, but as a woman.

What I really wanted was to be able to capture the complexity of our relationship in all its grime and glory. To lasso the fullness of its love and the depth of its pain. I wanted to show the truth of my loss in a scream or a sob, I wanted to shout my respect in long eulogies, and spill my anguish in hard, hot tears just like everyone else. But I couldn't. For my father gave me Spartan tools of survival. He taught me how to hide my tears, stand tall in silence as branches bit my skin, and surrender without giving up or giving in. So now I couldn't even cry for him. I hated that.

But if my father was right, and we were Siamese twins who always knew what the other was thinking, I was willing to bet that his hidden agenda was to give me what he thought I needed, while he gave my sister and my son the courage to face their biggest fears and the recognition he could finally see they deserved.

He must have known what losing him would mean to me. For once, he must have been able to acknowledge my vulnerability, and even his own. And maybe he could see now, that while he had taught me to conquer my fears, he had never been able to teach me to enjoy life the way he had. So after all those years of responsibility, he wanted to give me freedom.

What my father didn't understand, with as much as he had learned in his last three months, with everything he had learned in his life, was that freedom can't be given. And that while he had *trained* me for leadership, it was my own heart that led the way.

In the DNA of my soul, my place in my family had already been written. It was traced on my cells, from the time I came to be. Their well-being was my own, and helping them my pleasure. Freedom? Real freedom for me wasn't having no responsibility, it was doing what I was born to do. And I was born to this.

I left that night. I hopped a plane. I consciously walked away from my family . . . so my sister and my son could claim their power, know their worth, and face their fears. And so my father could die in peace in the way that he had chosen.

But even more, so I could honor my feelings to keep him immortal and not have to watch him die a real human death. Because there are human experiences worthy of tears, and woundings deep enough to break the human heart. And I knew this was one of them.

The following night I was sitting at the table on the deck in Malibu when I called home. To my surprise, my father answered the phone. I could hear his breath rattling in his chest. "Daddy?" I said. "It's me."

I heard him say, "How!"

I didn't understand. So I asked, "What's going on, Dad?"

He whispered, "Baby, the Indians are out on the front lawn." Then he laughed a soft, funny laugh.

I wondered what kind of medicine my sister had given him, or if the cancer had gotten to his brain. He had never sounded confused before.

"What are the Indians doing?" I asked tentatively.

He laughed again, real joy. "They're dancing and singing," he said.

"Daddy," I said, "let me talk to Barbara. Is she there?"

"Sure, baby," he said. "Just a minute. Are you having a good time?"

"Swell, Daddy," I said nervously. "Put Barbara on?"

He handed the phone to my sister. "Hi, Carol," she said.

"What medicine did you give Daddy?" I asked. "He sounds confused."

"He does?" she asked, surprised. "I'm not giving him anything different."

"He told me that there were Indians dancing and singing on the front lawn," I said.

Barbara laughed. "Brooke Medicine Eagle is here. Teri brought her over. She talked to Daddy and then they went inside to speak to Janith."

"We have a very crazy family," I said, relieved. I thought about Brooke Medicine Eagle showing up for my father. An amazing synchronicity, no doubt angel inspired. Brooke walked the Beauty Way; she honored the crossroads of life with ritual and ceremony. She made the transition we call death sacred, with chants and song and dancing, a calling to Great Spirit to welcome the Spirit of the one who was passing. I'd read her books, listened to her tapes, and loved that she was there, that she was singing traveling songs, songs of celebration, when I couldn't.

"Teri just walked in the door," Barbara said."Do you want to talk to her?"

"Sure, thanks," I said, shaking my head with relief.

Teri took the phone and said, "Hi, Mom."

"You had me thinking your grandfather was losing it," I said. "Why are you singing and dancing?"

"In Native American tradition, when someone is sick, singing and dancing and storytelling is used to help the person heal. So Brooke was telling Poppy stories. She says that ceremony helps them find their way home. It seems like a good thing to do . . . better than crying."

"Poppy sounds like he's having fun," I said.

"Mom," Teri said, "you know all those times you talked about the beauty and healing in death. Well, I have to confess, I thought you were crazy. Especially after Greggy. But watching Poppy, I can see it now."

"How's that?" I asked.

"Well, you know how controlled he always was," she said. "Watching him in these last weeks, as he allows all of us to help him, seeing how he can let go and surrender with such dignity, and hearing how much love he feels makes me feel completely different."

"The man has always been a hero," I said."Short, but still."

"Really, Mom," Teri said. "I can see so much more now. When death is allowed to be a part of life, and when someone can die at home with everything he loves around him, and he feels safe, it's a very special time. I can finally understand why God put death in life."

"How so?"

Teri tried to explain. "To give us a chance to become whole and loved and at peace," she said."I always thought death was ugly. But it's not. It's the fear around it that's ugly, and Poppy's not afraid."

"Why do you think that is?"

"Maybe because you showed him how to travel and he took so

many trips into the unknown that it became familiar. I know that's helped a lot," she said. "And having all the people he loves around."

"I hoped that would do it," I said.

"This whole process of dying is so healing," she said, "and Spirit is amazing. Isn't it great that Brooke is here?"

I said, "I would have liked to meet her."

Teri said,"She met Poppy, then we had a session and Brooke wanted to give a song of thanks to Janith, and sing a traveling song for Poppy . . . and he's having so much fun."

"Give Brooke my thanks," I said. Then I looked at my watch. "It's late. What are you still doing there?"

Teri walked inside with the phone. "I wanted to be with Poppy because he's having a lot more trouble breathing. I gave him an amethyst crystal to help. Jenny's here tonight, and Chris has been walking back and forth, looking worried."

"Did Janith say anything about Poppy in the session?" I asked.

"She said there are angels all around us at this time. Then she told us the baby would be coming very soon. Poppy asked about him again tonight," she said. "Gordon and I have to go into family court early tomorrow morning to get some more papers. We need to fax them to Romania right away."

"Good luck with the papers," I said. Then I asked, "Put Pop back on the phone?"

My father got back on. "Hi, isn't this wonderful?" he said. "Isn't it a real trip?"

"I guess the universe is watching out for you, Daddy."

"I have no doubt, baby."

That night I tossed and turned for a long time and couldn't fall asleep. Because though my head could comprehend it, my heart was having a very hard time knowing that I'd never see my father again. Who would challenge me, stretch me, be there for me to grab on to when I was afraid I'd fall? And then I remembered. . . .

I was only about four when my father first took me fishing. Those early mornings were always cold and damp. By dawn we'd get to the charter boat, a big boat. He had promised my mother that he would tie a rope around our waists, tie us together. The first couple of times we went, when the big boat rolled, I rolled with it, lost my balance, almost fell. I'd reach over and grab on to my father's pants, hold tight till I felt steady again. Soon I was able to walk around without losing my balance, without falling, hardly ever reaching out to grab my father.

The day that my father cut me loose, he made a big deal about it. He didn't just untie us, he took his fishing knife and cut me free.

"I'm scared, Daddy," I said, and tried to reach for him, but he moved away.

He smiled. "You'll be fine," he reassured me. "You've got your sea legs, Carol."

Finally, after what seemed like hours, I fell asleep.

But suddenly, as clearly as the day he first said it. I woke to hear my father's voice. *"You've got your sea legs."*

Now I was wide awake. I sat up. Looked at the clock. It wasn't even four A.M. I climbed out of bed quietly, trying not to wake Mario, and carefully opened the doors to the balcony. I walked out into the warm night air and leaned against the railing. It was so black out, I could hear the water but I couldn't see it.

I sat on the deck, my legs folded beneath me. For some time I focused only on the sound of the waves. Threw myself into that sound, became a part of it. But then I heard a whistle, a funny whistle, the kind of whistle my father made when he called me to come home. I opened my eyes. I looked around. But no one was there. When I closed my eyes again . . . I found myself somewhere else.

It seemed to be a valley I was in, a small enclave. And all around me there were people preparing for a celebration. There was an ox on a spit, women with earthen jugs upon their heads carrying fine wine. I tried to get my bearings. I looked around. Nothing was familiar. But from atop the mountain I heard a call. I turned my face up and saw a huge bird. A condor? Daddy?

I heard the phone ring, but it seemed to be coming from a distance. I struggled to get my bearings. When I realized it was coming from the house, I ran inside. Mario was just about to reach for it, but he let me pick it up. I glanced at the clock. Five-thirty.

I heard Bridie's voice. "Come home, Carol," she said. "Your family needs you. . . ."

It had happened just a few minutes before. It was Monday. My father was to go for his first radiation treatment. Bridie had come over with her van. It had a ramp for wheelchairs. They hoped that would make it easier for my father. He wasn't dressed yet but he had already taken his shower. Danny had gotten in with him, held him up, helped him out and then put him back in bed.

Barbara had gone inside to get ready to go with them. It caused her pain to watch her father's struggle to breathe.

My mother went inside to call the doctor. To let him know they'd be a little late.

Danny was standing at the foot of the bed. My father smiled at him, beckoned to him. Danny saw how hard his breath was coming. He walked over to the bed, leaned down, held his grandfather's hand, and said, "Let go, Poppy. Go on. I'll take care of Gram."

But my father was waiting. . . .

When Barbara came in she sat next to him on the bed. "What is it, Daddy?" she asked.

"If you want me to keep fighting, I will," he said. But it took such effort.

She had tears in her eyes as she smiled at him. And she struggled to keep her voice calm when she said, "No, Daddy, you don't have to fight any longer, not for me."

He patted her hand. He nodded his head and smiled.

My mother walked back into the room. My father smiled at her too. She got his socks, unfolded them, began to put them on him.

It was then my father saw the angel hold out her hand. . . .

By the time my mother looked up again, my father had gone.

And on that same day . . .

Far across the world, in the district of Tulcea, in a small court building in the country of Romania, a judge was reading some papers.

"Everything seems in order," he said. "Where is this child going?"

"America," the lawyer answered.

"Ah, America," the judge said. "His parents' names?"

"Gordon Andrew Griswold and Theresa Catherine Griswold," the lawyer said.

"Can they provide for this child?" the judge asked.

"They have a home that they own in a suburb of New York. There are schools close by, and many places for a child to play. He'll have food to eat. And children to play with. Three sisters . . ."

The judge smiled and signed the papers. "This child's American name?" he asked.

"They will call him Thomas," the lawyer said.

During our communication with Janith, Teri asked if we could have some steps to guide us in healing in order for us to arrive at the best outcome. We now offer them to you, in the hope that they serve you as well.

Eleven Steps for Healing Grief and Loss

1—Allow yourself your loss with all the components, with all the factors involved in this loss. Allow yourself to experience the loss fully, the pain fully. Accepting your loss is the first step to the beginning of healing.

2—The second step is to allow yourself the knowledge of emptiness; to understand that you have been emptied of all previous personality.

3—Once you have accepted your emptiness, and your loss, you may begin to fill up again with what you choose. Three is connecting to Spirit to begin to fill that emptiness with Spiritual knowledge rather than personality.

4—Four is to begin to relate to persons around you. Four is also about finding the nature of Oneness in the individual aspects of all of Nature. So it is not now a personal thing, it is an interactive experience. It is the beginning of the acknowledgment, "I am on earth and I still exist and there are others around me who still exist."

5—Five is to then experience the Oneness of family and friends, self and Spirit—to understand that now that you are an emptied out being, you can find your Spiritual aspect.

6—Six is to allow yourself the whole loss experience once again. To feel it—at this level—once again. To reaffirm your commitment to healing once again.

7—Seven is to speak to others about your experience of Loss. Not to minimize your loss. To tell them what you have learned from this experience is quite healing.

8—Eight is to begin to perceive a life after Loss. To begin to look for signs, signals, opportunities that will present themselves. Just to see them, not to act on them.

9—Nine is to begin to act on your future opportunities. To build again from your emptiness and spirituality rather than from your personality.

10—Ten is to begin to look back. Since you have process in your life, now that you have begun your opportunities, this step encourages you to look back to where you have been and how far you have come. It's a reaffirming place that "I have been," and "I will be."

11—Eleven is allowing yourself to be touched once again.

We wish for you to know that all the time you are developing your spiritual sense, with guides, prayer, meditation, or whatever you wish along the way, it is understood that you are connecting with your God at each one of these steps. And that you are never truly alone.

Love & Light,
Janith

NATIONAL RESOURCES

National SIDS Alliance   1-800-221-7437
1314 Bedford Avenue
Suite 210
Baltimore, MD 21208

The SIDS Alliance has over 50 chapters and other resources throughout the U.S. This organization provides bereavement support 24 hours
a day, educational materials and funds research in hopes of one day
eliminating SIDS. The Alliance can also provide resources in Canada
as well as internationally.

Alliance of Grandparent Against SIDS Tragedy   1-888-774-7437
A.G.A.S.T.
2323 Central Avenue
Suite 1204
Phoenix, AZ 85004

A.G.A.S.T. was founded by grandparents of SIDS babies and provides
support and information specifically for grandparents.

National SIDS Resource Center   1-703-821-8965
2070 Chain Bridge Road   ext. 249
Vienna, VA 22182

The SIDS Resource Center is a federally funded organization. The
center provides literature, catalogs and published articles on SIDS.